One Semester Economics

Rebecca Harding

One
Semester
Economics

An Introduction for Business and
Management Students

Copyright © Rebecca Harding, 1998

The right of Rebecca Harding to be identified as author of this work has been asserted in accordance with the Copyright, Designs and Patents Act 1988.

First published 1998

2 4 6 8 10 9 7 5 3 1

Blackwell Publishers Ltd
108 Cowley Road
Oxford OX4 1JF
UK

Blackwell Publishers Inc.
350 Main Street
Malden, Massachusetts 02148
USA

British Library Cataloguing in Publication Data

A CIP catalogue record for this book is available from the British Library.

Library of Congress Cataloging-in-Publication Data

Harding, Rebecca.
    One semester economics: an introduction for business and
management students / Rebecca Harding.
        p.   cm.
    Includes bibliographical references and index.
    ISBN 0–631–20025–8 (alk. paper)
    1. Economics.   I. Title.
HB171.5.H3253   1997
330—dc21   97–14137
                                                        CIP

Typeset in 10 on 12 pt Plantin
by Graphicraft Typesetters Ltd, Hong Kong
Printed in Great Britain by Hartnolls Ltd, Bodmin, Cornwall

This book is printed on acid-free paper.

Contents

Preface

A Guide to the Book: for the Student and the Lecturer

This book is intended as a one semester introductory course in economics for students on business-related courses. As a tutor of these 'non-specialist' economists for a number of years now, I have realized that this group of students has a particular need for a text that is simple, non-technical and logically structured, and which teaches them the key areas of the discipline in a way that will underpin other material that is covered on such a course. To this end, the book should be read as an overview rather than as a complete guide to the subject but, equally, as a text which will stimulate interest and, critically, demonstrate to students *why* they study economics on a business course.

Each chapter is mutually exclusive and will stand alone as a discussion, for example, of costs, markets, unemployment etc. However, it is highly recommended that the text is read in chapter order, rather than by taking one chapter in isolation. This is the case for several reasons. First, the text 'flows' logically from one area to the next and each chapter builds on the last. At the beginning the assumption is that the reader knows little or no economics; by the end of the book the discussion is more sophisticated, on the assumption that readers will now feel confident with the basic concepts. Second, the text is designed to complement a one semester course. Each of the twelve weeks corresponds to the areas that would normally be covered during the course of one semester. Third, approaching the text in progression ensures that a full picture of the subject and its uses for business is gained. It is this that distinguishes it from other texts currently on the market.

Finally, the approach taken is 'traditional' in that it covers the basics of an introductory course. Many 'pure' economists will find limitations in the subject material covered, but for business studies students the areas covered are enough to ensure that a degree of confidence and understanding of the subject is reached within the framework of a one semester course. It is also a deeply personal interpretation of the subject, in that it lends a particularly novel approach to the relevance for business. In my view the approach is a welcome and long overdue re-examination of a subject which *is* critical to everyday life and which underpins everything that a student will cover elsewhere on a business-related course.

Reading

Short and appropriate reading lists are given in chapters as appropriate so that the interested reader can take the investigation of a particular area further. In order to avoid the criticism that the lists are either too short or not inclusive enough it is worth pointing out that the text is written with a view to providing a basic understanding. It might further aim to stimulate some interest in the subjects covered. Having taught this subject in an era of modularization, however, I am inclined to be more pragmatic about recommending reading to students. It may be that articles and books listed are unavailable or inaccessible or simply that it is not practical to find the extra material.

I would suggest, however, that any students wanting to succeed in their studies read at least one 'quality' news publication a week and try to keep in touch with some of the excellent radio and television broadcasts which focus on business and economic issues. Following current affairs like this will enable the student to see that economics can be found in everyday life. Once a certain number of concepts have been grasped it is easy to criticize and appraise company behaviour and government policy in a clear and informed way.

Acknowledgements

There are so many people who have been involved with this book since its first inception many years ago that it would be impossible to thank everyone. It would be inappropriate, however, to allow the invaluable assistance of a few people to pass unnoticed. First, the book contains a number of 'real' cases. Rodney Dyer from Lucas Diesel Systems Sudbury provided vital information in chapters 2 and 4, but was also involved with my earlier research which is integrated elsewhere in the text. Jane Scott, the Worldwide Marketing Director of the *Financial Times* (FT), has provided full cooperation with my many enquiries. Without Sam Goonetilake, also from the FT, the ideas for chapters 2 and 3 would have been much poorer. The author and publisher are grateful to the FT for permission to reproduce the material in the case studies, which first appeared in FT editions as follows: case 1, 18 October 1995; case 2, 29 February 1996; case 3, 16 December 1993; case 4, 17 December 1993; case 5, 10 January 1995; case 6, 27 September 1995; case 7, 27 November 1995; case 8, 27 September 1995; case 9, 21 August 1995; case 10, 5 March 1996.

My thanks are also due to the first year BA Business Studies students at the University of Brighton between 1990 and 1997. Without their feedback and enthusiasm I would not have realized how poorly their needs were served. Particular thanks are due to Andy Sutherland, Mark Cox, Simon Richards and Lee Bunker (1994/5), whose excellent first year project formed the basis for the material in chapters 2 and 3. Thanks are also due to their contempories, who dutifully answered surveys for me and gave me useful feedback on the introductory chapter. Finally, the first years of 1995/6 compelled me to rush ahead with the text and also provided invaluable feedback.

Colleagues and friends have helped with the content and reading of the text. Paul Gower and Fabio Franchino tested the taught module and provided immeasurably useful feedback. Dennis Harding proof read and provided invaluable comments on numerous drafts.

Ultimately, though, the real thanks are due to the members of my family who have suffered my endless preoccupation with the text. To Dennis, I owe the space and time to think as well as the love, support and encouragement that enabled this book to be written. Jack and Charlie provided me with piano accompaniments and 'extras' to the text, which, by now, I hope have all been eliminated! Any errors of analysis or judgement remain, of course, my own.

Rebecca Harding
January 1997

# **Why Economics?**

An Economist is a man who once had a human being described to him, but has never actually met one.

(Henry Mintzberg, British Academy of Management Conference,
September 1991)

A city bank's economist visiting the Continent passed a butcher's displaying various types of brains including, not only those of animals, but one labelled 'Economist' and 'Sociologist'. After recovering from his initial shock, he noted that the economist variety was twice the price of the other. So he went in and told the butcher he was pleased to see his profession's grey matter was so valuable.

'It's the supply factor,' the man replied. 'Brains in Economists are very rare.'

(Financial Times, Observer column, 3 May 1991)

1 Introduction

Someone will no doubt have already said to you, 'Oh, you *need* to study economics, it's fundamental to the study of business.' And if they haven't already said it, they soon will. Economics is a subject which is covered at an introductory and intermediate stage on most business studies courses, so it must be important. But has anyone *really* told you why? Most of the people who have started this course with you are feeling confused. They are more than a little anxious that economics is going to be mystifyingly theoretical and difficult, or just plain boring. If this is you too, then read on.

Economics *is* fundamental to the study of business. There, someone has said it! Businesses make decisions daily about the way they spend their money, the way they sell their product (be it a good or a service), the way they market their product, the way they produce, the way they distribute, how they attract customers and so on. Other disciplines within a business studies course will tell us a little about each of these functions. Marketing will tell us about selling, advertising and branding a company's product to make it as attractive as possible.

Logistics and operations management will tell us about how companies organize their supply, production and distribution. Accounts will tell us how companies are spending and investing their money. Strategy will tell us how and why companies are making decisions to move into particular markets or spend their money in a particular way. Each is a necessary part of studying business, but none alone is sufficient to understand the whole context in which businesses operate.

Not one of these disciplines will give us this *complete* picture of the reasons why companies make decisions and the way in which they make them in the way that economics can. With each subject we can understand an aspect of business. We can apply it and we can make recommendations about the types of policy that a company should pursue. But to understand *why* we need to return to first principles and ask ourselves why a company is in business at all: what are the *human* aspirations behind any business that make it tick?

The answer, of course, has to be that business people are ultimately seeking to earn a good wage for themselves such that they can pay their bills. Money is scarce and people work in order to make it more plentiful for themselves. Then they have more to spend on the array of goods and services that exists in any economy. They can only do this if the companies themselves are generating enough sales revenue to cover their costs, including wages. So, in their turn, companies spend their 'income' on inputs to their production processes. Because their supply of money is not infinite, they must allocate these inputs as efficiently as possible to keep costs down, and thus to make as much profit as possible. They then spend this profit on wages to their employees and on investment so that they can continue to sell their product and pay their wages in the future.

This is the essence of business, but it is also the essence of economics. Most economics texts will start off with 'economics is about scarcity and choice'. To carry on this tradition, this text is no different (see section 4 below). But business is *also* about the allocation of scarce resources and the decisions that need to be made in order to allocate those scarce resources. In studying economics we learn about the basis on which business decisions rest and we learn about the factors that will influence those decisions.

2   Aims and Objectives

This book has an overriding aim for both students and tutors of economics. It seeks to demystify the subject such that it can be learned (and taught) within the framework of a one semester course as part of a business-related modular degree programme. Naturally its learning objectives are considerably more complex and numerous than that. Among these might be:

- to give you a basic grounding in the first principles of micro- and, where appropriate, macroeconomics, which are seen as underpinning other subjects in the business studies curriculum. The assumption here is that the 'end customers' of this text are studying economics for the first time and are either totally unfamiliar or only vaguely familiar with its tools and concepts. This does not preclude more advanced students of economics, however, who might find the approach refreshing.
- to enable you to use economic tools and techniques in the analysis of real world business problems – in short, to 'think economically'.
- to enable you to understand the interplay between the micro and the macro economies – the impact of government policy on business and the impact of business performance on the health of the economy.

Above all, however, the aim is for all students of economics to enjoy the subject and to realize its importance in the study of business. Economics and economists have had a bad press from academic business gurus, the media and the press recently. At the top of the chapter you saw just a sample of this. It is time that the subject reawakened itself, with confidence, to the fact that it does provide a useful framework within which to study the activities of business.

3 What Do Economists Study?

3.1 Investigation (1)

Very many readers of this text will admit either to knowing nothing about economics or to having found it tedious in the past. Whatever, many will be feeling scared or bored at the prospect of wading through a dense undergrowth of theory with little relevance to the practice of the business world. But take a little time now to think about 'economic' news items. Jot down some of the key words that you hear during these items. This is not a brain-teasing exercise, so you won't gain anything by cheating: there are no 'right' or 'wrong' answers, as you may well have heard different key words from me or some of your colleagues.

You will have come up with words like, 'balance of payments', 'supply', 'demand', 'income', 'interest rate', 'exchange rate', 'market', 'recession', 'Economic and Monetary Union', 'Single European Currency' and so on. You probably know what some of these concepts mean, have a vague idea about some of the others, and wrote the others down without having a clue about what they mean.

All of these concepts are important to economics, and every person, even if he or she is not conversant with the details of the subject, will have a lay-person's knowledge of them. So we all know some economics. The critical factor now is to turn that starter into a working knowledge so that it can be used in the study of business.

4 Economic Rationality, Scarcity, Choice, Opportunity Cost and the Allocation of Resources

We will start our journey through the discipline by looking at the basis on which the rest of the subject rests and by examining the key 'problems' which economics seeks to solve. We go on to look at the way in which economists research these problems.

4.1 Scarcity and Choice

Economics is about scarcity and choice.

Consider a man who has too many hats and not enough room to accommodate them all on his head. He has to make choices. Does he choose a bowler hat? A baseball cap? A sombrero? He may choose to wear several hats at once, but this is not necessarily a decision that gives him the best possible outcome. He has to ask himself questions like, 'Why do I want a hat?', 'What image do I want to portray?' and 'What function will that hat serve?'

Similarly, every student is short of money, which means choices have to be made: a club tonight or an economics textbook? A pair of jeans or two weeks' food? A new CD player or a term's rent? A coffee or a tea after a lecture? And even the richest people cannot have everything they desire because resources are scarce. Thus, while the richest people may not be short of money, the product they wish for may not be available and so they have to choose a substitute commodity.

Given that resources are scarce, how do we make our choices? Economics assumes that we make 'rational' choices. In other words, we will make decisions on the basis of our desire to maximize the amount of satisfaction that we gain from them.

4.2 Utility Maximization

For a *consumer* (i.e. a person buying or choosing things) this 'rationality' is said to be the desire to *maximize utility*. To return to the hat example above, this is the use, the value and the satisfaction that the man gains from his final choice of hat, i.e. the best possible solution to the problem of too many hats.

Very simply, utility is the amount of pleasure or enjoyment we gain from something. So, if you get a huge amount of enjoyment from an economics text as opposed to an evening in a nightclub, then you will spend your money on an economics text. Similarly, if you enjoy driving fast and powerful cars, you will wait until you can afford a Ferrari rather than making do with a Skoda now, because you would not maximize your utility by buying a product that you did not anticipate any pleasure from. Further, if you need a pair of jeans at all costs and are not bothered about the style, you will select a cheap, chain-store brand rather than a pair of Levi's, but if you would not feel good in a pair of cheap jeans, you will delay your decision to buy jeans until you can afford something that matches your tastes.

Utility is not always purely financial, as can be seen. But economists will *measure utility* through the price we are willing to pay for a particular good or service. This is because it is useful to have a tangible value attached to a particular concept. For example, if people are willing to pay high prices for reconditioned VW Beetle cars, then this must mean that they are gaining a high amount of utility (call it enjoyment, pleasure or street-cred!) from driving around in one. This acts as a signal to companies: if people are not paying high prices for their products then perhaps they need either to repackage what they are selling or to reduce the price or both in order to make it more attractive. Similarly, if a product is selling very rapidly and consumers are suddenly willing to pay higher prices, this indicates that tastes have swung in favour of a particular product and the company may need to produce more, and perhaps could charge higher prices.

4.3 Profit Maximization

Companies are said by economists to be behaving rationally when they are maximizing profits.[1]

Maximizing profits means keeping costs as low as possible and making sales revenue as high as possible. Companies will want to charge a price that is high enough to cover their costs but low enough to sell everything that they produce. All their decisions about how to allocate resources will be based on the desire to maximize profit. Thus, if a machine is inefficient using three workers, produces optimally using four workers and becomes inefficient again with five workers, it pays the company to allocate four workers to the machine. Each worker is effectively employed and the machine is producing optimally. This allocation of resources ensures that costs are kept as low as possible without losing any potential output.

4.4 Opportunity Cost

If we make a choice in favour of one good or service, we are automatically forgoing the chance of consuming the product we have rejected, at least for the time being. This is called *opportunity cost* or *the price of something in terms of forgone alternatives*.

This is an important, non-financial (non-pecuniary) cost to bear in mind, both for individuals and for companies. For you as a consumer opportunity cost is all about the cake that you want to have *and* eat. But, because resources are scarce, you can't: you can't go to the nightclub *and* the cinema, you can't eat this week *and* buy those new CDs, you can't go to the cinema *and* buy an economics textbook and so on.

For a company, opportunity cost is all about business potential: an example serves to illustrate the point.[2] Lucas Industries PLC is a large group with interests in automotive components, aerospace and industrial technologies. In the 1980s it decided to restructure its operations in order to stem the tide of losses that it had been making. During the process of strategy formulation it decided on how it would reallocate its internal resources in order to make the organization more effective. It placed greater strategic importance on aerospace and industrial technology and rationalized the automotive division by cutting the workforce and simplifying its structure. It had taken the decision to concentrate on two areas and let the other fend for itself. The opportunity cost was that it was no longer able to put strategic resources behind the automotive division: thus any potential business had to be found by the greater competitiveness of the division itself.

In the case of Lucas this was a good short-term opportunity cost to have incurred. The automotive division duly became more competitive in world markets and has re-established itself as a major player in the automotive industry. Ultimately the company has accrued opportunity *benefits* from the decision to incur opportunity *costs*.

4.5 The Allocation of Resources

Businesses and individuals make decisions about how to *allocate resources* daily. The outcome for the economy is *the allocation of resources*. Lucas allocated its managerial and financial resources to aerospace and technology. You, during the course of this chapter, have allocated your time to economics rather than to marketing or accounts. You may have decided to go out tonight instead of watching television. You may have decided to buy more economics books instead of chocolate. Your colleagues will similarly have made their decisions about how to allocate their scarce resource of time and their scarce resource of money. Companies will also have decided on which products to supply to which markets in response to the signals provided by you, the consumers, and how to organize their managerial resources in order to ensure that they are cost-efficient and so maximizing profit.

4.6 Summary: Deriving a 'Testable' Model

This may seem a little confusing all at once but it can be summarized neatly in the decision tree in figure 1.1.

At a very simple level, the basic 'problem' which economics seeks to resolve is how resources are allocated. Figure 1.1 illustrates the process by which an individual or a company might arrive at a decision to allocate scarce resources. We assume from the outset that people are 'rational'. They will make decisions consistently on the basis of the desire either to maximize profits or to maximize utility. This rationality

 Figure 1.1 An economic decision path derived from the existence of scarce resources.

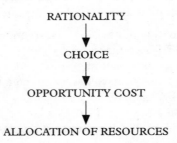

RATIONALITY

↓

CHOICE

↓

OPPORTUNITY COST

↓

ALLOCATION OF RESOURCES

lies at the heart of everything they do, and they make choices accordingly. In making these choices they incur an opportunity cost, which is the cost of what they have chosen in terms of that on which they have missed out. The outcome of their choice is the allocation of resources.

This is a very simple economic model but it shows us how useful economics can be in predicting or interpreting our own actions or the actions of business. The arrows between concepts represent the decision path or strategy that is being followed. We could use this model to structure our analysis of a company's activities. For example, Lucas was making losses – its resources were scarce so it had to make choices. Its aim was to return to profitability, i.e. maximize profits, so it had to reduce its costs. It incurred an opportunity cost: it could no longer sustain the number of employees and the organizational structures in the automotive division. So it allocated its managerial and financial resources to boosting aerospace and technology and allowed automotive the autonomy to return itself to competitiveness.

Economic models are useful tools, then, for analysing business decisions. A business person, for example, will want to know how customers respond to changes in the price of a product, what prices can be charged, how cost changes will affect prices (and, hence, demand) and how competitors are behaving in the market place (the prices they charge and the products they sell). These are the central pillars of company strategy. But they are also the basis of economics. As John Kay has argued, most business people think economics is about forecasting, and, because of the poor track record of economic forecasts, think that it is not a particularly useful discipline.[3] However, *microeconomics* (the economics of individuals, companies and markets) is about identical issues to those of strategic management: prices, demand, supply, markets, costs and competitor behaviour.

5 Investigation (2)

Read the material in the BMW–Rover case studies (cases 1 and 2) carefully and then think about the following questions.

1   In what sense do you think BMW was acting rationally in 1994?
2   What choices did Rover make up to 1995?
3   What opportunity costs have they incurred?
4   Were these opportunity costs less or greater than the opportunity benefits that BMW gained?
5   By 1996 how had BMW decided to allocate its resources globally? What are likely to be the long-term outcomes of this decision?

Rover Heeds Its Master's Voice

The UK carmaker is striving to become a more upmarket brand under its new German owner, says Haig Simonian

Neither the glitz nor the glamour of the competing displays at this week's London Motor Show will distract onlookers at the Rover stand, drawn by the surprise appearance of a modest, but crucial, new car.

Rover's new 200 series – originally expected early next year – is the company's challenger in the biggest and most competitive segment of the European car market: the small family-car market, dominated at present by Volkswagen's Golf and General Motors' Astra.

The decision to bring forward the launch of the 200, the last of the cars developed during Rover's former collaboration with Honda, could be interpreted as a sign of the company's confidence in its future under BMW, the German executive carmaker which bought it in 1994.

However, it may more accurately reflect the pressure facing Rover because of its sharply falling sales and hints of its new German master's growing impatience at the group's disappointing performance.

'BMW can't let a short-term decline in sales turn into a long-term collapse,' says Professor Garel Rhys, professor of motor industry economics at Cardiff Business School in Wales. 'So they're trying to take pre-emptive action to prevent things deteriorating further.'

One of Rover's biggest problems is its falling market share. In the first eight months of 1995, it sold 179,000 cars in the UK, including the Land Rover four-wheel drive brand. This is almost 9 per cent less than in the same period last year, and leaves the company's market share at 11.3 per cent, down from 12.4 per cent for the first nine months of last year.

The company has fared little better in continental Europe. Sales in the 17 west European countries tracked by the European Automobile Manufacturers' Association have fallen almost 12 per cent in the first nine months of this year. That has cut Rover's European market share to 2.9 per cent from 3.3 per cent in the same period last year.

Mr John Towers, Rover's chief executive, professes to be unworried by the falls, however. They are in line with the company's strategy of repositioning itself as a prestige brand rather than a volume producer, he says.

Rover's strategy in the past few years has been to produce a wide range of cars, but to pitch them above competing models from volume manufacturers such as VW and Ford by offering buyers higher specifications and a more exclusive image.

For several years before being bought by BMW, Rover used the German company as its model. Talk at the group's Birmingham head-quarters was of becoming a 'British BMW', combining traditional UK motoring strengths, such as wood and leather interiors, with the advanced engineering and improved quality and reliability gained from its association with Honda.

According to Mr Towers, the 'correct' UK share for a brand corresponding to Rover's aspirations could be as low as 9 per cent. That, he says, would broadly reflect the true level of demand for a prestige marque.

The company is similarly relaxed about its falling registrations in continental Europe – an area it identified until relatively recently as its target market. Rover attributes the decline partly to the disruption caused by its four new model launches this year: a revised version of the Metro compact hatchback (renamed the Rover 100); the MGF sportscar; the 400 Series of lower mid-range models; and the 200 Series.

Moreover, the company's focus, says Mr Towers, is now on world-wide sales. This year, US sales have risen by an impressive 77 per cent to nearly 14,000, while registrations in Japan are up 45 per cent to just under 17,000. That has prompted many analysts to forecast that the group's overall international registrations will reach a record in 1995.

Critics claim the decline in Rover's market share in the UK and continental Europe stems from fundamental misjudgments in its product strategy. They say Rover's vehicles often fall between two stools, rather than being pitched at a particular market segment. The recently launched 400 hatchback, for example, is little bigger than a Golf, but priced

and marketed as a rival to the appreciably larger Ford Mondeo.

Some argue that the problems with Rover's products stem from its relationship with Honda. The company has taken basic Honda designs, and customised them to its own requirements. However, Rover was not able to alter basic factors such as the cars' dimensions or overall design. That inevitably handicapped the company, especially after Honda, once Japan's most innovative carmaker, started to lose direction in its model programme in recent years.

Problems with Rover's dealers have exacerbated its sales difficulties. These are a legacy of Rover's steady decline from being the UK's biggest car company (as British Leyland), when it accounted for about one in three of all new UK car registrations, to its present size.

Rover has culled its dealer network to eliminate many of the smaller garages which no longer meet its new, upmarket image or its higher requirements for facilities and service. However, the process is incomplete. Mr Towers recognises the company still has a long way to go.

However, he stresses changes are under way. In some key markets Rover is building a new network based on bigger, service-oriented distributors, better suited to its present model range.

According to Prof Rhys, Rover's transformation from a mass producer to one concerntrating on upmarket versions of a variety of vehicles will be complete and convincing only when it tackles another of the legacies of its past. In spite of its achievements with Honda in renewing its range, the company is still identified with cheap and compact cars such as the Mini and the Rover 100.

Such workaday vehicles, highly successful in their day, now compromise the prestige brand image Rover is trying to develop. The Metro (dating from 1980) and the Mini (which celebrated its 36th birthday this year) are woefully long in the tooth. Even with BMW's backing, Rover probably lacks the resources to renew the two compact cars and its bigger models at the same time.

On the other hand, many think Rover and BMW would be foolish to let the compact cars wither away. 'BMW would be crazy to let that knowhow and heritage go,' says one stock market analyst.

The probable solution, according to senior executives, is that Rover's com-pact cars will eventually be marketed as a separate brand. 'Mini' is likely to become the trademark for a family of new, BMW-inspired sub-compact hatchbacks built by Rover.

The Mini and Metro replacements would be consciously different cars, trying to capture the same sense of surprise and radical engineering that greeted the original Mini back in 1959.

The splitting of the Mini brand would meanwhile free Rover to concentrate on bigger, distinctively 'British', models, pitched as cheaper, but occasionally overlapping, alternatives to BMW's own upmarket vehicles. This would in turn leave the German marque free to concentrate on the sportier, high-technology saloons which have become its hallmark.

BMW takes the long view

The fall in Rover's sales figures has been interpreted by some rival manufacturers as a factor behind last month's announcement that Mr Wolfgang Reitzle, BMW's head of research and development, would replace Mr Bernd Pischetsrieder as Rover's chairman.

The suggestion was that the change demonstrated BMW was losing patience with its UK subsidiary.

But Mr Reitzle says the move had long been planned and had nothing to do with Rover's sales performance.

He lays emphasis on BMW's long-term approach to the car business, highlighted by its transition from a manufacturer of Italian bubble cars under licence to one of the world's most admired and profitable car manufacturers. Given that back-ground, Mr Reitzle argues, Rover's short-term performance is of marginal importance to BMW's strategy for the company.

Credited as the man behind many of BMW's most successful vehicles, the new chairman will devote much more of his time to Rover than Mr Pischetsrieder, BMW's chief executive and the architect of the Rover acquisition.

He has identified four crucial areas on which the UK company will have to concentrate if it is to meet BMW's expectations.

He expects Rover to achieve relatively rapid improvement in two of these: quality and reliability, and competitiveness. 'Rover's quality and reliability have improved very substantially thanks to Honda. But they are still not up to BMW standards,' he says.

Over the longer term, Rover must expand the geographical range of both its sales and its dealerships. Particularly promising for Rover, according to Mr Reitzle, are markets such as south-east Asia, where BMW's own sales will remain limited because of its relatively high prices.

Finally, Rover must develop new models to complement BMW in the marketplace. This means finding it a distinct niche as a premiumbrand producer, not trying to make the UK company into a 'British BMW'. While some Rovers may be dearer than BMWs, he says, the 'centre of gravity' for Rover's pricing will be below its German parent.

Mr Reitzle foresees Rover evolving along the lines of Audi, the executive-car subsidiary of VW. Audi is a prestige marque, with a strong brand image, which is, however, different from that of BMW. 'Someone who buys a BMW would not buy an Audi,' he says. While BMW tends to appeal to the sportier motorist, Audi remains slightly more conservative.

There are some similarities between Rover and Audi. Both companies specialise in front-wheel drive cars and have a reputation for four-wheel drive technology – although their four-wheel drive vehicles are very different. And both have been innovative with the use of aluminium, rather than steel, for body panels.

Mr Reitzle and Mr Pischetsrieder know they cannot squeeze much more volume out of BMW without starting to take it downmarket. By developing Rover into a complementary brand, they can gain volume while reaping economies in terms of shared components, research and engineering.

One senior motor industry executive from a rival manufacturer believes the Audi model has its merits. He warns, however, that Audi reached its present position as a respected executive carmaker only after nearly two decades of heavy financial support from VW.

'It's very, very difficult to do,' he warns. 'You have to pitch the price and level of the intermediate product just right, and you need someone with enough money to see you through your mistakes along the way.'

The head of motor industry strategy at a leading management consultancy asks whether BMW's shareholders – notably the Quandt family which controls the company – are ready to see BMW to forgo part of its profits (and their dividends) for however long it takes to bring Rover up to Mr Reitzle's standards.

'These things take a lot of time. How will BMW's investors react?' he asks.

From this straightforward example, you have learned how some of the 'jargon' within economics is actually quite useful to understanding the processes by which companies might arrive at a decision on resource allocation.

CASE 2

BMW to Invest $200 Million More in South Carolina Plant

By John Griffiths

BMW, the German carmaker, is to invest a further $200m in its Spartanburg, South Carolina, car plant – its first outside Germany – to expand capacity from 75,000 to 100,000 cars a year.

The expansion will create 500 more jobs at the plant, the sole source of supply for the new Z3 sports car which BMW plans to sell around the world. It also produces 3-Series saloons for the North American market. Current employment is 1,700.

It also adds strength to recent BMW warnings that it would consider increasing output outside Germany to compensate for the rise in the D-Mark and other high costs of producing in Germany.

The additional capacity on the 1,000-acre site will bring BMW's total investment in its South Carolina facilities to more than $800m.

It also indicates that the company is becoming more confident about quality standards at the plant, in a region of the US which has few motor industry traditions.

US executives of the company do not rule out a further expansion of the facilities, to 120,000–130,000 units a year, in the longer term.

Mr Berndt Pischetsrieder, BMW's chairman, says the Spartanburg plant could be 'only the first' of several manufacturing sites outside Germany. BMW already owns Rover Group of the UK.

BMW, whose success in its chosen executive sector market niches is strongly dependent on high quality standards, has taken a cautious approach to building up production levels while training its greenfield site work force.

Initial output when the facilities first opened 18 months ago was only a few dozen cars a week.

The plant is continuing to increase production rates steadily but is not expected to reach 200–250 cars a week until the end of this year. After the expansion the weekly output rate is will reach 400.

The expansion primarily entails larger body production and final assembly areas. Paint plant capacity is already adequate for the higher output. It was described yesterday as 'a vote of confidence' in the South Carolina work force.

6   How Do Economists Study?

6.1   Normative and Positive Economics

You have already encountered the qualitative (or subjective) means by which economists might begin to gather information on a particular issue. The material contained in a case study, such as the example of Lucas or the cases of BMW and Rover, allows us to formulate a preliminary opinion on a particular issue. In your analysis of the case you may well have come up with opportunity benefits like access to the UK market, purchase of Land Rover allowing BMW to widen its product range and even access to the Honda technology which Rover was using until the deal with BMW was struck. You might have come up with opportunity costs like less money available to locate in other areas such as North America, or less freedom to influence manufacturing strategy at Rover than would have been the case had it established a BMW manufacturing subsidiary as opposed to purchasing an existing manufacturing site. You might have decided that the benefits outweighed the costs.

However, you may find that someone else comes up with a different interpretation of the case and comes to the conclusion that BMW misallocated its resources in the purchase of Rover. Neither of you would be wrong, although, of course, the companies concerned would have a lot to say about either interpretation, particularly any inaccuracies or misguided conclusions you may have reached.

In reading a case and drawing some conclusions on the basis of limited data you are being *normative* or subjective. Normative economics is an area of the discipline in its own right. Indeed, the study and interpretation of business decisions is essentially normative in that, without asking very sensitive questions, we cannot be certain from the outside about the real reasons for a particular decision.

Positive economics, in contrast, allows us to be definite about a situation. Let's take our decision-path model as an example. We want to test *empirically* (i.e. on real world data) whether or not people really do behave according to that model. We set up a 'testable' hypothesis; for example, that people will always make choices and allocate resources (a) on the basis of economic rationality and (b) after having weighed up the opportunity costs involved.

We could start our investigation in a normative way by looking at newspaper articles and secondary material on consumer behaviour patterns. This would give us a feeling for the subject and might allow us to make our hypotheses a little more sophisticated.

Having developed our ideas on the basis of this we could then look at some national data on consumer expenditure patterns and published information on the response of consumers to advertising campaigns for example. At this point we could be *positive* in our approach. We could look at the relationship between, say expenditure patterns and advertising campaigns and see if expenditure was altered in any way (suggesting that, perhaps, people's ideas of their utility maximization might be malleable). Using simple statistical techniques we could test our hypotheses using actual data and develop them accordingly.

If we still felt that there were questions that needed answering, we could design a questionnaire asking people about their expenditure patterns. We would derive both normative and positive conclusions from this because the survey would be qualitative (i.e. asking people's opinions on things) but could be numerically classified, allowing us to use statistics.

This type of approach is that taken by many marketing departments when they analyse their sales figures. It is also the approach taken by economists in looking at a very wide range of specific problems. Perhaps this very simple fact gives an indication of why we study economics and why economists are often employed in companies!

6.2 Developing a Methodology

Essentially, then, the 'method' of investigating a problem in economics is exactly the same as for any area of business. The flow chart in figure 1.2 illustrates how we can design a methodology that allows us to be both positive and normative.

Figure 1.2 is only designed as a rule-of-thumb process by which economists and businesses might go about investigating a particular problem. It is perhaps useful at this stage to mention that a good, analytical student project or assignment will also go through a similar methodological process.

6.3 Note of Caution: Using Data

During the course of this book and your wider studies you will come across a wide range of data, some of which will be useful, others of which will not. A summary of these might help you to structure your own thoughts when you have assignments to do, so some of the key types are displayed in table 1.1.

 Research design.

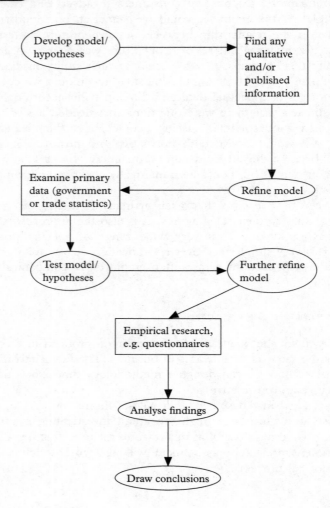

6.4   Investigation (3)

On the basis of the methodological material in the past few pages you might like to look at the following problem.

A large German company is suffering from a lack of motivation among its workforce on the shopfloor. Its level of absenteeism is high and it is finding that its productivity is suffering as a result.

Table 1.1 A quick guide to data

	Use by business	Use by economists	Use in student assignments
Primary data Interviews, questionnaires, 'raw' unpublished statistics – can be either qualitative or quantitative	Identifying market trends and/or testing hypotheses as strategic inputs	Testing models and hypotheses	Supporting information and model testing – essential for research-based project
Secondary data books, published statistics, journals, newspapers, company reports and accounts	Raising awareness of activities of competitors/ establishing background information	Background information and central to formulating hypotheses	Essential to establish a picture of subject area
Qualitative data: opinion surveys, interviews, subjective material	Gauging opinions – for example, of customers – and acting accordingly	Normative: used as support for positive analysis – establishes possible trends	Useful as guide – but use carefully and support with secondary data
Quantitative data: statistics, accounts – no value judgements involved	Used to support qualitative research	Positive: used to test hypotheses and support normative assertions	Use as strong support for any assertions you are making

Examine table 1.2 and then answer the questions below. Some of the questions are positive in scope, others ask you for normative judgements. You might like to think about which are positive and which are normative.

1 Where does the critical problem in absenteeism lie?
2 Is there a difference between genders?
3 What might be the resource implications of such a level of absenteeism?
4 From where might the problems originate?
5 How would you design a research project to investigate this problem further? Think of both positive and normative techniques.

| Table 1.2 | Absenteeism among the workforce at a large manufacturing site[4] |

Type of employee	Absenteeism (% of full allocated time in workplace)
Salaried staff	0–1
Hourly paid – men	10–15
Hourly paid – women	24

7 Conclusions

Economics is a subject which concerns the real business world. It does not need to be heavily technical or boring, as I hope this chapter has demonstrated. We have learned some basic economic concepts which you will be able to apply to your everyday life and to any business cases about which you might read.

Above all in this book we will be trying to construct a picture of business and the environment in which it operates (consumers, government policy and the international context) through elementary economics. The approach is to cover those areas of economics which are necessary to understanding the subject's importance to business, rather than taking an exhaustive (and exhausting!) gallop through every aspect of the discipline. Each of the chapters will cover enough theoretical material to enable you to do this and will provide you with enough data and applied information to see its application in the real world. You will be given case studies and examples throughout, and encouraged to 'think economically' through questions in the text and investigations. Each chapter will conclude with indicative supportive reading so that you can make the most of the material contained in this book.

What should be clear by now is that we study economics because its approach is very similar to that used in business. Its central problem is how resources are allocated, which, of course, is the central problem of business in a highly competitive world. Economists can use both positive and normative techniques to arrive at an answer to this problem, as can business analysts. The main distinction between economics and business is that in economics we use models to formulate our methodology. Economics then becomes useful as a way of describing and understanding business behaviour. And, by using these models as 'tools', economics can act as an organizing framework for strategic analysis *and* as a tool of strategy. The remainder of the chapters in this book examine these models and how they can be used as tools for business as well as tools of analysis.

8 Further Reading

Easterby-Smith, M., Thorpe, R. and Lowe, A. (1991) *Management Research: an Introduction*. London: Sage.
Kay, J. (1996) *The Business of Economics*. Oxford: Oxford University Press.
Ormerod, P. (1994) *The Death of Economics*. London: Faber and Faber.

Notes

1 Company objectives are considerably more complex than this, as mentioned in chapter 6. For the time being, however, it is reasonable to assume that companies will desire to make as much money as possible in order to cover their costs.
2 This case is based on primary research conducted between 1989 and 1992 reported in Harding, R. (1995) *Technology and Human Resources in Their National Context: a Study of Strategic Contrasts*. Aldershot: Avebury.
3 Kay, J. (1996) *The Business of Economics*. Oxford: Oxford University Press.
4 This is a real example, although for obvious reasons the name of the company is not disclosed. See Harding, op. cit., note 2, for further details.

2 Demand and Supply

Teach supply and demand to a parrot and you've got an economist.

(Anon)

1 Introduction

'Buy two, get one free!', 'Taste the paradise!', 'New! Improved!', 'Could you be seen without one?' The advertisements scream at us from posters in the street, from television, radio, newspapers, magazines, sportswear and even our clothes. No one is immune to the pressure to spend money, dress fashionably, drive the fastest car or eat the healthiest foods. Advertising is part of our daily lives, but why do companies undertake it and what do we as consumers gain from it?

Look at how important advertising spend was as a percentage of national income (or gross domestic product, GDP) in a number of European countries between 1987 and 1992, as shown in table 2.1. The table shows some quite stark differences between expenditure on advertising among the European countries listed. For example, Spain spends the most on advertising and saw an increase in advertising expenditure even in the recessionary period of the early 1990s. The UK has one of the highest levels of advertising as a proportion of GDP. It fell during the recessionary period, but was still higher than in the major economies of France and Germany.

Newspapers like the *Financial Times* gain 70 per cent of their total revenue from the space they sell to companies for the purposes of advertising; companies, what's more, are willing to pay £40 000 for a full-page advertisement (or £65 per square centimetre). Prices for prime-time television space go even higher than this. In short, as Porter found in 1990, the marketing industry is one of the major strengths, and drivers, of the UK economy.[1]

Total consumer expenditure in the UK between 1983 and 1993, which showed an increasing trend throughout the period, was as follows:

Year	Expenditure (£ million)
1983	261 200
1985	276 742
1987	311 234
1989	345 406
1991	339 915
1993	348 688

In order to allow for the rate at which prices are increasing (inflation) the figures are adjusted and all expressed in terms of price levels in 1990. This shows a big overall increase in expenditure between 1983 and 1993 of £87 488 million over ten years. It also shows a small fall in expenditure between 1989 and 1991 which is accounted for by the fact that the country was in a recession. In short, we could interpret from these data the fact that individuals are consuming more.

This is not a chapter on marketing, but it is a chapter on the two most basic models of economics: demand and supply. These two concepts are central to the whole of the discipline. Much of what follows

Table 2.1 Advertising as a percentage of GDP

Country	1987	1988	1989	1990	1991	1992
Austria	0.59	0.64	0.73	0.75	0.77	0.77
Belgium	0.48	0.50	0.51	0.51	0.52	0.55
Denmark	0.78	0.82	0.82	0.84	0.77	n.a.
Finland	1.03	1.03	1.06	1.00	0.91	0.90
France	0.67	0.72	0.76	0.78	0.73	0.70
Germany	0.87	0.90	0.92	0.91	0.96	0.99
Greece	0.39	0.46	0.52	0.63	0.68	0.92
Ireland	0.94	0.97	1.03	1.05	1.04	1.07
Italy	0.58	0.60	0.61	0.61	0.60	0.62
Netherlands	0.85	0.85	0.87	0.94	0.92	0.93
Norway	0.94	0.84	0.77	0.74	0.73	0.63
Portugal	0.44	0.55	0.62	0.67	0.74	0.83
Spain	1.01	1.15	1.28	1.37	1.50	1.75
Sweden	0.77	0.83	0.85	0.81	0.72	0.71
Switzerland	1.06	1.09	1.07	1.04	0.95	0.94
UK	1.22	1.28	1.29	1.20	1.09	1.09

Source: Pan European Market 1994.

in this book is based on an understanding of the models of supply and demand. They are also the models that underpin most of marketing. Companies try to change our attitudes to what we wish to buy through their marketing, particularly advertising and branding. They change what we are willing to pay, they create fashions and trends, they make their products seem like necessities while we might have been willing to 'do without' them just last year.

So why do we need a *theory* of demand or a *theory* of supply? Surely it is simple enough: companies produce goods and services to fulfil our needs and wants and we buy them. If we have no money left over at the end of the week then we go hungry, don't we? Buying and selling need be no more complicated than that.

If the answer to this question were, 'we don't need a theory' and, 'yes, buying and selling is simple' then there would be no need for any of the business-related disciplines (for example, marketing, economics, sociology, psychology), and certainly no need for politicians to impose taxes on our income so that we have less money to spend on the things that we really want – like alcohol, tobacco and petrol. We would not necessarily spend money on goods and services that produce a socially or economically desirable outcome for the economy as a whole: would we spend money on education or on health; would we always buy food that is good for us or cars with the most efficient engines; would businesses spend money on the most environmentally friendly production processes, or the cheapest?

There are many questions that arise when we start looking at what we buy and what we sell. The models that are presented here might seem highly abstract and theoretical but they do have their application in business. They are extremely important as tools for marketing as well as for understanding the allocation of resources in the economy. As was discussed in chapter 1, and as will be argued elsewhere in this book, if we use the models in a practical sense to illustrate what is going on in the real world, we can examine the key influences on company and consumer decision-making. Indeed, they become and important aid to company strategy. With that in mind, we turn to the models now.

2   Aims of the Chapter

There are two principal aims of this chapter.

- To give you a basic understanding of two very important theoretical concepts which underpin the rest of economics.
- To give you an understanding of why these concepts are important – in theory and in practice.

By the end of the chapter, you should be able to draw demand and supply curves and use them to make pricing policy recommendations to a company. You will be familiar with terms such as price elasticity and will understand their implications for company decision-making. Above all, it is hoped that you will see the models of demand and supply in the strategic framework within which they operate in business, and realize the contribution that economics can make to understanding company decisions about what to produce, how to produce it, at whom to target it, what price to charge and how to sell it.

3 Interlude: Actors in the Economy

Everyone has needs and wants. You need to eat, you need clothes, you need to drink, you need to have a roof over your head and so on. In order for you to be able to consume the items that are essential to your well-being, you have to choose between the goods and services on offer and allocate your money accordingly, *and* those goods and services have to be available. Similarly, in order for companies to provide the goods and services that people want, they have to buy inputs into their production processes *and* they have to be certain of a basic level of market demand in order to guarantee revenue.

There is thus an interaction between two groups in the economy which is the basis of everything else that happens. These groups are called 'buyers' (in business-speak, consumers or customers) and 'suppliers' (alternatively, companies, firms or businesses). They interact with one another in the market place through their buying and selling activities. At any one time anybody can be both a buyer and a seller (for example, you *buy* a newspaper to read on the train, for which you have bought a ticket to go to work, where you are, effectively, *selling* your services as a factor of production).

But this is moving on too quickly. We will return to markets in the next chapter and we will look at the role of individuals and buyers and sellers in the context of macroeconomics later in the book. For the time being, divide the economy up into just two groups of 'actors': those who buy and those who sell.

4 The 'Buyers': Consumer Demand

4.1 Investigation

Think about the last time you bought something in a shop. Perhaps it was before breakfast this morning when you realized that you had no coffee but that you could not survive for the rest of the day without some caffeine. You walked round to the local corner store and saw an amazing array of coffee in front of you: ground coffee for filters, percolators, cafetieres, coffee beans, Camp coffee, coffee bags, one-cup filter coffee and, of course, instant coffee in all shapes, sizes and prices. How did you make your choice? Make a note of a few factors which might have influenced your decision.

You will have come up with factors like the fact that you had only brought £1.50 with you (income), you only like instant coffee (tastes), you went for the cheapest (price) or you chose tea because it was cheaper and just as full of caffeine, and you would have had to have bought some sugar as well as coffee (the price of substitutes). Think also of the *one* factor that would be most important to you and again compare it with the list. Try isolating one factor for people with different levels of income: would a millionaire be as worried about the price of a jar of coffee as a student?

4.2 Consumer Demand: towards a Formal Model

There are a number of factors that will influence your *individual* demand for a product, as you will have found when you thought about your own demand for coffee first thing in the morning. Among these we can include:

- *Price of the product itself* (P_c) is, perhaps, self-explanatory. Usually, you will buy more of it if it is cheap and less of it if it is expensive, depending on the value that you attach to it.
- *The price of other goods* (P_{n-z}) can be divided into two parts. First, *substitutes* are those goods which compete directly with the product that you want to consume. This might mean real coffee instead of instant or it might mean tea, hot chocolate or even a cold drink if we are talking about your consumption of drinks generally. Second, *complements* are those goods which are consumed with a product in order to enhance the utility that you get from it. The obvious example is coffee and milk and sugar. An interesting point to note

here is how companies will sell complements alongside a product in order to make it seem more attractive – Cadbury's chocolate eggs alongside Tetley tea bags, for example.

- *Your income* (Y) is the reward you get for the performance of a particular task and is usually paid to you in the form of money. In later chapters we will look back at this definition. But for the time being, the important point is that what and how much you demand is determined by your income: there is very little point in demanding a Jaguar if your income will not even stretch to a second-hand push bike!
- *Tastes* (T) are a critical part of what you demand. Your utility is, in part at least, affected by what you like and what you don't like. Fashion influences your tastes, so through their advertising companies are able to influence your demand for goods and services. How many people looked back at pictures of the 1970s and swore that they would never wear flared jeans or platform shoes?
- *Your expectations:* would you buy something if you expected the price to fall? MMX technology enhances the power of the Pentium chip; do you buy a computer without MMX as its price comes down, or do you buy the slightly more expensive MMX computer? Your expectations will be determined both by company advertising and by trends in the economy as a whole. For example, if house prices look set to increase by 7–10 per cent in 1998, and you are thinking of buying a house, it makes sense to buy at the beginning of the year rather than at the end.
- *Actions of government:* government policy affects your attitude to what you buy. Through its actions, a government can influence levels of unemployment (would you buy something expensive if you thought you might lose your job?) and the level of inflation (your attitude to a purchase will depend on whether you think prices will rise in relation to your income, for example). Your income as a student is determined to a large extent by levels of grant and student loan allowed by the government. You may supplement your grant by working in order to buy the things you want.

As economists, we use a shorthand to represent these factors and write demand as a function, or equation, as a checklist for reference. The demand function is often represented by means of the shorthand equation in the middle of figure 2.1. All the equation says is that demand for coffee (or any product for that matter) is a function of the price of coffee, the price of other goods (substitutes and complements), your income, your tastes, your expectations and actions of government.

Figure 2.1   The demand function.

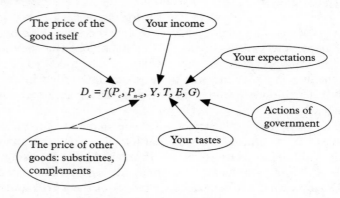

Key: D_c, demand for coffee; f, a function of (or is determined by).

Many people are frightened at the sudden use of abstract symbols like this in an equation. Think of it as a list of items where each item has a shortened form. It then becomes a useful tool for working out what influences demand.

The balance between each of these factors represents an opportunity cost: if the coffee is more expensive, then perhaps you have less of your income to allocate to the purchase of other products (such as milk, sugar or biscuits). In choosing coffee rather than tea you have decided that your utility is maximized by drinking coffee and that you will forgo the other goods in the interests of consuming it. Perhaps it is your tastes that have been most influential in this instance.

4.3   Drawing the Demand Curve and the Concept of *Ceteris Paribus*

There are many factors that will influence your choices; some will be more important than others depending on your level of income. However, for many people, the overriding factor in influencing demand will be price. This is particularly the case for necessities like basic food-stuffs, but even for luxury-type items, the price will determine the quantity that you are able to buy given your level of income. The price that you are willing to pay for a product will reflect the value (or utility) that you place on it – the price of a pair of Levi's jeans is high compared to that of many substitute products but many people pay that price because they maximize their utility by wearing Levi's and will be prepared to forgo other products (more clothes, food or economics textbooks) in order to wear them.

So, we know a little bit about the major influences on demand, and we know that price will be very important for most people. As economists, we like to get a picture of what demand looks like in order to be able to use it as a tool for analysis. To do this, we look simply at the relationship between price and the quantity demanded of a particular good and 'hold all the other aspects constant'. This means that we assume that, at any one point in time, your income is the same, your tastes are the same and the prices of other products are the same (a reasonable assumption for a single shopping trip!).

We call this *ceteris paribus* (or holding all other things equal). The concept is central to economic theory. It is used in order to examine the exact effects of one factor on a situation. Thus, for demand, we assume that the prices of other goods, income and tastes remain the same while we examine the effects of price on quantity demanded. It is a tool in *comparative static analysis*, i.e. where snap-shots of particular situations are taken for comparison with other, similarly static, situations. 'Freezing' the analysis like this is especially useful for projecting the effects of a strategic change (such as in pricing) on the market as it stands at any one point in time.

Generally the relationship between price and demand is seen as negative:[2] as the price goes up, less will be demanded; as the price goes down, more will be demanded. This can be illustrated as in figure 2.2.

Figure 2.2   The demand for a product (e.g. jars of coffee).

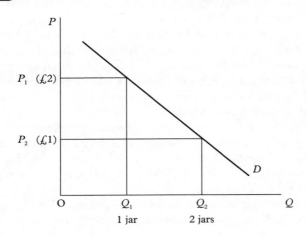

This shows the downward sloping relationship between price and quantity demanded for a normal product (such as a jar of coffee). If the price of a jar is high, say at P_1, consumers will only want to buy a small quantity: one jar, for example. In contrast, if the price of the coffee is low, say at £1, you will be able to buy more, say two jars. The downward slope of the curve is logical: it stands to reason that for anyone with normal expenditure patterns the ideal is to buy as much as possible for as little as possible.

Retail companies have been quick to harness this basic and rational consumer desire with expedient marketing. Electronic Points of Sale (EPOS) allow the quantity of a particular product that has been purchased by a consumer to be counted through at the checkout. This means that a store can not only add up what is being spent, but can also deduct an amount for 'bulk-buying'. You will see this in the supermarket as 'multi-buys', where we are collectively lured into buying more yoghurt or coffee than we actually want because we get the third one free: as it is swiped through the checkout an amount is automatically deducted from your bill. As a customer, you feel good because, on average, you have spent less per jar of coffee and have bought more. Of course, the supermarkets are similarly happy because we have actually bought, and spent, more than we would have done!

4.4   Demand Schedules and Demand Elasticity

It could perhaps be argued that the shape of the demand curve is, generally speaking, intuitive and determined by the nature of the product (but see also note 2). It is economically rational to try to spend as little as possible and obtain as much as possible, and thus, if prices rise, consumers will wish to buy less.

But for any company it is particularly useful to know exactly how demand will change in response to a change in price in order that the effects on revenue can be ascertained. In other words, companies will want to know the price responsiveness (or elasticity) of their product, as this will give an indication of the freedom that the company has to follow pricing strategies through.

In order to establish the price responsiveness (or elasticity) the company can construct a *demand schedule*. This graph plots the exact relation between price and quantity and could be drawn as the result of market research or sales data. Figure 2.3 is a demand schedule for the *Financial Times* (FT) newspaper.[3]

What figure 2.3 shows is the impact on demand of its pricing strategy to charge different prices to different markets. 65 pence represents

Figure 2.3 Demand schedule for the *Financial Times*.[4]

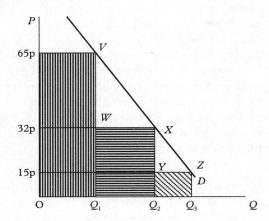

the full cover price of the newspaper. At this price quantity Q_1 is demanded. If the FT were to drop its price to 32 pence a day its demand would be Q_2. The consumers who would have paid 65 pence for the paper are now paying a lower price.

Similarly, if the newspaper were reduced in price to 15 pence a day to the whole market (making it competitive, for example, with other broadsheet newspapers such as *The Times*) its demand would increase to Q_3. But in charging a lower price, it would run the risk of not covering its costs through the amount of revenue it received.[5]

This comes about because the demand for the newspaper is *price inelastic*, i.e. the quantity demanded will increase proportionately less than the corresponding reduction in price. The company is therefore not in the position where it can reduce price significantly in order to increase demand. A more detailed analysis of elasticity is undertaken below, but for the time being, it is sufficient to note that the rate at which demand will change relative to price is an extremely important input into company pricing strategy.

In contrast, *The Times* newspaper has seen its market share increase by 33 per cent following price reduction. Demand for that newspaper is *price elastic*: in other words, it is highly price responsive.

4.5 Summary Features and Strategic Implications

The demand curve, then, has the following features.

- *It is downward sloping to the right for all normal goods*: this means that as the price falls more will be demanded. How much more, as we have seen from the above discussion, will be determined by the price responsiveness, or elasticity, of demand.
- *At higher prices, less will be demanded*: how much less is again determined by the price elasticity of demand.
- *The slope of the demand curve reflects the rate at which demand changes relative to price*: a steep curve, i.e. with a slope greater than one in one (or 45°), shows inelastic demand; that is, the level of demand will not respond much to changes in price. A flat curve, with a slope of less than one in one, illustrates elastic demand; that is, the level of demand will respond greatly to a change in price.

Why is all this important to business? Demand analysis is central to the marketing function of any business and pricing strategy is one of the key implements of an effective marketing strategy. It stands to reason, therefore, that any company will need to know how its level of demand (and hence its market share) will change if the price is altered in any way.

Think again about the case of the quality newspaper market discussed above. How is it that the FT and the *Guardian* managed to maintain a roughly constant market share throughout the price war without reducing their prices? The answer lies in an analysis of the price elasticity of demand. By undertaking this analysis we can see how demand will change if there is a strategy to change price, and thus, the effectiveness of a price change can be evaluated.

Price elasticity is the price responsiveness of demand. For the time being, we will calculate it as shown in exhibit 2.1. Try a calculation of price responsiveness using the data in table 2.2.

This calculation shows that the price elasticity of demand for, say, *The Times* is highest at 1.23 while demand for the FT is highly inelastic at 0.03:

- By reducing its price from 45p to 20p *The Times* increased its demand from 361 991 copies to 528 388 copies. In other words, the newspaper gained market share by reducing its price.
- If the FT were to reduce its price from 65p to 15p for all copies sold it would not see a proportionately large increase in its market share. Its demand rises by only 5823 copies even on special schemes and, as 15p would be a price only slightly above break even, this would not ensure the newspaper's profitability.

Exhibit 2.1 Calculating Demand Elasticity[6]

Price elasticity (i.e. price responsiveness of demand)

$$\pi = \frac{\text{Percentage change in quantity demanded}}{\text{Percentage change in price}}$$

Income elasticity (i.e. income responsiveness of demand)

$$\yen = \frac{\text{Percentage change in quantity demanded}}{\text{Percentage change in income}}$$

Cross elasticity (i.e. responsiveness of demand to changes in the price of other products)

$$\ddot{E} = \frac{\text{Percentage change in quantity demanded of one product}}{\text{Percentage change in the price of another product}}$$

Table 2.2 The price elasticity of demand for the *Financial Times* and *The Times*

Newspaper	Change in demand (%)	Change in price (%)	Responsiveness
The Times	68.50	55.56	1.23
Financial Times	1.75	50.00	0.03

So, if any company is to review its pricing strategy, it has to be aware of the price responsiveness of its product as well as its overall level of demand (or market share). The demand schedule and analysis of price elasticity become key marketing tools. Income elasticity will similarly tell a company how dependent its demand is on the 'feelgood' factor in the economy, while 'cross-elasticity' will tell the company how likely the product is to be replaced by a competitor product if the price is comparatively high. The FT, for example, would have a high income elasticity at the full cover price – consumers would buy the product if they have high incomes but would be less able to buy it on lower incomes. The cross-elasticity, on the other hand, would be low because there is no exact substitute for the product.

Price elasticity and the domestic gas market[7]

The analysis of price elasticity undertaken above is still inexact and will not tell a company much about the profitability of a particular marketing strategy. The slope of the demand curve, even if the demand curve is a straight line, will only give us an indication of the rate at which demand is changing. It will not tell us the exact rate at which demand is changing at different points on the demand curve. The following example of the newly deregulated gas market in the South West of England demonstrates just how useful a more exact calculation can be.

The supply of gas to homes was, until spring 1996, controlled almost exclusively by one company, British Gas. For reasons discussed in later chapters, the market was opened up to competition in April 1996, which allowed customers to choose from nine companies supplying the market, instead of just one. The new companies in the market offered significant price reductions (an average of 20 per cent) and, by December 1996, some 17.24 per cent of the total number of customers in the region had switched to alternative gas supply.

We can calculate the rate at which demand is responding to price changes using these figures and the formula given in exhibit 2.1:

$$\pi = \frac{\% \text{ change in price}}{\% \text{ change in demand}}$$

$$= \frac{17.24}{20}$$

$$= 0.85$$

From this, we can legitimately draw a straight line demand curve with a slope of 0.85, reflecting the aggregate rate at which demand is changing in the market as a whole. This is shown in figure 2.4. The distance between P_1 and P_2 is greater than the distance between Q_1 and Q_2. In other words, the decrease in price (10 per cent) is greater than the proportionate increase in demand (8.5 per cent).

However, this does not imply that it is unprofitable for a company to enter the domestic gas market in the South West on a price cutting strategy. Indeed, at some price reductions it may be that the market is extremely profitable even though consumers are not switching at a particularly fast rate.

Figure 2.4 The rate at which customers are switching to alternative gas supply in the south-west of England.

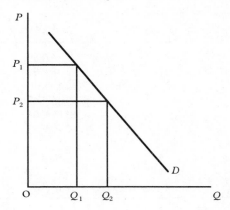

We can conclude this by looking at price elasticity in more detail at each point on the demand curve. In other words, we are simply looking at the rate at which demand is likely to switch at different prices given an overall switch rate of 0.85. To do this we need a formula which will give us the rate at which demand is changing relative to demand *proportionately* at each point. The formula for this is:[8]

$$\frac{\Delta \text{ Demand}}{\Delta \text{ Price}} \times \frac{P}{D}$$

where Δ is 'change in'.

From this, we can derive a table of different elasticities at various price reductions, given an overall switch rate of 0.85, as shown in table 2.3. For a company considering entry to the domestic gas market, this table gives some important information.

- At price reductions between 10 and 30 per cent the elasticity of demand is substantially greater than 1. There will be more customers switching supply than the proportionate reduction in price. At a 10 per cent price reduction, for example, the elasticity is 5.77. That is, 57 per cent of customers may be prompted to switch for an anticipated price reduction of 10 per cent. This is clearly worthwhile in terms of market share and potential revenue gains.
- By the time the price is reduced by 40 per cent, however, the elasticity of demand is approaching unity. This is, for a 10 per cent

Table 2.3	Calculation of elasticity of demand at the switch rate of 0.85

Percentage reduction in price	π *at switch rate* $= 0.85$
10	5.767857
20	3.284091
30	2.125000
40	1.453947
50	1.016304
60	0.708333
70	0.479839
80	0.303571
90	0.163462
100	0.103659

reduction in price, there will be a 10 per cent increase in custom. With this switch rate, any gains that the company makes in terms of market share will be equal to the loss in revenue caused by the reduction in price. There are still some gains to be made at 40 and 50 per cent price reductions, but a company would have more difficulty sustaining the advantages at this price.

• With price reductions above 50 per cent the elasticity of demand is less than 1. Any gains in terms of market share would be offset by greater losses in revenue and it would not be profitable for the company to cut prices by this amount.

4.6   Investigation (2)

The newspaper industry is not the only one to have embarked on an aggressive price war in the past few years. If you have found this analysis interesting and relevant, you may also like to examine pricing in two other industries: the car industry and the supermarket sector of the retail industry.

You might like to think about the following questions on the basis of your investigations:

• How threatened by low-price suppliers like Cost-Co or Aldi are the major supermarkets?
• Do you think the Rover Group was correct to stay out of the price war embarked upon by the major Japanese and American producers in Britain?

• Why could economic theory have predicted the end to the price war in the newspaper industry?

Data for this type of investigation would be both qualitative (based on newspaper articles) and quantitative (based on market reports, such as those published by Mintel).

Once you feel comfortable with the theory of demand and its applications, read on. Take care that you have fully grasped the concept of elasticity and the importance of a demand schedule. This will help you understand the theory of supply.

5   The Suppliers: Company Supply

Economists assume that all companies will behave 'rationally' by maximizing profits. Profit is the difference between revenue and costs:

$$\text{Profit} = \text{Revenue} - \text{Costs}$$
$$\pi = R - C$$

So, if a company is maximizing profits it will seek to keep costs as low as possible (minimize costs) and sell as much as possible (maximize revenue); this concept will be returned to in chapter 5. For the time being, it is a reasonable assumption that most companies will want at least to cover all their costs with the revenue from the sale of their products and will produce at a level to ensure that this is the case.

If companies are to accrue as much revenue as they can, it would seem logical that they would want to charge as high a price as possible for the products that they produce. This obviously contradicts the desire of consumers to spend as little as possible on the products they buy. In the next chapter we examine the market mechanism, which is the means by which this conflict is resolved. Again we, reasonably, assume that companies will want to sell at the highest possible price.

5.1   Investigation (3)

Put yourself in the shoes of the managing director of a small business manufacturing the 'trend' children's toys (Turtles, Mighty Max, Power Rangers, My Little Pony, Polly Pocket etc.) that fill shops around Christmas time. Your product is made of plastic and easy to produce;

it is also fairly easy to switch production from one range to another depending on what is fashionable, as it only involves changing the moulds.

As with consumer demand, your supply will be influenced by a number of factors, such as prices, costs and technology. And, as with demand, you could make your own list of these potential factors, and write them down. Your list might include the price of the product, the price of any substitute or complementary products, the budget of the firm, the aims of the firm (i.e. what it is attempting to do in entering into production), the costs of inputs and the type of technology it employs.

5.2   The Supply Function – towards a Formal Model

Economics says that the following factors will influence individual company supply:

- *The price of the product* (P_a): producer rationality is to maximize profits. In pursuit of this objective, companies will seek to sell as much as possible for as much as possible.
- *The price of substitutes and complements* (P_{b-z}): the price of competitor products is important. For example, if the price of a substitute rises, it will pay the producer to switch production to production of that substitute, thereby reducing supply of product itself. 'Trend' children's toys are a good example of this. Conversely, if the price of a complement rises, producer rationality would be to supply more of the product in anticipation of higher profits.
- *Costs of factors of production* (F): these are central to the analysis of supply. If costs rise then the producer supplies less in anticipation of lower profits. We will return to this in more detail in chapter 4.
- *Goals of the firm* (G): neo-classical economics (i.e. what we are studying here) assumes that the company will have as its main goal the maximization of profits.
- *Technology* (T): the technology employed by the firm will affect costs and productivity and, thus, supply. If technology improves, we can predict that the company will want to supply more.
- *Budget of the firm* (Y): in the long term the company cannot produce beyond its budget or income. While in the real world many companies borrow in order to be able to produce at higher levels, this position is unsustainable if the increase in production volume is not met by an increase in sales revenue.

Figure 2.5 The supply function.

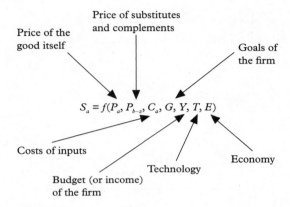

$$S_a = f(P_a, P_{b-z}, C_a, G, Y, T, E)$$

Key: S_a, supply of toys; f, a function of (or is determined by).

- *The economy (E):* as we have already noted in this chapter, the economic health of the nation will have a profound effect on the company's ability to supply to a market. If interest rates are high, for example, this makes the cost of borrowing higher and will tend to depress supply (we return to this in chapter 10).

The supply function equation is given in the centre of figure 2.5. Again it is simply a shorthand to demonstrate the complexity of factors that might influence supply.

5.3 Drawing the Supply Curve

As with demand, we show the relationship between the price of the product and the quantity supplied of that product, holding all other aspects constant for the time being (figure 2.6). This shows an upward sloping relationship between price and the quantity supplied – in other words, as the price rises, the company will want to supply more to the market in anticipation of greater revenue.

If the price is set at P_1 (say, £3.99 for one plastic pony), the company will produce (and hence try to sell) the quantity Q_1 of the product. If the price rises, say to P_2 (£4.99 for each), then the company will supply (and try to sell) Q_2, i.e. more than Q_1. In other words, the higher the price, the more the company will produce in anticipation of higher profits, *ceteris paribus*.

Figure 2.6   The company supply curve.

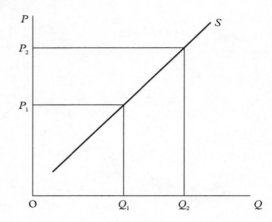

5.4   Supply Schedules and Supply Elasticity

Any company will want to know exactly the relationship between the amount it supplies and the price in order to calculate its anticipated revenue. It is likely, then, that the supply schedule showing an exact relationship is likely to be of most use to the company.

Using our FT example again, we can illustrate how a company, quite rationally, will want to supply more at higher prices than at lower prices (figure 2.7). At 15 pence per copy the FT will only supply Q_1 copies, at 32 pence Q_2 copies and at 65 pence Q_3 copies. It supplies more at a higher price because it wishes to maximize profits.

5.5   Supply Elasticity[9]

As with demand, the extent to which supply changes as a result of a change in the price of the product (i.e. the price responsiveness of supply) is called the price elasticity of supply. As with demand it is calculated by dividing the percentage change in quantity demanded by the percentage change in price. It might seem that this is of lesser importance, but an example will demonstrate how supply elasticity changes as company strategy changes.

Look again at figure 2.6. It shows the elasticity (or prices responsiveness) of the supply curve for the FT. In this diagram it is shown as fairly elastic; in other words, a relatively small reduction in price will result in large amounts less being supplied to the market.

Figure 2.7 The supply curve for the *Financial Times*.

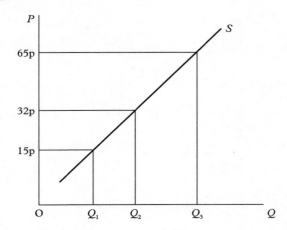

However, the company launched its Higher Education Programme (HEP) in 1993/4. Under this scheme the newspaper was sold at 15p a copy to students in higher education establishments. This scheme was aimed at creating customer loyalty among a group of people who would not normally be able to afford the full cover price of the newspaper. Normally, this strategy would be approached entirely from a demand perspective, and this text takes that approach in chapter 6.

However, there are some important supply considerations in this decision as well. The company has effectively changed its strategy and, in so doing, has incurred opportunity costs, as we saw in chapter 1. Its goal has not changed (it still wishes to maximize profits) but its strategic means of achieving that goal has changed – it now supplies a slightly larger niche at three separate prices. Its supply becomes more inelastic – a small reduction in price will only result in a small reduction in the amount supplied to the market.

The decision to launch this scheme was driven by good marketing considerations and involved a change in the strategies of the newspaper. Instead of concentrating entirely on a niche market, it was attempting to widen that niche by accessing a group of people who would not normally be able to read the newspaper, but who might be future readers. It had changed its strategies and, hence, had changed the readiness with which it supplied newspapers at a lower price.

In attempting to increase its circulation it is, effectively, making its supply curve more inelastic, as shown in figure 2.8. The company is

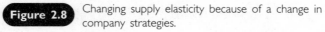

Figure 2.8 Changing supply elasticity because of a change in company strategies.

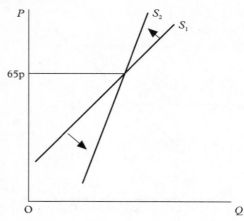

initially operating on a supply curve S_1, which is fairly elastic. Because of the increased emphasis on the marketing of the HEP programme, the company has, effectively, changed its strategies towards its own profit maximization. It has decided that, in the interests of creating brand loyalty among a group that would otherwise only read the paper sometimes, it is prepared to sell more at a lower price where previously it would not have reduced its prices, in order to protect its niche image. Its supply curve has changed its elasticity from S_1 to S_2.

However, the company wants to ensure that it continues to sell the same number of copies at its full cover price of 65p, as this guarantees that its costs are covered. The two curves will therefore intersect at that price.

Let's look now at an example of supply which became perfectly elastic because of pressure from its competitive environment.

During the 1980s Lucas Diesel Systems at Sudbury went through some major organizational changes in order to reduce overall costs, including more than halving the size of the manufacturing site and the total workforce. Simultaneously, the company was subjected to changes which were occurring in the industry as a whole, whereby automotive assemblers were able to dictate the prices (as well as quality and quantity) at which a component manufacturer supplied to them. If the component manufacturer failed to supply at the correct price and quality, its contract with the assembler would not be renewed – thus undermining its market share.

Figure 2.9 Perfect elasticity of supply.

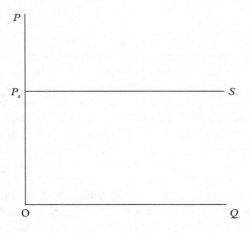

What Lucas, and other components manufacturers, experienced was enforced perfect price elasticity, as shown in figure 2.9. In other words, the company had to supply at the price set by the automotive assembler, P_a, and had to supply the amount specified. It had little or no flexibility to change its strategy without fundamentally undermining its own market position.

5.6 Summary Features and Strategic Implications

The supply curve has the following features:

1 It is upward sloping to the right for all normal goods, reflecting the producer's desire to sell more at higher prices and less at lower prices in order to maximize revenue.
2 At higher prices more will be supplied.
3 The slope of the curve reflects the price elasticity, or price responsiveness, of the product.

As we will see later in the book when we discuss markets and costs, the supply of a product is considerably more complex than simply the price at which it is desirable to sell. However, the relationship between price and quantity supplied presents the marketing departments of companies with useful information about how much can realistically be produced at particular prices in order to guarantee that costs are covered. Without this information the marketing department would risk undermining profitability through pursuing a pricing strategy.

5.7 Investigation (3)

Supply elasticity is extremely important because it gives an indication of how profitable the company is likely to be. If, as in the FT case, supply can be made more inelastic without actually losing revenue from the full price of the product, the company can accrue a number of advantages. The 'opportunity cost' of such a decision might be that profitability at the full price is slightly eroded but there is a gain in long-run customer loyalty, which eventually will increase profitability. On the other hand, the Lucas case demonstrated that sometimes companies might have to supply any amount of the product at a constant price simply in order to remain in the market. The 'opportunity cost' of doing this might be making a loss for the duration of this strategy.

Select an industry with a large advertising profile (the automotive industry or the financial services industry are good ones). Using data from the Marketing Yearbook, Mintel and government publications (the Central Statistical Office publishes data on consumer expenditure), examine the following:

- Trends in consumer demand.
- Pricing: have prices gone up or down?

What can you conclude about the responsiveness of supply and demand to price changes? What do companies gain and lose from changing their prices?

6 Conclusions

The cases used for demand and supply elasticity show just how important the two concepts are in the overall business strategy of a company. Demand analysis is a central pillar of the marketing function; analysis of the demand curve will tell a company a lot about the nature of demand for its product; for example, its price responsiveness, income responsiveness and how tastes are changing. And, as a result, the company will be able to formulate short- and long-term pricing strategies. As we saw from the case of the newspaper market, a company can follow a price-cutting policy to gain market share if its demand is price elastic. But we also saw that this type of policy would erode profitability and, therefore, only be sustainable for a short period.

Similarly, no company's strategy is complete without an analysis of its internal capacity and, particularly, the responsiveness of supply to price changes. It was seen that a company can manipulate its elasticity of supply by changing its goals, perhaps to become more sales-driven with the long-term goal of increasing profitability. While this is not a prediction that would be derived from orthodox neo-classical economics, it is a valid use of the model to analyse actual trends and strategies in business.

7 Further Reading

Read the article which looks at attempts by Hindustan Lever to increase its sales in India (case 3), then think about the following questions. While the article will not enable you to make exact calculations, say of elasticity, it will give you the scope to think about the models discussed in this chapter in the context of a real business problem.

1 How price elastic do you think consumer demand for household products is in rural India?
2 What other factors are important in the consumption of household products in rural India?
3 How elastic is the supply of these goods to rural India?
4 Do you think the nature of demand or the nature of supply is the more important factor for Hindustan Lever in making decisions about how to supply these products?

CASE 3

Mapping out Sales to India

Stefan Wagstyl examines a computer system which is set to transform marketing to rural communities

Farming families living in the dusty village of Chajjahpur on the plains of northern India only buy a few dozen bars of soap and packets of detergent a week from Haresh Kumar's shop.

It is five miles from the dirt tracks of Chajjahpur to the nearest metalled road and ten miles to the nearest town. But 700 miles away in Bombay a man with a computer is keeping tabs on Mr Kumar's sales.

With a few taps on his keyboard, Rajendra Aneja can call up a map of India on his computer screen. A few more taps and he gets a blow-up of a single state, then a district, then a group of villages and the roads and tracks which connect them. Points show the location of individual shops. If he chooses, Mr Aneja can pick out Chajjahpur and the small store Mr Kumar inherited from his father as a blob on the map.

As general sales manager of Hindustan Lever, India's largest consumer goods maker and the local affiliate of Unilever, the Anglo-Dutch combine, Mr Aneja is putting the finishing touches to a system which he believes could transform rural marketing in India – and in other large developing countries. By displaying individual villages and roads on an electronic map, he and his colleagues can plot the best way to supply and service a vast network of rural outlets.

Hindustan Lever, which has developed the system over the past three years, is gradually extending the use of computerised maps. Unilever group executives are so impressed with the scheme's potential that they have already offered it to Unilever affiliates elsewhere. 'Ours is the only system of its kind in the world,' claims Mr Aneja.

Details of the mapping techniques are a commercial secret. But, in general, the information for the maps is gathered mainly by the company's 2,300 stockists – self-employed wholesalers who often work exclusively for Hindustan Lever. They file handwritten sales reports which form the basis of the computer data. The crucial advantage of the map displays is that they enable managers to see at a glance information which would otherwise be buried in separate files.

If the network operates as planned, it will reinforce the crucial bridge between head office managers and the customer – a link which is particularly difficult to maintain in developing countries with large rural populations and poor communications. It will also help Hindustan Lever to bring to bear a formidable range of marketing techniques as – following the partial liberalisation of the Indian economy – the company prepares for full-blown competition with its international rivals, notably Procter & Gamble of the US. Rural markets are mushrooming in India for basic household goods such as packaged foods, soaps, detergents, and cosmetics. In Chajjahpur, population 8,000, there are now 25 shops. With over 600m of India's 900m people living in the villages, the potential demand is enormous. The actual demand is growing fast as some 15m people a year are entering into the cash economy, according to Hindustan Lever. The company estimates rural sales are growing twice as fast as urban – or at about 15 per cent a year.

Hindustan Lever has the country's largest sales network, serving 40 per cent of the population. By 1995 it hopes to serve 70 per cent – reaching every village with a population of 1,000 or more, via its network of stockists. The stockists visit outlets weekly in urban areas and once a fortnight in the villages, bringing goods mainly by van or scooter. In remote roadless districts, suppliers resort to donkeys, camels and even elephants. In urban districts, marketing is mainly carried out through television, radio and newspaper advertisements. But Mr Aneja estimates 400m people, mainly those in small villages, have little or no access to the mainstream media. To reach these people, marketing executives rely heavily on word-of-mouth. Mr Aneja says that when Mrs Indira Gandhi was assassinated news of her death reached even remote villages in six hours. Product information will not travel nearly as fast, but it will be conveyed, for example, by shopkeepers like Mr Kumar in Chajjahpur who travel frequently to buy goods from wholesalers.

Hindustan Lever supports its retailers with direct campaigns in the villages. The group has 1,200 promotion vans, mounted with loudspeakers and painted with advertisements for its best-selling brands such as Lifebuoy soap and Rin laundry soap. When one called in Chajjahpur recently, the salesman's job was to promote Rin. He produced a dirty handkerchief and proceeded to launder it in front of about 20 bored-looking villagers. When he had finished he offered Rin for sale, with a free box of matches. He sold about 10 bars and moved on.

Hindustan Lever also has a fleet of 115 cinema vans, each equipped with a projector and screen. The vans show clips of Indian films interspersed with advertisement films. Mr Aneja says these films are specially-made for rural audiences. The 10-second long television advertisements are too short; villagers need films of at least a minute or two if they are to get the message.

A typical advertisement shows two village wrestlers grappling, one in a snow-white loin cloth the other in a greyish one. Needless to say, the man in white wins. The loser's wife scowls at the winner's and says: 'You must have washed his clothes twice.' The winner's wife answers: 'No. I just used Rin.'

Mr Aneja says rural advertisements must carry simple messages. He argues that villagers, like anyone else, will quickly associate with familiar images – scenes from popular cinema films, from religious stories, from dances and folk customs, all work well.

Among the advantages of the new computerised maps is that Hindustan Lever will be able to target its marketing campaigns more accurately.

Executives will be able to plan the routes for the promotional and cinema vans more effectively and to judge the results more easily. As Mr Aneja says: 'We have to combine twentieth century methods with the needs of eighteenth century village life.

Notes

1 Porter, M. (1990) *The Competitive Advantage of Nations*. London: Macmillan.
2 The analysis here is kept as simple as possible. However, economists identify different types of goods that exhibit different relationships between price and quantity demanded. Thus, for example, the negative relationship between price and quantity demanded holds for 'normal' and 'inferior' goods, but not for 'Giffen' goods. With a Giffen good, a rise in price actually makes it more exclusive and hence more attractive; the relationship between price and demand is positive. Further, as a household's income rises, it is likely to buy more 'normal' goods (shifting demand) and fewer inferior goods (for example, choosing butter rather than margarine).
3 Data in this section were compiled as part of a student project supported by the *Financial Times* in conjunction with its Higher Education Programme. The author is grateful to staff of the FT and to students on the BA Business Studies and BA International Business at the University of Brighton for comments on drafts of this chapter.
4 Based on 1995/6 prices.
5 Total revenue at any one price is represented by the shaded area under the demand curve (this is the price charged multiplied by the number of customers buying the product). Thus for the price 65p, the revenue received by the FT is the shaded rectangle, $O65pVQ_1$. At 32p the revenue is the rectangle $O32pXQ_2$. At 15p, the revenue is $O15pZQ_3$.
6 These calculations give demand elasticity at any one point on the demand curve (point elasticity). As is shown in the gas industry example, actual elasticity is different at different points on the demand curve and this is in itself an important indicator of the profitability of a given price strategy.
7 This section is based on consultancy work undertaken between 1996 and 1997. The author is grateful to Lynda Dunford and Dennis Harding for their input.
8 A proportionate figure for price and demand is used in this calculation, i.e. $(P_1 + P_2)/2$ and $(D_1 + D_2)/2$, i.e. taking the midpoint between two points on the line.
9 As with elasticity of demand, the elasticity at each point on the curve will be different. The analysis here relates to an overall rate of change in order to explain the strategic importance of elasticity of supply.

3 The Market Mechanism

You can't buck the market.

(Rt Hon. Margaret Thatcher MP, 1979)

I Introduction

The bedrock of government policy since 1979 has been the faith in the idea that 'markets work'. In essence, this is the belief that demand and supply, as described in chapter 2, describe accurately the 'rational' behaviour of individual consumers and individual companies. We can therefore look at how demand and supply interact with one another to determine prices in individual markets and assume that this can be aggregated to the level of the national economy as a whole. From this a *laissez-faire* (or non-interventionist) model of economic management develops where economic power rests in the hands of businesses and consumers through their demand and supply decisions.

We will return to the issues of economic management in the second half of this book, but it is useful to realize that, even at this early stage, we can already explain much of what has been happening in the country over the past 18 years. By the end of this chapter you will understand how prices are determined and how this model has been used as a basis for government policy in preparation for a more detailed study of policy later on.

1.1 Interlude: the Micro and the Macro Economy

Some readers may be puzzled by the sudden leap into policy that is being made here. After all, this is surely a book about economics and business, so why is the whole economy important?

As economists we make a distinction between the 'micro' economy and the 'macro' economy. The micro (or 'small') economy means individual markets and industries. We look at the interaction between the buyers and the suppliers, say of cars or newspapers, initially in terms of the determination of the prices of particular products, but also in terms of changes in the market such as a rise in overall levels of income, a change in tastes or an increase in the costs of production. We can also look at the competitive structure of the industry (i.e. the number of firms producing substitute products) and predict how that will affect the freedom of the individual company to make strategic choices over how much to supply to a market and the price it should charge. The micro economy is at the heart of the study of business and, as a result, the focus of the first seven chapters of this book is on that.

The macro economy (meaning 'large' or 'whole') is no less important to the operations of business, however. As macroeconomics is about the sum of all the individual markets in the economy (*aggregate* demand and *aggregate* supply), the operation of each individual market place obviously has an impact on the health of the whole economy. Many will have read commentaries on the recession of the early 1990s which argue that problems originated in the housing market, where prices were rising out of proportion with prices elsewhere.[1] Indeed, if you conducted the investigation at the end of chapter 2 you may have found a similar trend. Others will have watched the car industry with interest and observed that, as unemployment rises and mortgage payments on homes increase, 'luxury' items like brand new cars are difficult to purchase. It is clear that the actions of individual businesses and consumers will, added together, have an effect on the whole economy.

But it is similarly clear that the health of the nation as a whole will affect the ability of companies to operate effectively. High inflation (loosely meaning rapidly increasing prices) can push up costs of supplies and even of labour. A firm producing cars, for example, cannot be certain of the link between price and the quantity that it is profitable to supply to the market, because costs are rising. High unemployment might reduce the disposable income of consumers, which, in turn, can affect individual market demand severely (the housing market is a particularly good case in point here).

2   Aims and Objectives

This chapter has the overall aim of introducing the model of the market mechanism to you so that, by the end of the chapter, you will understand how prices are determined. Under this general aim are a number of objectives:

1 To enable you to reproduce and understand the model of the market mechanism.
2 To give you a basis for understanding the interaction between the micro and the macro economy through the market mechanism and, hence, through the operations of business.
3 To enable you to understand the importance of this simple theoretical model in dictating economic policy at micro and macro levels around the world.
4 To enable you to understand the practical application of the model to different economic systems around the world.

3 Investigation (1)

Assume for a moment that you are a craftsperson selling small ceramic pots at fairs around the country. There are, obviously, other people selling craft products at these fairs and it is a reasonable assumption that there will be similar pots for sale at each one you attend. You will want to set a price that will both guarantee that you cover your costs and make enough money to live on. Having set a 'best possible' price, you will then decide how much to take to each fair to sell. Think about the following questions.

• What will happen if this price is too high and no one buys your pots?
• What will happen if the price is too low and you sell out quickly?

What is important here is to realize that you as a producer cannot make the decision to supply at a particular price without taking into account the nature of your demand. Unilaterally setting a price that is too high will mean that people chose the pots at another stall while if your price is too low, you will sell out and then customers will go to the other stalls to spend their money.

4 Formal Presentation of the Model

The model of the market mechanism dates back to the classical economics of Adam Smith.[2] It is the model upon which the rest of

economics rests; understand this and you can also grasp the end objectives of some of the other, more complex, areas of economic theory.
Very simply, it tells us that buyers and suppliers will 'meet' in the market place, i.e. the place where a particular good or service is bought
and sold. In the market place buyers and sellers of a product communicate how much of a product they want to buy or sell through
prices: firms want to sell large quantities at high prices while consumers will want to spend as little as possible and buy as much as
possible. If the price is too high, they will not buy! The price will have
to come down if producers are to shift unsold stock.

Effectively, then, the interaction of buyers and sellers is telling us
how resources will be allocated: the level of consumer demand in a
particular market tells producers how much will be demanded at different prices and therefore tells them how much to supply to that market in order to ensure that all produce is sold.

Check that you are familiar with the models of consumer demand
and producer supply covered in chapter 2 by answering the following
questions:

1 For a normal product (say an item of clothing) what will happen
   to demand if prices rise?
2 For the same product, what will happen to demand if prices fall?
3 Will producers tend to supply more or less to a market at higher
   prices?

Your answers to these questions will have given you an apparent paradox: that producers want to supply at high prices and consumers want
to buy at low prices. How can we reconcile this difficulty and come
to a solution where all that is produced is sold?

The answer, of course, lies in putting the two curves on one diagram and locating the price at which the price charged is equal to the
price that consumers are willing to pay. Chapter 2 drew up curves for
individual demand and supply. If we add up all the individual demand
curves for a particular product we arrive at the market demand for
that product. Similarly, if we add up all the individual supply curves
of firms producing a particular product we derive the market supply
of that product.[3]

Take, for example, the market for electric fans during the summer.
You will want to keep cool and will buy a fan in order to assist you.
Other people will think the same way and will make purchases accordingly. All the demand added together is the total market demand for
fans at any one point in time. Similarly, you can buy an electric fan

Figure 3.1   Supply of and demand for electric fans.

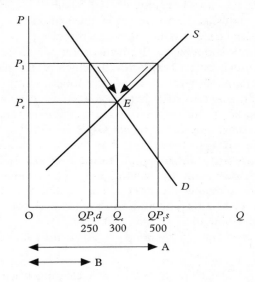

from a variety of manufacturers, but they all perform essentially the same task; the sum of all the electric fans produced in the market is the market supply.

Consumers will want to pay a price for them that is reflective of the utility that they gain from buying them: a cooler workplace or home might mean greater efficiency in performing the tasks of the day, for example. However, if the price rises too high, consumers of electric fans will find alternative ways of keeping cool; for example, opening the window, drinking iced water or buying ice cream. The demand curve is downward sloping to the right, as shown in figure 3.1.

Suppliers of electric fans would anticipate that consumer demand would be highest in the summer and less price elastic (in high temperatures rational behaviour is to keep cool, perhaps at the expense of shorter-term measures). The supply curve will be upward sloping to the right. They will want to charge as high a price as possible in anticipation of greater profitability in the summer months (shown by the price P_1).

At P_1 the amount that the company will want to supply is greater than the amount that consumers will want to buy. At price P_1 the company will supply QP_1s fans. In this particular market that is 500 electric fans. However, at this price only QP_1d fans will be demanded. In this market that is 250 fans. The difference between the quantity supplied and the quantity demanded (i.e. 250 fans) is the excess supply to the market. There is a surplus of 250 fans.

The same point can be made using the symbols on the diagram. Arrow A represents the distance between the origin, O, and QP_1s, i.e. the total quantity supplied by the firm producing electric fans at the price P_1. It is much bigger than arrow B which represents the distance between the origin, O, and QP_1d, i.e. the total quantity demanded of electric fans. In other words, there is a surplus of supply of electric fans in the market place: supply is greater than demand. The excess supply is represented by the distance $OQP_1s - OQP_1d$.

To return to the real case again, it is clearly unsatisfactory for the company to have a surplus of supply to the market, especially in summer when demand should be at its highest. The company can resolve the situation by reducing the price it charges for the electric fans. If it reduces the price to P_e, then companies will supply 300 fans and 300 fans will be bought.

Point E is called the *equilibrium point*. At it, the following conditions will be met:

1   The price will be equal to the market clearing price of P_e.
2   The quantity supplied (Q_e) will equal the quantity demanded (Q_e).
3   The market will clear: there will be no excess demand and no excess supply.
4   The price mechanism (i.e. the interaction of supply and demand in the market place) will have allocated resources to ensure that supply equals demand and that the market clears.

Now look at the market for electric fans where the price is too low, as shown in figure 3.2. As can be seen from the diagram, this time the price that the producers are charging in the market place is too low. At that price they do not want to provide particularly large quantities – only 250 fans – but consumers, thinking that the price is cheap for the utility they will gain from the fans, demand 500 units. The difference, 250 units, is the excess demand in the market place. The level of demand is not satisfied at price P_1.

Again, we can express this in terms of symbols. Arrow A represents total market demand for electric fans, the distance OQP_1d. It is much longer than arrow B, which represents total market supply, the distance OQP_1s. The difference between the two, $OQP_1d - OQP_1s$ is the excess demand in the market place.

In this situation, where there are shortages of supply in the market place, there will be upward pressure on prices. As prices rise some

Figure 3.2 Interaction of supply and demand: price too low.

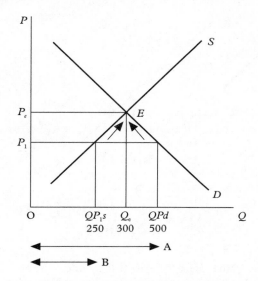

consumers will not consider the purchase necessary in order to max-imize their utility and will decide not to buy electric fans. At the equi-librium price, P_e, again, demand will equal supply; prices will have risen to a level where the market clears at 300 units. There is no unsold stock and no excess demand.

5 Shifts in Demand and Their Effect on the Market

Until now we have looked only at the relationship between demand, supply and price. There are, of course, many complicating factors that make it unrealistic to keep our discussion simply to this. For example, many of you will have experienced the heat of the summer of 1995 and wanted to keep cool at any price. The market demand for electric fans rose substantially, but it was not because prices of electric fans fell. Throughout the whole period, the prices on aggregate remained the same.

How can we explain this? The answer is that demand *shifted*. In other words, the level of demand increased irrespective of price. At the prevailing market price for electric fans more were demanded. Looking back at the demand curve, we argued that demand was a

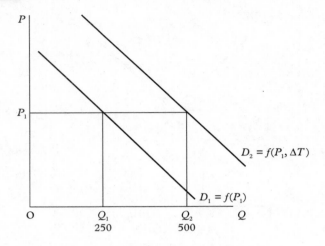

Figure 3.3   A shift in the demand curve.

function of price, the price of substitutes and complements, income and tastes. To draw the demand curve we looked simply at the relationship between price and quantity demanded, as with the curve D_1 in figure 3.3.

Demand curve D_2 is identical to D_1 in every respect except its position on the diagram. Its elasticity is the same (the two lines are parallel). This means that the price responsiveness of demand will be exactly the same – people will decide that the price does not reflect their utility in exactly the same way as they will for demand curve D_1. So why is D_2 further out on the chart?

D_2 represents a shift in demand for electric fans when one of the other factors in the demand curve has changed. The change could be in the price of substitutes – perhaps ice cream has suddenly become very expensive, for example, and provides only a short-term solution to the problem of over-heating. Indeed, on 21 August 1995, the *Financial Times* reported that 'the equivalent of a litre of Häagen-Dazs ice-cream costs £10.90, or £2.24 more than the same supermarket's vintage port'.[4] It could be a change in income – perhaps the saving accrued over the year for the summer holiday could be spent on fans instead. Perhaps it was simply a change in tastes: people will always want to keep cool in hot weather, but prolonged periods of hot weather meant finding long-term solutions to the problem. Whatever happened, the total market demand for electric fans shifted from D_1 to

Figure 3.4   A shift in demand for electric fans in a heat wave: the effect on the market.

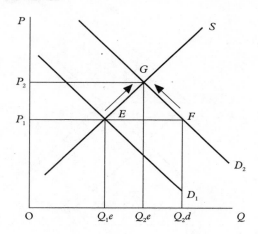

D_2. At each prevailing price (P_1), more fans were demanded (Q_2 as opposed to Q_1).

Look now at figure 3.4 to see how this affects the whole market for electric fans. The diagram shows the two demand curves in relation to the prevailing market supply. Initially the equilibrium was at E where the price P_1 guaranteed that the quantity supplied and demanded was equal, so the market cleared (Q_1e). There is a shift in demand because of the hot weather which makes substitute methods of cooling down seem expensive and tastes change to favour long-term methods of keeping cool. The curve now moves to D_2. At price P_1, Q_2d will be demanded. Q_1e is still being supplied so there is a shortage in supply of $OQ_2d - OQ_1e$. On 21 August 1995 the 'fan famine' was such that some shops were selling out.[5]

Economics predicts that in the short term the pressure would be on suppliers to increase prices in order to reduce demand. Demand elasticity remains the same, so increasing the price to P_2 reduces the demand for fans to Q_2e and creates a new short-term equilibrium.

In the longer term, however, there would be a large number of consumers who do not have their demand satisfied at price P_2. There is every incentive for producers to supply more to the market in anticipation of yet higher profits. This scenario is shown in figure 3.5.

In reality, firms are likely to try to meet the market demand for a product like electric fans, as this increases their potential for maximizing profits. They will do this in preference to increasing prices in

Figure 3.5 The market for electric fans after a shift in supply.

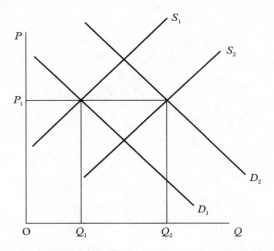

the short term, not least because it creates a bad 'image' for them if they are seen to be exploiting a situation. As quickly as possible the supply curve will also shift, this time downwards to the right, such that more is supplied at each prevailing market price. A shift in supply cannot happen overnight – it involves increasing the numbers that are produced, which might, in turn mean altering tooling on the shopfloor and shifting personnel around. In the very long term it might even involve employing more machines and people.

6 Summary and Relevance to Business

From all of this we can draw out the following summary points to remember

1 The sum of individual demand and individual supply decisions for a particular product is the market demand and supply of that product.
2 For a normal product, with a demand curve that slopes downwards to the right and a supply curve that slopes upwards to the right, consumers and producers will interact in the market place to determine the price of a product.
3 The equilibrium price of a product is that price at which the market clears: it is the price at which the quantity demanded is equal

to the quantity supplied. There is no unsold stock and no un-satisfied demand so prices will be stable in the long term.

4 The equilibrium price for a product is found through the inter-action of supply and demand and is the point at which the two curves cross, or intersect.

5 Demand will shift if a factor in the demand function other than price changes. If the price of substitutes rises relative to the prod-uct, or if the price of complements falls, or if incomes rise or if tastes change in favour of the product, more will be demanded at each market price. The demand curve will shift outward to the right.

6 If demand shifts outward to the right then there will be a short-term shortage of the product. If this happens, prices might rise to restrict demand during the period of that shortage, but ultimately companies will prefer to increase supply in the long term.

All this may seem quite theoretical and abstract so we should take a closer look at how businesses might use the model of the market (or price) mechanism.

The first point is that companies will always want to look at the nature of demand in the market place. As was argued in chapter 2, examining the price responsiveness of demand and the level of demand is a key task of any marketing department. Charging the 'right' price for a product is an extremely difficult business problem. As the model tells us, if the price is too high consumers will not buy; if the price is too low consumers may buy too much. It is not good business prac-tice to set a price for a product which does not reflect supply poten-tial, as this will lead to high storage costs if supplies are unsold, and unsatisfied and frustrated customers if there is no surplus capacity to meet high levels of demand from low prices. Only by examining what the 'market' will take can a company set an accurate price for its product.

Look at this now in relation to the example of the newspaper indus-try discussed in chapter 2. The total market demand for the broad-sheet newspapers was 2.35 million copies a day in 1994. Table 3.1 shows how the total market changed between 1986 and 1994.

What is interesting here is that over an eight-year period the total size of the market has changed very little. Indeed, despite changes in price of three of the major suppliers (*The Times*, the *Daily Telegraph* and *The Independent*), the market has shrunk. This might suggest that total demand for quality newspapers is highly *price* inelastic, but that other factors (particularly income) might play an important role.

Table 3.1   The broadsheet newspaper market, 1986–1994

Year	Total size of broadsheet market (million copies)
1986	2.500
1987	2.535
1988	2.524
1989	2.492
1990	2.448
1991	2.354
1992	2.289
1993	2.257
1994	2.226

6.1   Individual Demand and Supply for The Times

The Times had 17.13 per cent of this market in 1986. By 1991 this had fallen to 15.67 per cent. But by 1994, after it had implemented its price cutting strategy, it had 22.34 per cent. By reducing its cover price it has taken a larger share of the total market, but it has not actually managed to increase total demand in the industry as a whole. It has created a *movement* along the original demand curve but has not made market demand *shift*. This is represented graphically in figure 3.6.

Marketeers at *The Times* have looked at its market demand and realized that it is price responsive relative to other newspapers in the industry. If you are uncertain of this look back at chapter 2, which contains the analysis of demand in the industry. By reducing its price to 20p it anticipated higher demand at Q_2, which represents the higher market share that it now enjoys. In anticipation of higher sales (i.e. in terms of the supply curve, a change in the goals of the firm) it has shifted its supply downwards to the right to meet the increase in demand. The shift from S_1 to S_2 illustrates that the company is now prepared to sell more at each prevailing market price.

6.2   Market Demand and Supply for the Newspaper Industry as a Whole

Similarly, we can draw a demand curve for the total market which is downward sloping. Unlike the demand for *The Times*, total market

Figure 3.6 Demand and supply for *The Times*.

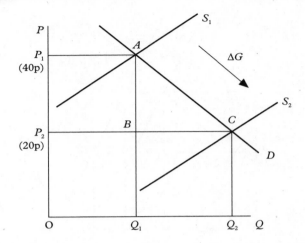

demand is highly price inelastic. As can be seen from table 3.1, total demand has not shifted significantly over the period despite the price war that has gripped the industry. In other words, demand is influenced strongly by other factors in the demand curve.

- *Close substitutes*: radio, television, magazines and, increasingly, computers (via the Internet) may substitute for reading a newspaper. This may cause the demand curve to shift to the left (D to D_1 in figure 3.7).
- *Tastes*: if individuals want or need to buy a newspaper they will do so irrespective of price, but as other substitutes become more available, total demand may fall (D to D_1).
- *Income*: disposable income, arguably, has fallen since 1989, owing to a wider recession in the British economy. This may have caused total demand to shift to the left (D to D_1).

In figure 3.7, P_1 is average price in 1986. By 1994 the average price of a newspaper had fallen to P_2. *Ceteris paribus* (assuming demand conditions to have remained the same) this would have meant that demand would have increased to Q_2'. However, the total newspaper market shrunk, representing a shift in demand to the left ($D - D_1$). Had prices remained at P_1 this would have represented a considerable drop in demand to Q_1'. However, three quality newspapers dropped their prices to P_2: demand only fell to Q_2. The strategy of reducing prices, then,

Figure 3.7   Total market for quality newspapers.

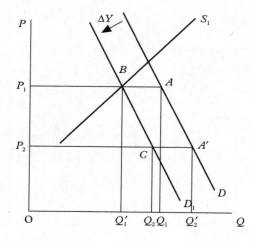

ensured that the fall in the total size of the market was limited to 127 665 copies per day by 1994.

We can also predict the overall level of profitability for companies in the industry using this diagram. If demand is at Q_1, then the area under the demand curve (the rectangle OQ_1AP_1) represents the level of revenue received. If demand is at Q_2 then the area under the demand curve at the new price is the new level of revenue received (OQ_2BP_2). But the second rectangle (where prices are lower and supply only slightly lower) is smaller than the first. In other words, total revenue into the industry has fallen. Where a newspaper has not entered into the price war – for example as is the case with the *Guardian* or the *Financial Times* – revenue levels will not be severely affected. But for a newspaper charging lower prices, this represents a serious drop in revenue. In 1994, for example, *The Times* was making large losses. As a result, pricing policy can be sustained for a short while but, because of reduced profitability, cannot be sustained in the long term.

What does this tell a marketing department of a quality newspaper? If demand is inelastic (as is the case for the *Financial Times* and the *Guardian*), the company has very little to gain from reducing prices because of the reduction in revenue *and* the increased costs of supplying greater quantities of newspapers. A company with inelastic demand has to increase demand by use of longer-term measures and seek to *shift* demand out overall.

Figure 3.8 The demand schedule for the FT, showing price discrimination.

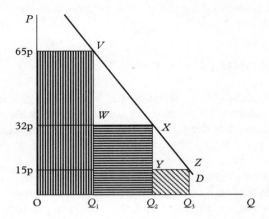

The Higher Education Programme of the *Financial Times* was an attempt to do just this. As we saw in chapter 2, three different prices were charged to three different markets. The market was *segmented* into three separate and almost mutually exclusive divisions; there was no real possibility of a commuter being able to purchase a copy of the FT under the Higher Education Programme at 15 pence so there is unlikely to be any resale between the three divisions. The newspaper can therefore charge different prices to each segment. In other words, it can *price discriminate*. This is a very common tool and increases the overall sales revenue of the company without reducing profitability. This is shown in figure 3.8, which is a copy of the same diagram from chapter 2.

The reason why this schedule is important is that it shows us the extra revenue that the company gains from selling the product at different prices. At its first price (65 pence) its revenue is the horizontally shaded rectangle – in other words, total sales at that price multiplied by the price. This price ensures its profitability, so that any extra that it gains is a 'bonus'. It then charges a separate price to a separate market. This separate market cannot sell its newspapers to the people who are willing to pay a full cover price because they are mutually exclusive groups. The people paying 32 pence might be part-time students or lecturers who wish to have the paper delivered to the door. The extra revenue gained is represented by the vertically shaded rectangle – in other words, the additional copies sold multiplied by the price they were sold at. Finally, the scheme to sell newspapers to students in college at 15 pence represents more additional revenue to the company, this time of the diagonally shaded rectangle, or the additional copies multiplied by the price at which they were sold.

7 Investigation (2)

All this should have demonstrated just how useful the model of the market mechanism is to business. In marketing the tools are used constantly to ensure that the price is reflective of the product being sold and that the price is one that consumers are willing to pay.

1 You may like to try the techniques developed in the context of the newspaper industry on the industries that you chose to examine in chapter 2, the car industry and the supermarket sector within the retail industry.
2 Draw diagrams to illustrate how supply and demand are affected by changes in price. Has demand shifted overall or are price wars simply creating a short-term increase in the level of demand? Can the techniques used in analysis of demand elasticity similarly be applied to these industries?
3 Using the data sources that you may have covered in the investigation at the end of chapter 2 look at the aggregate output figures for the whole economy and then at aggregate expenditure data. Is there a mismatch between demand and supply? If there is overproduction, where does the surplus go? If there is excessive demand, how is this met?

8 Conclusions: from Micro- to Macroeconomics through the Market Mechanism

This chapter started off with discussion of policy issues and a promise that you would understand the nature of the policy link between the micro and the macro economy by the end of the chapter. You should by now be familiar with the model of the price mechanism and understand that the determinant of an equilibrium price will dictate how resources are allocated to a market.

In order to see how this links to the macro economy, we assume that we can add up all demand and all supply in all markets of the economy (you may have seen this link if you conducted investigation (2) above). The total at which we arrive will be the *aggregate* demand and *aggregate* supply of that economy. We will return to this later in the book when we examine macroeconomics in more detail.

What is important, though, is that the economic health of the nation is the sum of its activities in individual markets. If prices are rising in individual markets, prices will, on aggregate, also rise. If there is a deficit of production to meet demand in individual markets, either prices will rise or supply will be increased by imports from abroad. As prices rise in one market, there is a knock-on effect through the economy, as was discussed in the context of the housing market at the beginning of this chapter. This manifests itself in inflation. Of course, this has profound implications for economic policy which are also discussed in more detail later in the book.

9   Further Reading

Hutton, W. (1995) *The State We're In*. London: Jonathan Cape, chapter 4, 'The revolution founders'.
Lazonick, W. (1992) *Business Organisation and the Myth of the Market Economy*. Cambridge: Cambridge University Press.
Michie, J. (ed.) (1993) *The Economic Legacy 1979–1992*. Harlow: Harcourt Brace Jovanovitch.

Notes

1   See, for example, Michie, J. (ed.) (1993) *The Economic Legacy 1979–1992*. Harlow: Harcourt Brace Jovanovitch.
2   See Adam Smith (1776) *An Enquiry into the Nature and Causes of the Wealth of Nations*. Harmondsworth: Penguin.
3   A note may be useful at this point. The demand and supply curves are used in this text to explain buyer and producer behaviour – as strategic tools of analysis. This means that we can use the interaction of supply and demand through the market mechanism as a way of explaining the signals that these two groups of actors in the economy send to one another. Hence, our use of the models is to explain how prices are set in a real context rather than a theoretical context.
4   *Financial Times* Observer column, 21 August 1995, p. 13.
5   *Financial Times*, 21 August 1995, p. 6.

4   Costs

Britain cannot afford the minimum wage or the 48 hour working week because it would increase costs to our manufacturers and make us uncompetitive.

(Rt Hon. John Major MP, November 1996)

1   Introduction

Chapter 3 ended with a discussion of the link between the micro and the macro economy through the price mechanism. It was argued that government policy has rested on the assumption that we can explain the whole economy in exactly the same way that we can analyse individual markets. Therefore, we can use an aggregate model of supply and demand to describe what is happening and, as is the case of monetary economists, also use it as a policy tool. The area of macroeconomic policy and its interplay with business is complex and so warrants separate treatment. It is, however, sufficient for the time being to hold the idea of the link through the market mechanism between the macro and the micro economies in order to see the importance of business performance for the health of the whole economy. This is a theme to be developed in this chapter.

Throughout the 1970s and into the 1980s commentators and analysts of the British economy argued that manufacturing costs (particularly wage costs) were too high. Companies were urged to shed workers, introduce new machines and tighten up on inefficiencies like unnecessary tea-breaks in the interests of making industry generally 'leaner and fitter'.

Look at table 4.1, which compares competitive positions as measured by relative unit labour costs in Britain with those of its major competitors between 1984 and 1994. Comparative labour costs are important because they give a measure of competitiveness: they are a critical part of a company's supply decision, as we saw in our analysis of supply in chapter 2. And, if labour costs are rising comparative to major competitors, this signals problems for indigenous industry.

Table 4.1   Relative unit labour costs

	1984	1985	1986	1987	1988	1989	1990	1991	1992	1993	1994
USA	157	161	132	113	105	107	103	100	94	95	94
Japan	84	83	114	117	120	106	93	100	112	138	141
FR Germany	83	81	89	100	99	97	101	100	104	113	113
France	105	107	109	109	104	100	102	100	102	105	103
UK	101	101	94	91	96	94	97	100	96	80	80
Korea	66	68	57	62	74	102	101	100	96	98	103
Taiwan	85	80	73	83	94	108	104	100	103	99	98

Source: CSO Blue Book 1995.

Table 4.1 shows an *index* of labour costs over a ten-year period during which world industry became more 'global'. This meant that companies, realizing that they were experiencing comparatively high domestic labour costs, located manufacturing in other countries around the world where labour costs were cheaper. An index can only show us the rate at which labour costs in a country are changing. It cannot tell us anything about comparative real wage levels. This means that we cannot conclude from looking at the table that in 1994 America was more competitive than, say, Korea. This is because US wages are compared with the level of wages in the USA in 1991. It might be that American wages started from a much higher level than those in Korea.

We can conclude, however, that wages were following a generally downward trend in the USA, in contrast to its Japanese, German, French and Korean competitors. This might indicate that attempts were being made at a government level as well as an industrial level to improve competitiveness.

From table 4.1, we can also point to periods in different countries when labour costs were increasing and when companies might have followed globalization strategies. For example, American and British companies expanded abroad significantly in the early 1980s, when domestic costs were particularly high. Japanese companies started to increase their levels of manufacturing operation abroad in the mid-1980s, again when labour costs were increasing. We are now beginning to witness an expansion in the global manufacturing activities of German companies, which arguably corresponds with their increasing domestic costs incurred since unification with Eastern Germany.[1]

There are many institutional and political reasons why labour costs were reduced through the decade in both Britain and the USA. In the UK these include both government incentives and legislation to reduce trade union power, with the end objective of reducing wage claims. For example, by the end of the 1980s trade unions no longer had the power to call strikes at will in support of wage claims; unemployment was high and inflation low, so that individual workers were easily persuaded that low level pay increases, static pay or, at times, pay reductions were the only alternative to redundancy. A detailed discussion goes beyond the scope of this chapter,[2] but it is worth mentioning that such forces were influential at this time to show that the pressure to reduce costs was ubiquitous in both countries.

Lack of competitiveness was a real threat to the manufacturing base of the economy.[3] Three factors were particularly important in exacerbating this trend:

1   Companies were entering the British market with cheaper products because their real costs of production were lower and because the exchange rate was favourable (see chapters 8, 11 and 12 for a further discussion of this).
2   The entrance of low-cost, low-price competitors was part of a wider process of globalization in industry generally. During the late 1980s and into the 1990s we have seen a massive expansion in the worldwide activities of, particularly, large companies.[4] The pressure was (and is) on companies to produce and sell all around the world.
3   The advance of new, microelectronics-based technologies (such as computer numeric control machine tools, flexible manufacturing systems, management information systems and robotics) put renewed pressure on companies to use the most advanced and productive machinery as effectively as possible, and, therefore, to keep costs as low as possible. This meant that companies had to look at the way in which people were employed, the types of work they did and the quality of work performed in the interest of making the whole organization 'lean'.[5]

So, in order to be competitive with companies reacting to these three trends, other companies had to reduce costs, in terms of their labour, in terms of machinery and production processes and in terms of quality. And as this is a text about business, we need to look at the real measures that companies took to reduce costs in order to restore competitiveness and how these can be explained using basic economic techniques.

2   Aims and Objectives

Costs are, perhaps, the most complex area of economics. Where there is an element of common sense in the analysis that we have conducted thus far, the work we do with costs makes us encounter some elementary maths for the first time. A large number of readers will suddenly feel frightened; others will be saying to themselves, 'There, we said economics was difficult', and shutting off completely. The reply to that is that this is the area of economics that is of particular use in the rest of your business studies course. Accountancy, logistics, operations management, personnel and strategy all rest on an understanding of what costs are and why they are important to business.

So the aim is a simple one: to ensure that, by the end of the chapter, you have met all of the cost curves used in introductory economics and that you can draw them and use them to analyse real business situations. As always, there are some specific objectives which the chapter also aims to meet.

1   That you will feel confident to use terms like average, total and marginal cost in your discussions of business situations.
2   That you will understand wider, macro, pressures on companies to reduce costs and, therefore, to allow you to understand some of the difficulties with which the British economy was faced in the 1980s and into the 1990s.
3   That you will also understand the pressure on companies to reduce costs because of the process of globalization in industry generally.
4   That you will also understand the importance of the advance of microelectronics-based technologies for cost structures in companies and the impact on strategies for competitiveness that that had.

3   Introductory Investigation

Assume you are going shopping in a supermarket with a limited amount of money, say £50. You need to buy all your food, toiletries, cleaning products and so on for over a week, so you will spend all of that money. Think about that expenditure as the *cost* of your shopping spree and imagine that you are wandering around the supermarket with a calculator. Now try to answer the following questions:

1 What is the total cost of your shopping trip?
2 If you buy 50 items, how much, on average, has each of those items cost?
3 You can buy one can of baked beans at 25 pence. But you can buy a pack of four cans for 92 pence. What is the average price of the four cans of beans? Why do you think the average cost of something decreases as you buy more of it?
4 You have been adding up the costs of everything as you walk round the shop. You are half way through your trip and have already spent £30. Next you buy a loaf of wholemeal bread for 95 pence. What is the total cost of your shopping bill at this point in your trip? What is the additional cost of adding the loaf of bread to your shopping trolley?

4 The Cost Curves

If you have answered these questions you will not have any great difficulty in understanding cost curves. Of course, we will be talking about production costs rather than shopping costs, and, of course, there are more factors than just spending money to take into account. The above investigation served a purpose of introducing you to total, average and marginal costs and realizing that any maths involved is, actually, quite simple.

4.1 The Supply Curve Revisited

You will remember that the supply curve was drawn simply to show the relationship between the price of the product being produced and the quantity of the product supplied. For a normal product it would slope upwards to the right, indicating that, other things being equal, the company would want to supply more as the price of the product rose. This would be a *movement* along the supply curve.

Supply curves, like demand curves, can shift if any of the determinants of supply except the price of the good itself change. If costs of factor inputs (the land, labour, machinery or raw material used, for example) rise, then less will be supplied at each prevailing market price. This is because companies anticipate lower profits.

Diagramatically this can be illustrated as in figure 4.1. S_1 is the supply curve before a change in the costs of factor inputs. S_2 is the curve representing an increase in costs. At the price P_1 less is supplied $(Q_1 - Q_2)$.

Figure 4.1   A shift in the supply curve after an increase in factor costs.

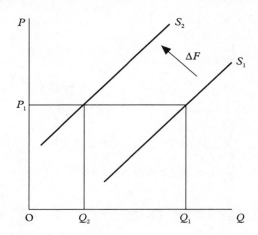

There are many reasons why costs might increase. These can be grouped into two sets:

1   *External shocks*: these are changes that occur outside the company, or even outside the economy. Examples might include the four-fold increase in oil prices in 1973, followed by the doubling of oil prices in 1979. These represented huge increases in input prices over which companies had no control and which took a long time to work through the system.
2   *Internal factors*: these are the increases in costs brought about by changes in the organization itself. Examples might include the introduction of a new machine which enhances productivity or the removal of an administrative loop, making processes simpler and therefore cheaper.

The rest of this chapter really focuses on the latter kind of cost changes, as these are the ones over which companies have most control. They are the costs of production and the costs of organization which are faced by one company only. All companies in an economy would face the effects of a rise in oil prices. Internal costs affect only the company concerned.

This chapter, then, takes a close look at cost curves and how companies in the real world have sought to make improvements in cost structures and efficiency when faced with the competitive problems discussed briefly at the beginning of the chapter. For many years

Figure 4.2   The production function for a product: the optimum combinations of capital and labour to produce a given quantity of output (Q_x).

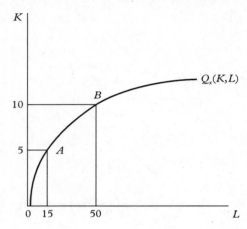

technological advance and increased competition from Japanese companies have increased the importance of low-cost, high-quality and effective production systems. Attempts to emulate the Japanese success have been structured around total quality and continuous improvement programmes. These programmes have been particularly successful in manufacturing, although they have more recently also extended into the service sector as well.

4.2   The Nature of Production and Production Decisions

A company makes a decision to supply a product on the basis of how much revenue it expects from the sale of its product and how much it expects production to cost. The difference between expected costs and expected revenues is expected profits. It will set a level of desired output given its expected (or anticipated) level of profitability. It will then employ machinery (or capital) and people (labour) in proportions that ensure that the level of output can be produced efficiently.

The short term and the law of diminishing returns

The ratio between the capital employed and the labour employed is called the production function, which is shown diagramatically in figure 4.2. The diagram shows the combinations of machinery and people necessary to produce a particular level of output at any one point in time, i.e. the short term; for example, 50 people and 10 machines, or 15 people and 5 machines. Any point along the production function is efficient: it implies that the capital and the labour is employed optimally to produce a given level of output.

The shape of the production function illustrates the *law of diminishing returns*. This law tells us that as we increase the inputs of one factor, say labour, it will become less efficient; the 'returns' it gives 'diminish'. Another way of looking at it is as the 'Too many cooks spoil the broth!' law. This is a useful tool for a company, in that it projects the effective combinations of machinery and people to produce the desired level of output. The slope of the curve reflects the comparative efficiency of labour compared to capital. For example, at point A it only takes 15 people to operate 5 machines. But at point B it takes 50 people to operate 10 machines. This demonstrates to the company that labour becomes less efficient as the quantity of machinery expands.

The production function in figure 4.2 shows a ratio between capital and labour where at least one factor is fixed in the short term. This gives the *law of diminishing returns* (also called the *law of variable proportions*), i.e. that, with one factor fixed – for example, capital – the variable factor, labour, will become progressively less efficient as more of it is used (just think of trying to make a cup of tea 'helped' by five people!).

While such an analysis may seem theoretical, this does not stop it from having its application in the real world. Take a company like Lucas Diesel Systems at Sudbury in Suffolk.[6] It is part of Lucas Automotive, which in turn is a part of Lucas Industries PLC. Its role is as a manufacturing centre producing fuel injection systems for diesel engines. As a manufacturing centre it incurs costs but does not accrue profits. In the early 1980s it began the process of making itself more effective because of the pressure on it to reduce its costs. The budget given to it by its holding company was sufficient to cover costs but not sufficient to introduce new machinery. Any new machinery had to be justified in terms of efficiency gains *after* improvements in productivity had been achieved.

The company set about this by reorganizing its production. Demand in the industry was slack, so the level of output remained the same throughout the period *and*, critically, capital was fixed. This means that we can assume that the intention was to improve the efficiency of labour (i.e. to reduce costs) without increasing output or capital input. As economists we would call this a 'labour-enhancing' improvement. The company reorganized its shopfloor. It spent no money at all on new machinery and instead concentrated on making people work its existing machinery better. The improvement in productivity meant that after the changes the workforce had reduced by more than a half, but production had remained the same and productive *capacity* had increased.[7]

The importance of this analysis is that it shows how, in the short term, without increasing expenditure on capital, a company can increase its efficiency by altering the way in which capital and labour are employed. In the short term, where a company is trying to make relatively fast cost savings and productivity improvements, this is a useful strategic insight. The company can continue making improvements and changes at a given level of output until there is no extra productivity to be reaped from the variable factor, in this case labour. In other words, it makes changes until returns are constant.

The long term

In the long term, of course, a company can vary both capital and labour. Of importance, then, are two things:

1   Expanding the size of the plant such that the efficiencies are retained (in other words, no extra productivity can be gained from the factor which was variable in the short term).
2   Gaining any 'extra' advantages that might accrue from size (for example, bulk buying or distribution deals). These are called 'economies of scale' and we return to them later in the chapter.

A brief critique

This type of economic analysis has been severely criticized by people who study technology and technological change.[8] They argue that technology is dynamic and evolves from the cumulative experience of production that a firm develops. Static analysis such as this, comparing a 'before' and 'after' situation, can do little to predict the effects on production that a new technology will have or the way in which that new technology would develop.

Some economists have criticized the approach as a 'black box' approach. They argue that it sees the firm as a conflict-free structure which simply converts inputs into outputs, as shown in figure 4.3. Put simply, they argue that there is no scope for strategy or research and development in this model. Inputs are converted into outputs and distributed to the market, where their price is determined by the market mechanism as described in chapter 3. They argue that the dynamic process by which a product reaches a market is not explained sufficiently.[9]

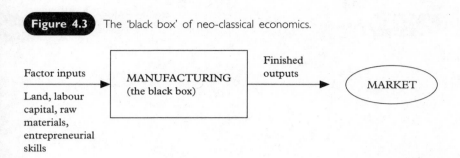

Figure 4.3 The 'black box' of neo-classical economics.

It is certainly true that the economics of technology is a discipline in its own right. Only through looking at the dynamic evolution of technology can we ultimately say anything about how that technology develops and how companies themselves develop around it. However, it is also true that the conventional tools of neo-classical economics (those being covered here) can explain and describe the new technology itself, in particular its impact on costs structures at any one point in time. And, as in the case of Lucas, it can provide an input into strategy by demonstrating how to make short-term productivity improvements and longer-term efficiency improvements. We develop this further now by looking at cost curves.

4.3 Total Cost

The total costs of production are all the costs involved in producing a particular product. They include the heating and lighting of a building, the canteen facilities, the maintenance of the building, the administrative costs, the machinery replacement costs and, of course, the costs of employing people directly in the production process. As such, then, total costs are composed of two parts.

1 *Total fixed costs* (*TFC*): these are the costs that are the same no matter how much is produced. Even if nothing rolls off the production line at all there will be costs of maintaining the factory, heating and lighting buildings, employing accountants, analysts and personnel managers and so on. Sometimes companies will refer to these as the indirect costs (that is, not directly associated with the production process). Diagramatically, total fixed costs are a straight line, which shows that they are the same, no matter the level of output (see figure 4.4).

Figure 4.4 Total fixed costs (*TFC*).

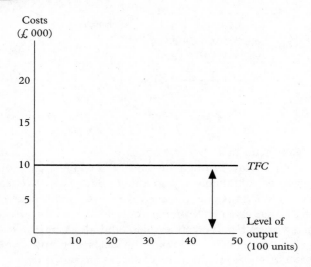

2   *Total variable costs* (*TVC*): these are the costs that are directly associated with the level of production and their slope reflects the law
of variable proportions (or diminishing returns). For example, if
the company wanted to produce a small quantity, say 100 units a
month, it would only be necessary to employ a few people and a
few machines. This level of production will not require much to
be bought in the way of supplies, and will not require a large distribution network. However, if production rises, say to 100 000
units, it will be necessary to operate on a much larger scale, with
more people and machinery, more supplies, more space for storage and more lorries for distribution. This is shown by an S-shaped
curve, as in figure 4.5. The S-shaped curve illustrates how, as output increases, factor efficiency rises sharply to start with (from the
origin to point A reflecting increasing returns), then rises at a
decreasing rate (line *A–B*) and then starts to increase rapidly again
(after point *B*, diminishing returns). At point *B*, where the curve
turns, the curve is flat and returns are constant.

Total costs are the sum of total fixed costs and total variable costs.
In shorthand we can write this as an equation:

$$TC = TFC + TVC$$

Figure 4.5 Total variable costs (*TVC*).

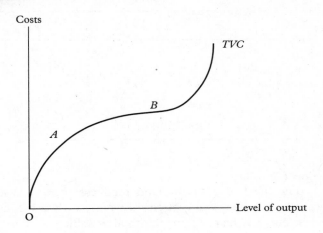

Figure 4.6 Total costs (*TC*).

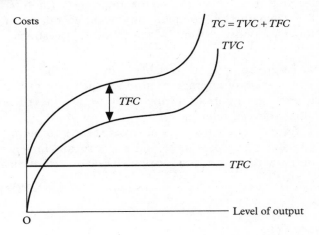

This is intuitively the case. It stands to reason that the total cost of something is the sum of all component costs. As economists we group these into two parts: fixed costs (the costs which exist regardless of the level of production) and variable costs (the costs directly related to the level of production). We can illustrate total costs diagramatically as in figure 4.6.

Table 4.2 Fixed, variable and total costs for a hypothetical company

Level of output	100 units	150 units	200 units	250 units	300 units
Total variable costs (TVC)	85	95	100	103	110
Total fixed costs (TFC)	15	15	15	15	15
Total costs (TC)	100	110	115	118	125

Investigation (2)

Figure 4.6 puts the fixed, variable and total cost curves together so that you can see how the total cost curve is derived. You will note that the total cost curve is higher than the total variable cost curve by an amount equal to total fixed costs. A numerical example might help to show you why this is the case.

Examine table 4.2, which shows the total costs (in thousands of pounds) for a hypothetical company producing an output of a product, X. Now try to answer some of the following questions:

1 At what level of output are variable costs rising the least quickly?
2 What is it costing on average to produce each unit of the product at each level of output? (You might like to add these below table 4.2 so that you can refer back.)
3 What is the rate of change of total costs relative to output at each level? (Again, you might like to add an extra row for reference.)
4 Can you draw the costs at the various levels of output on the total cost diagram?

4.4 Average Costs

As the name suggests, average costs are what it costs the firm, on average, to produce one unit of a product. It is the total cost of production divided by the total level of output:

$$AC = \frac{TC}{X}$$

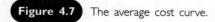

Figure 4.7   The average cost curve.

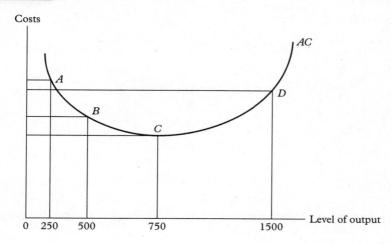

The average cost of production for our hypothetical company can be found by dividing total costs by the level of output. So, for example, we divide total costs of 100 by output of 100 to arrive at an average cost of 1000 per unit (remember the costs were shown in thousands).

Average costs are the costs, on average, of one unit of a product; in other words, what it usually costs to produce one washing machine or one car or one video recorder. You will often hear accountants and companies referring to this as unit cost. We can represent average costs diagramatically as shown in figure 4.7. The graph simply plots the figures given in table 4.2. It shows that, as output expands, costs, on average, fall. It is cheaper, for example, for the company to produce 500 units of a product than it is for the company to produce 250 units.

The reason for this lies in the shape of the average cost curve. Its U-shape reflects the fact that, as the level of output increases, costs, on average, decline up to a point where returns are constant. In the short term, as argued above, this is caused by varying the input of one factor with increasing returns until it becomes as efficient as it can be (at point C). Beyond point C the factor has become less efficient: returns are decreasing and average costs rise again; the more of the factor that is used, the less efficient it becomes. The curve slopes upwards.

The U-shape of the curve reflects both diminishing returns and economies of scale, but we must take care to distinguish between the short and the long run.

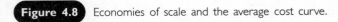

Figure 4.8   Economies of scale and the average cost curve.

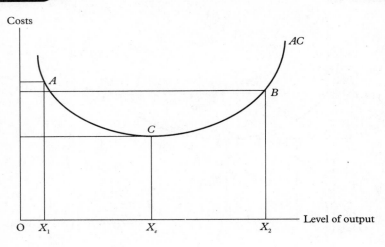

The short run and diminishing returns

If we redraw figure 4.7 without the numbers, using symbols, we can re-examine the way in which a company aims to produce where returns to scale are constant, and we can look at the significance of the minimum (or lowest) point on the average cost curve in terms of organizational efficiency. We can look at what happens to companies if they expand output beyond that minimum point. We do this in figure 4.8.

Producing at the level of output, X_1, is not efficient for the firm. It can reduce costs further by expanding output to X_e. At this point it is experiencing increasing returns to scale; that is, as it gets bigger, its costs reduce, on average. At the point X_e it cannot reduce its costs any further. It is at an efficient (or optimum) size. Returns to scale are constant. In fact, if it expands output any further its costs will rise. An example would be the point X_2, where it has expanded output significantly, perhaps because it anticipates rising demand in the future. However, it has not expanded such that the utilization of its factors of production is still efficient. It experiences diminishing returns to scale, in that its organization has become less effective as it has expanded output at that scale of plant. The only way of returning to a point where it is operating at optimum levels is by reducing output to the level X_e.

Figure 4.9 The envelope curve.

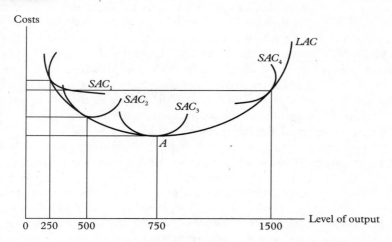

Key: short-run average cost curves consistent with a plant scale producing 250 units (SAC_1); 500 units (SAC_2); 750 units (SAC_3); 1500 units (SAC_4).

Average costs in the short and long term

Remember, all this assumes that the firm cannot expand its overall level of plant. In other words, it uses existing machinery and existing employees and cannot utilize extra floor space, expand its premises or even buy new machinery and employ more people. It is only operating in the *short term*.

In the longer term, of course, a company can increase the scale on which it operates and aim, in the very long term, to reach a position where all possible economies of scale (or the cost advantages of size) have been reaped. It aims to reach the minimum point on its *long-run average cost* curve. The means by which it does this is shown in figure 4.9.

Each of the short-run average cost curves represents the average costs of expanding output given a scale of plant. For example, if the plant is on SAC_1 it will produce at an optimum level of output where returns are constant and costs are as low as they can go, at 250 units. This point is the minimum point on SAC_1. If it expands beyond that level in the short term without expanding its scale of operations (buying new machinery etc.) it will experience diminishing returns to scale.

In the longer term, the company might well decide that it would be able to operate profitably producing 500 units. It will increase the size of its plant accordingly, and while this will incur higher total costs, on average the cost of producing each unit of output will have fallen. If the plant operates at the minimum point on the short run average cost curve (SAC_2) it will have constant returns and it will be operating efficiently in the long term, with average costs at C_2.

Figure 4.9 draws the short-run average cost curves consistent with four levels of output: those given in table 4.2. It would of course be possible to draw the intermediate curves in between as well. The long-run average cost curve (LAC) 'envelops' all these minimum points. At point A, for example, long-run and short-run average costs are equal. The slopes of the two curves are identical to one another. This 'envelope curve', which is derived from the minimum points of each of these curves, is the *point of optimum efficiency* (constant returns) for each scale of plant. So the long-run average cost curve is the location of all possible points of efficiency for a firm wishing to produce a particular product.

To return to our Lucas example above, the company aimed to achieve constant returns to scale in the short term by its improvement measures. In the long term, however, it did introduce new capital (in the form of robots and computer numerically controlled machine tools), carefully selected to ensure that it could be used efficiently given the returns to scale achieved in the short term. In that the company wanted to be efficient, it was, arguably, expanding its production along the path of the long-run average cost curve and reaping economies of scale as it expanded.

4.5   The Strategic Implications of This for Business

As with many of the models covered in this book, the U-shaped average cost curve represents a theoretical 'ideal' rather than an actual situation. Economists have argued long and loud about the empirical shape of the curve. What they want to know is whether or not the U-shape is found in the real business world. Some argue that theories assuming a U-shaped curve are realistic: a firm does experience diseconomies of scale as it expands output without expanding scale. Others argue that the long-run average cost curve is L-shaped: firms will not experience diseconomies of scale as they grow. No doubt much to the relief of some readers, there is no intention to enter into this debate here. What is important for our purposes is the use of the model in understanding business activities.

The first factor to highlight is the importance of average (or unit) costs as an indicator of competitiveness. For example, in a major study of the automotive industry, it was found that productivity levels impact on costs so significantly that they can undermine the worldwide competitiveness of the company.[10] In 1989 it took a Japanese plant around half the effort of an American luxury car manufacturer to produce a similar vehicle. Comparisons with Europe were even more revealing. The best European plants needed four times as much effort to produce a similar vehicle, and the worst over six times. Such stark differences in unit costs were used by UK companies as indicators of falling competitiveness and pointed to the need for strategic change in order to compete 'on a level playing field'.

The second factor to highlight is the means by which companies attempted to redress the balance in costs. The comparative average (unit) cost figures were (and still are) used as benchmarks of an ideal which had to be achieved and even surpassed. Companies looked at what they were producing relative to stock levels (unsold stock represents a cost to companies) and relative to levels of present and forecast demand. In the car components industry this meant a downscaling in output to ensure that production was for customers and not for stock. In other words, the assumption was that many companies were experiencing diseconomies of scale and needed to rationalize before they could operate optimally. Having found the 'ideal' level of output by reducing wastage and stock levels, companies could then concentrate on reducing costs in management structures (for example, by reducing hierarchies and simplifying communication channels) and making individual workers responsible for their quality, thereby reducing the costs involved in producing goods which were not up to required standard.

4.6   Marginal Costs

The final cost curve which has to be covered is the marginal cost curve. Marginal costs are the costs of extra units of production. In terms of the first investigation above, they are the amounts added to your shopping bill each time you added an extra units of shopping to your basket. The second investigation demonstrated how to calculate marginal costs – by dividing the rate at which costs are changing by the rate at which output is changing. Refer back to table 4.2 if you still feel uncertain on this.

Table 4.3	Total, average and marginal costs for a baker's first five batches of bread

Batches (Q)	Total cost (£)	Average cost (TC/Q)	Marginal cost (ΔTC/ΔQ)[a]
1	10	10	10
2	18	9	8
3	24	8	6
4	32	8	8
5	50	10	18

[a] The marginal cost of, say, the second batch is calculated by subtracting the total cost of the first batch from the total cost of the first two batches.

From this you can see that marginal costs are the extra costs of production for each extra unit of the product that is produced. You will find marginal costs defined formally as, 'the incremental change in costs caused by a unit change in output'.[11] You can calculate marginal cost using the following equation:

$$MC = \frac{\Delta TC}{\Delta Q}$$

This calculation is given in table 4.3, which shows the relationship between total, average and marginal costs for the first five batches of bread produced by a baker each day.

The marginal cost curve is again U-shaped: as drawn in figure 4.10. It is the slope of the total cost curve (in other words the rate at which costs are changing relative to changes in output) and, therefore, illustrates diminishing returns to scale. Up to the minimum point, for example at X_1, units of the variable factor are increasing and units of output cost less: returns to scale are increasing. Beyond the minimum point on the curve, X_m, diminishing returns are apparent: as the variable factor increases additional units of output cost more.

Yet it will always pay the company to produce on the upward sloping part of the marginal cost curve. Remember that the curve refers to rates of change of cost and not absolute cost levels. Thus, for example, if the company is increasing its output at the rate X_1, its costs increase at the rate MC_1. However, if it increases the rate at which it is expanding output, for example to X_2, its costs are increasing at the same rate, MC_1. It therefore pays the company always to produce on the upward sloping part of the marginal cost curve.

Figure 4.10 The marginal cost curve.

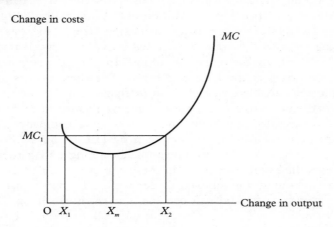

Average costs and marginal costs

The relationship between average costs and marginal costs is an important one, which warrants a little extra attention. You will recall that both curves are derived from the total cost curve and, in the short term, both demonstrate diminishing returns. It therefore follows that if marginal costs are less than average costs, additional units of output cost less than average to produce. Thus average, or unit, costs must be falling. Similarly, if marginal costs are greater than average costs, additional units of output cost more than average and thus average costs must be rising. As a result, a company will always produce on the upward sloping part of the marginal cost curve *and* will always cut the average cost curve at its minimum point, such that additional units of output are equal to the average costs of production (returns to scale are constant).

In the long run, if marginal costs are less than average costs, there are economies of scale to be reaped, because extra units of output cost less than average to produce. If long-run marginal costs are greater than average cost, any extra units of output produced result in diseconomies of scale because they cost more than average to produce.

4.7 The Strategic Importance of Marginal Costs

Kaizen or continuous improvement

There is no denying that this analysis is abstract in the extreme. Very few companies would be very interested in calculating marginal costs, because of the difficulty of assuming that production had only increased by one unit and then projecting the effects on total costs.

What is important about marginal costs, however, is that they show the rate at which costs change with output. Mathematically this is the slope of the total cost curve (a slope rising steeply suggests rapidly increasing costs with output, while a flat curve suggests that costs are rising slowly relative to increasing output). In order to gauge what this means, look back at the total cost curve. The slope of it is identical to that of the variable cost curve. So marginal costs are derived from the rate at which variable costs are changing relative to output.

This is extremely important information for a company. Through rationalization, such as that undertaken by Lucas, the company can reduce its fixed costs. It can subcontract catering and gardening; it can reduce the number of levels in the hierarchy; it can make reporting and communication simpler. In reducing these fixed costs it also reduces average costs and can become efficient in so doing. But if it wishes to make itself more effective it also has to reduce those costs directly related to output levels: the variable costs and, more particularly, the rate at which variable costs increase. In other words, it must seek to achieve constant returns to scale by improving the efficiency of a variable factor of production: here, labour.

This is reducing marginal costs: the marginal cost curve demonstrates diminishing returns in the short term. Similarly, continuous improvement programmes such as those implemented at Lucas reduce marginal costs rather than average costs by enhancing the productivity of a factor of production without incurring any capital expenditure. Take a case as an example. At Lucas Diesel Systems, Sudbury, one production cell was experiencing considerable difficulties in packing the filters it was producing into boxes. The boxes were flimsy and unstapled, so, as soon as they were lifted, the filter fell out. One manufacturing employee suggested that the process would be improved if the boxes were stuck together in some way. He bought a stapler in order to do this. Now, as the filters are put into boxes, the boxes are stapled and their contents stay inside them. This prevents the time wasted while filters are rescued from the floor and has greatly improved the 'job satisfaction' of people working on the shopfloor.

The example is a simple one but it serves a point. Costs have fallen only slightly, but each filter is now slightly cheaper to produce than before because not only is no time wasted, but job satisfaction has improved.[12]

Investigation (3): marginal costs and marginal benefits
A company seeking to alter its strategy in any way will always weigh up the costs and benefits of a particular decision path. In the decision

to follow a particular strategy through, the benefits have to outweigh the costs, and a means of ensuring that this is the case is by examining minute changes such as those represented by marginal costs.

A small baker, for example, decides whether to produce one extra unit of output a day (say one extra batch of bread). That extra batch of bread is worth £10 in extra (or marginal) revenue if it is sold at full price (50p per loaf). The marginal revenue (marginal benefit) is equal to £10 *ceteris paribus*. The baker can sell the bread at full price in the early afternoon, and there is always a rush of customers around lunch time (when he usually experiences a shortage). But by 4 p.m. the price has to be reduced to 25p a loaf, resulting in a marginal revenue for the whole batch of only £5 and less than that if only a proportion of it sells.

In order to produce that extra batch, the baker incurs a marginal cost dependent on the time of day the batch is baked. If it is baked in the early morning his marginal costs are £6, which are the costs of ingredients. Machinery is operating and staff are available – there is some slack in the operations to allow the extra batch to be baked. However, although he can sell the bread at its full price, it has usually been sold by lunch time and the problem with the increased lunch time demand remains.

If the baker waits until mid-morning, a member of staff is paid an hour's overtime and marginal costs rise to £10. However, the bread is sold at its full price and the customers arriving at lunch time are supplied with the fresh hot loaves that they want.

If the baker waits until after lunch, the overtime paid rises to two hours and marginal costs are now £14. Even if the loaves are sold, the baker does not cover the costs with the extra revenue received, and the likelihood is that the price will have to be reduced at the end of the afternoon.

What would you recommend as a strategy for this baker? What should be the balance between marginal costs and marginal revenue (the benefits in this case)?

5   Further Investigation (4)

Much of the material that has been covered in this chapter is highly theoretical, but it does have its application in the real world. Any company will want to compare its cost structures with those of its nearest competitors: low costs mean that low prices can be charged without affecting profit margins. And, as the example of Lucas showed, high quality can also mean low costs and greater competitiveness.

New Just in Time Zone

Guy de Jonquières reports on a plan by US supermarkets to integrate the supply chain

When Taiichi Ohno, then Toyota's chief engineer, visited the US in the late 1940s, he was more impressed by the country's supermarkets than its car industry. Their organisation and expertise, he said, inspired the just-in-time production system pioneered by Toyota and since adopted by manufacturers worldwide.

Today, it is the supermarkets which are scrambling to catch up. Beset by mounting competition, shrinking market share and meagre profit margins, they have launched an ambitious joint project to modernise their business by adopting the latest just-in-time techniques.

Known as Efficient Consumer Response, the project aims to squeeze $30bn (£20.1bn) in costs out of the $360bn-a-year US grocery trade through co-ordinated action by retailers and suppliers to slash stocks and speed up distribution.

If all goes to plan, the efficiency gains will not only enable supermarkets to cut prices by as much as 11 per cent; ECR will also transform their relations with suppliers and may hasten restructuring by consumer goods manufacturers.

Although supermarkets in much of Europe – notably the UK – are more efficient than in the US, the project is arousing interest across the Atlantic. Several large supermarket groups, such as Ahold of the Netherlands, Delhaize of Belgium and Britain's J. Sainsbury, own north American chains.

ECR was hatched earlier this year by five retailing and manufacturing associations. It is backed by supermarkets including Kroger, Safeway and Shaw's, and suppliers including Coca-Cola, Kraft General Foods and Procter & Gamble.

The driving force is the US supermarkets' growing alarm at losing business to discount chains such as Wal-Mart and warehouse clubs such as Costco, which charge 10–15 per cent less for many grocery lines.

Their lower costs reflect superior productivity. At Wal-Mart, for instance, tight links with suppliers and extensive investment in computerised technology allow sales to be monitored continuously and ensure that products are made and delivered when they are needed.

While US supermarkets installed electronic point-of-sale scanners more than 20 years ago, they have used them mainly to speed up check-out transactions, rather than to generate information about their business or manage it better.

Furthermore, their relations with suppliers remain antagonistic, partly because US food and household goods manufacturers have not faced the competitive spur of cheap imports which prompted makers of textiles, toys and consumer electronics goods to co-operate closely with chains such as Wal-Mart.

Things have been made worse by a uniquely American system of short-term promotional discounts on manufacturers' list prices. This encourages bargain-hunting supermarkets to purchase as much as three months' stock at a time and store it in warehouses.

So common is the practice that more than 80 per cent of some grocery lines are bought in this way. As well as undermining producers' pricing policies, it has led to uneven distribution flows and a costly build-up of finished products, while draining funds from advertising and marketing.

Although manufacturers originally launched promotional deals to drum up sales, many have grown disenchanted. Some, such as P&G, have recently tried unilaterally to restore price stability. But such efforts have been patchy and yielded mixed results.

ECR aims to end this anarchy through an industry-wide effort by retailers, wholesalers and manufacturers to integrate the supply chain by installing advanced electronic systems and sharing detailed information about sales, orders, production schedules and payments.

Kurt Salmon, an industry consultancy, estimates ECR could cut stock levels by 37 per cent and reduce the time taken by a typical grocery product to move from factory gate to checkout counter from 104 days to 61.

Industry co-operation would also improve supermarkets' use of sales space, speed stock replenishment and enhance the quality of product innovation and marketing by freeing suppliers and retailers to concentrate on consumers instead of fighting each other.

'We have to move from a "push" approach, which relied on putting products in a warehouse and hoping they would sell, to one where the industry is pulled forward by consumer demand,' says Phil Marineau, president of Quaker Oats.

Quaker began applying some principles of ECR in the late 1980s, shaking up its sales and marketing effort and working with supermarkets to eliminate surplus stocks and streamline distribution. It has been rewarded with increased margins and market share.

ECR's sponsors have set a tight timetable. Trials of the techniques and information systems involved are already under way.

The aim is to have the project operating throughout the industry by the end of 1996.

But some observers think the really tough issues have yet to be tackled. 'Everyone is still just picking the low-hanging fruit,' says Douglas Adams, an ECR expert with Nielsen, the market research firm. 'From now on, progress will be more difficult,' says Winston Taylor, a vice president of Campbell's Soup.

The biggest obstacle is not the technology, which is already widely used in other industries, but getting supermarkets and suppliers to behave as partners, not adversaries.

Even ECR's most enthusiastic backers admit they will need extensive reorganisation and staff training to overcome ingrained mutual mistrust and the urge to seek short-term advantage at each other's expense.

Further hurdles are uncertainty among wholesalers about their future role and manufacturers' anxiety about the impact of the planned elimination of surplus stocks from the supply chain.

David Rabinowitz, of stockbrokers Kidder Peabody in New York, estimates that adjustment could cut food manufacturers' production by 40 per cent in a single quarter. Even if phased in over two years, it could still depress manufacturers' sales growth during that period.

Yet the supermarkets' continuing loss of market share provides a powerful incentive to press ahead, as does manufacturers' concern that if they miss the bandwagon, they may lose to competitors.

Those with the most to fear are manufacturers of weak brands. Many have survived largely because US supermarkets lacked the tools to measure the performance of individual grocery lines.

Once ECR provides that information, it seems certain to add to the pressures for a further shake-out of products which are failing to earn their keep on supermarket shelves.

Lucas is one company within one industry that has become very focused on the need to drive down costs over the past 15 years. You may also like to try out the example for the American supermarket sector (case 4). Read the case carefully and then try to answer the following questions.

1 How will total costs be affected by the measures being taken by US supermarket chains? Include an analysis of fixed and variable costs.
2 How will reductions in average costs create efficiency gains for the supermarkets?
3 How will the prices charged by US supermarkets be affected by the changes in costs in (a) the short term and (b) the long term?
4 Is the move towards integrating the supply chain likely to be an enduring trend affecting the long-term competitive structure of the industry? (You might like to return to this question after reading chapters 5 and 6.)

As a further investigation into the importance of technology and its effects on industries and competitiveness, you may find it useful to examine the impact of a new technology of your choice on an industry of your choice. You could focus on the following areas:

1 The impact on cost structures for individual companies.
2 The impact on the competitiveness of individual companies.
3 The impact on organizational structures of individual companies.
4 The impact on the concentration of industries (e.g. are there more or fewer companies operating in it?).
5 The impact on supply relationships in the industry (are component suppliers being 'bought out' or are strategic alliances forming?)

6 Summary of Theories and Strategic Implications

Costs are a vital part of a company's operations because they dictate its competitiveness and profitability. No apology is made for the complexity of the models presented here; they are central to economics *and* to business. We could not study a course purporting to explain either without covering them. The following summary may help you to remember the key points.

1 The total cost curve shows the total costs of production as output increases. Its shape shows us diminishing returns as it expands its output. Any company will have to know what its total costs are in order to project its expected levels of profitability.
2 The average cost curve shows us what, on average, it costs to produce a unit of output. It is calculated by dividing the total costs of production by the amount being produced. Unit costs (in economics called average costs) are central indicators of competitive performance to companies. They show a company how it can become more effective through altering its factors in the short term and its scale in the long term to reduce costs.
3 Marginal costs are the incremental costs incurred by increasing costs by one unit. They are the rate at which variable costs are changing and, as such, also illustrate how economies of scale can be reaped. While companies may not make marginal cost calculations as such, any company that has embarked on total quality or continuous improvement programmes will want to look at how variable cost increases can be kept to a minimum as output rises.

7 Conclusions

Companies throughout the world are becoming more cost conscious and cost competitive. It is hoped that this chapter has given you a taste of how cost analysis can be used in many (of the 'trendy') areas of management science – particularly logistics and quality management. Indeed, without a thorough knowledge of its cost structures a company cannot satisfactorily form strategies to achieve competitive advantage. In order to facilitate this understanding of costs, companies have broken themselves up into separate, often competing, business units (SBUs), each responsible for minimizing average (or unit) costs in exactly the ways described above. As technology improves and

organizational structures become leaner, this focus on costs, and therefore the importance of the tools above, can only increase.

8   Further Reading

As background on costs and competitiveness at a national level you will find
the following of interest.

Hutton, W. (1995) *The State We're In*. London: Jonathan Cape, chapter 2.

Michie, J. (ed.) (1993) *The Economic Legacy 1979–1992*. Harlow: Harcourt
Brace Jovanovitch.

Stoneman, P. and Vickers, J. (1996) The economics of technology policy. In
T. Jenkinson (ed.), *Readings in Microeconomics*. Oxford: Oxford University
Press.

As an international comparison of competitiveness you might find useful
Porter, M. (1990) *The Competitive Advantage of Nations*. London: Macmillan.

As a discussion of the car industry, you may find useful Roos, D., Womack,
J. and Jones, D.T. (1990) *The Machine that Changed the World*. New York:
Rawson Associates.

Notes

1   This is the subject of ongoing research by the author. See also Michie,
J. and Grieve Smith, J. (eds) (1995) *Managing the Global Economy*. Oxford:
Oxford University Press.

2   If you are interested in this some extra reading is listed at the end of the
chapter.

3   For a historical discussion, see Blackaby, F. (ed.) (1979) *De-industrialisation*,
NIESR series, no. 2. Oxford: Heinemann. For a more recent discussion
see Michie, J. (ed.) (1993) *The Economic Legacy 1979–1992*. Harlow:
Harcourt Brace Jovanovitch; or Hutton, W. (1995) *The State We're In*.
London: Jonathan Cape.

4   See chapter 11.

5   'Lean and mean' is a term that was used by politicians to describe the
shake out that was taking place; also a term coined by Krafcik and
McDuffie to describe a truly effective organization with no operational
slack.

6   See Harding, R. (1995) *Technology and Human Resources in Their National
Context: a Study in Strategic Contrasts*. Aldershot: Avebury.

7   Based on research by Harding, R. (1994) CI is a way of LIFE at Lucas.
Works Management, February 1994; ibid.

8   See Rosenberg, N. (1982) *Inside the Black Box*. Cambridge: Cambridge
University Press.

9 For the pioneering work in this area, see ibid. This was one of the first attempts to integrate the dynamic evolution of technology into economics.

10 See Roos, D., Womack, J. and Jones, D.T. (1990) *The Machine that Changed the World.* New York: Rawson Associates, based on the Massachusetts Institute of Technology's International Motor Vehicle Programme (IMVP).

11 More technically, the marginal cost curve is the first derivative of the total cost curve: $\mathrm{d}TC/\mathrm{d}X$.

12 See Harding, op. cit., note 6.

Competition and Market Structure 1: Perfect Competition and Monopoly

You can have any colour you like, so long as it's black.

(Henry Ford on the Model T Ford, 1908)

The basic actor in a market economy is the firm. It brings material, money and labour together to produce goods and services. It is the firm that supervises the process of adding value – from buying in raw materials to organising the marketing and distribution of the final product. It is the firm that puts new techniques and ideas to practical use; and it is the firm that harnesses human capital to the best advantage. The vitality of a capitalist economy depends upon the vitality of its firms.

(Will Hutton, *The State We're In*, p. 111)

1 Introduction

What is it that economic theorists and policy makers have found so attractive about the model of supply and demand that they want to base models of the macro economy on it? Why is it that business people blithely talk about the 'rigour of the market' and praise 'healthy competition'? And why, as world markets become larger, are companies breaking themselves into smaller autonomous business units?

The answers to these questions again lie in an analysis of very simple economic models. These models, as this chapter will show, demonstrate powerfully the theoretical strength of competition over monopoly in creating advantages for consumers and producers alike. For example, prices will be lower and output higher under a more competitive structure, which represents a welfare gain for all those who are buying the product. Similarly, if a company is producing in a competitive market, it will be under pressure to keep its prices as low as possible, meaning that it will also have to keep costs low in order to guarantee that it makes profits. Arguably this makes the company more efficient in the long run, despite the loss in revenue of having to charge lower prices.

One small proviso is worth mentioning here before we embark on a close examination of the models. The two models covered in the chapter seem a far cry from what happens in the business world and many students struggle to understand 'the point' behind the analysis. They are both based on limiting assumptions (such as no product differentiation and no advertising). This means that their applicability to real situations is at best dubious, and some authors have bitterly criticized the market-driven economics and economic policy that the blind adherence to these assumptions creates.[1]

However, we are covering the models for a number of reasons, not least because they allow you to understand how economists see the links between the decisions that individual businesses make, the markets in which they operate and the economy as a whole. Further, modern businesses compare their performance against an industrial 'ideal' and we can do the same. We can take the 'ideal' of a perfectly competitive market structure, compare it against what really happens and predict how prices and output might change if the market became more competitive. Such a 'competitor analysis' – i.e. an analysis of what competing companies are producing, what it costs them to produce it and how they are formulating their strategies – is a linchpin of any company's business strategy. Finally, of course, an introductory economics text would be incomplete without making a thorough examination of these models, and they do allow us to make predictions about the freedom of companies autonomously to follow through their strategies, particularly over pricing and output.

It is this link with strategy that makes the models of particular interest to us as students of business. We can define strategy very broadly as the means by which the company harnesses its internal capacity in order to compete in the market place. A company has to analyse its own demand and cost structures in order to be able to maximize its profits – these are central to an effective analysis of its internal (organizational) strengths. But in order to compete it will also have to be aware of the behaviour of other companies that are producing a close substitute – not least because if costs are lower, they will be able to make more profit. It makes strategic decisions on the basis of this analysis of its 'internal' and 'external' environment.

This chapter will show you that the freedom that a company has to follow through key strategic decisions over what price to charge and how much to produce is fundamentally determined by the number of other companies producing a close substitute product. As analysts of companies we are therefore able to predict and anticipate their behaviour under different market conditions: this is a powerful analytical and strategic tool.

2   Aims and Objectives

The overall aim of the chapter is to show you how to put all the curves that we have studied so far on to one diagram, to establish the price and output levels of firms under perfectly competitive market structures and monopoly market structures. By the end of the chapter you will be able to draw accurately and understand the equilibrium position of firms operating in these situations.

The specific objectives are as follows:

1   To allow you to understand why the number of firms in an industry is an important factor in the pricing and output decisions of a company.
2   To enable you to predict how firms will behave and markets will change under the market conditions of perfect competition and monopoly.
3   To help you understand the uses of these models in benchmarking actual industries against a theoretical 'best practice'.
4   To give you an understanding of the limitations of the models in preparation for discussion of 'real world' factors elsewhere in the book.
5   To introduce a 'strategic matrix' which relates the key predictions of the models covered to decisions which companies must make.

3   Investigation (1)

Please make sure that you are fully familiar with all the models that we have covered so far. If you do not feel confident, then try the exercises and read the text again until you are. Quite simply this is because the models of this chapter put all of the curves we have studied so far on to one diagram.

Once you have reassured yourself, jot down some thoughts on the following.

1   Think about the petrol stations in your area. Are there a lot of petrol stations near to one another? If so, what is the price range (roughly) of the petrol they sell. If one petrol station puts its prices down significantly, what do the nearest stations do with their prices? If there is only one petrol station nearby, how do its prices differ from those of its nearest competitor?

2 Why do you think that the prices that a petrol station charges are affected by the number of competitors in the area?
3 Think about other markets where products are very similar and prices vary only slightly between retail outlets. Jot some of them down and think about why companies have very little leeway over the prices they charge.
4 Why can a small village petrol station charge higher prices for its petrol than its counterparts in the town?

4 Pulling It All Together

Thus far we have examined demand, supply, the market mechanism and cost structures. We have covered all the major curves of economics at this level and, while you might find variations of the curves and different approaches elsewhere, in essence you will have learned sufficient by now to grasp the basics of why economics is important to business.[2]

But, as students of business, we are really interested in how companies make decisions and the factors that influence those decisions. To keep the analysis simple for the time being, we can assume that the two major decisions that a company makes are over how much of a particular product it produces and the price it charges for that product. In reality, of course, the decisions that companies make are considerably more complex, particularly if the company is producing more than one product. But as we saw in our analysis of demand, the pricing decision is extremely important, and our analysis of the market mechanism demonstrated that companies could not afford to have unsold stock, so the assumptions are a sensible basis for starting our analysis of company behaviour under different market structures.

5 Perfect Competition

We start our discussion with a reminder that this model is a theoretical ideal, and that it would be extremely difficult to find it replicated exactly in the real business world. With that in mind, we go on to make a number of assumptions about market conditions in a perfectly competitive structure as follows.

A perfectly competitive market structure is one where:

1 *The product is homogeneous.* This means that all companies are producing an identical product: loaves of identical size, weight and
taste, silicon chips for computers, petrol for cars etc. There are no
differences at all between the products that each company sells and
the company cannot attempt to differentiate its product in any way.

2 *There are a large number of buyers and sellers.* This is an important
assumption because it means that no one person has significant
power in the market place. If one company puts its prices up too
high, its customers will simply buy elsewhere. Similarly, there are
no dominant consumer groups which distort the market by paying
disproportionately higher (or lower) prices.

3 *Firms are price takers.* This means that the firm concerned will
have to accept the price that is set by the interaction of supply
and demand in the market place. Because there are so many producers of exactly the same product no producer has the capability
to increase prices without losing custom.

4 *Freedom of entry and exit.* This assumption is critical to the model.
If a firm is not covering its costs with its sales revenue in the long
term it will go out of business; there is no restriction to it leaving
the market at all. Similarly, if an entrepreneur looks at a market
and decides that profits could be made by operating within that
market, then he or she is free to do so.

5 *No government intervention.* The government will not assist entrepreneurs or intervene in any way that affects the free operation of
supply and demand in the market place.

6 *There is perfect knowledge of the market.* For simplicity it is assumed
that all consumers and all producers know exactly what is going to
happen in the market place in terms of prices, competitor actions
and so on. This is so that the model can arrive at an equilibrium
smoothly.

7 *Consumers and producers are 'rational'.* All consumers will be seeking to maximize their utility and all producers will be seeking to
maximize their profits.

These are obviously limiting assumptions, but are necessary in order
to make the model 'work'. We can relax these assumptions and look
at situations as they occur in the real world in the next chapter.

5.1 The Equilibrium Position for a Firm in a Perfectly Competitive Market

In a perfectly competitive market we assume that there are so many
consumers and so many producers, all selling an identical product,

Figure 5.1   Demand, revenue and price under perfect competition.

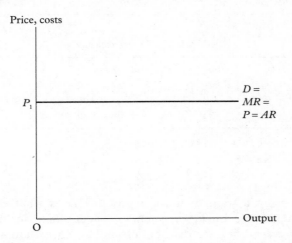

means that consumers can buy from anywhere and gain the same level of satisfaction from purchasing the product. For example, if you like thick-sliced white bread, you gain the same satisfaction from buying a loaf of it, no matter whether you buy it from a large supermarket or a small baker.

This makes demand perfectly price elastic, or a horizontal line, as shown in figure 5.1. What this line tells us is that if the price changed at all demand would completely change as well. You buy your loaf of white bread from the same shop every time, and it costs 45 pence. Suddenly the shop puts its price up to 55 pence. As you budget carefully on the basis of a 45 pence loaf, you are not willing to pay the extra 10 pence and so you buy your loaf from another shop, where the price has stayed a 45 pence. All the other consumers of white sliced bread will do the same, creating an infinitely large change in the demand faced by the shop that has put up its prices.

Price

Demand is perfectly elastic at price P_1, which is the price set by the market interaction of supply and demand for the product. The individual company has to accept this price. If it puts up its prices it will lose all of its demand, as the example of white bread showed above. If it puts down its prices then the company will be so swamped with demand that it will not be able to cover its costs. In addition, there is the danger that it will not be able to cover its costs in the long term with the increased demand and the lower prices.

Table 5.1 The average daily revenue of the FT: July–August 1995

Price	Total sales	Total revenue (no. copies × price)	Average revenue (TR/price)
65p	285 742	£186 732.30	65p
32p	5 175	£1 656.00	32p
15p	5 823	£873.45	15p
Average daily sales	295 740	£189 261.75	64p

Source: Data supplied by the *Financial Times*.

Revenue

Any business will want to make a profit. This is what enables it to continue operating: buying in supplies, paying for machinery, paying for employees, paying for distribution and so on. These are costs, as we saw in chapter 4, and the company will always try to keep these at a minimum. In order to cover these costs, the company has to receive revenue. All the money that the company receives in return for the produce it has sold will be its *total revenue* (*TR*). So we can write the equation for profit in a company as follows:

$$\pi = TR - TC$$

where π is profit; TR is total revenue; TC is total cost.

In order to know exactly the relationship between the volume sold and the revenue received, a company might calculate average revenue (*AR*), which is the total revenue divided by the total quantity sold. In other words, it is the average price that the company charges for a unit of its product and can be given in symbols as follows:

$$AR = \frac{TR}{X}$$

where AR is average revenue; TR is total revenue; X is total quantity sold.

Table 5.1 returns to the newspaper example of earlier chapters. It calculates the total revenue of the *Financial Times* from the sale of its 295 740 copies per day. You can see that the average revenue that the company receives from the sale of the FT, including its low-price schemes, is 64 pence a day. As long as average revenue is equal to or greater than average cost, the company will make a profit.

This is an essential calculation for a marketing department, as it will give an idea of the flexibility over pricing strategy that it has. In the case of the FT, its strategic use is to show the minimum price that can be charged in order to cover costs. It can then guarantee that, by segmenting the market, it has covered costs even at the lowest prices.[3]

Marginal revenue is a similarly important concept for a company, as it is the change in total revenue brought about by the sale of one extra unit. In symbols it is shown as follows:

$$MR = \frac{\Delta TR}{\Delta X}$$

where MR is marginal revenue; Δ is the change in; TR is total revenue; X is total amount sold.

As with average cost, it gives an indication of the profitability of the company. If marginal revenue is less than marginal cost the firm will not be making a profit in the long term. If marginal cost and marginal revenue are equal the firm at least covers the costs of producing that level of output.

Under a perfectly competitive market both average revenue and marginal revenue would be equal to the price set by the market. This is because the company is unable to influence demand at all by altering its price: it has to accept the price that is given by the market, which means that no matter how much the quantity sold changes, both average and marginal revenue will be the same. Look back at figure 5.1 and you will see that average revenue, marginal revenue, demand and price are all equal.

If you find this difficult, try the example in table 5.2 for a hypothetical loaf of white sliced bread costing 50 pence per loaf. Cover up the final three columns and calculate the total, average and marginal revenues using the equations above.

Costs
We looked at length at costs in chapter 4 and you should now be comfortable with the shapes of all of the cost curves. When we are drawing the equilibrium position for a firm under a perfectly competitive market structure we need to make use of the marginal cost curve and the average cost curve. We put them on the same diagram, as shown in figure 5.2.

Table 5.2   The total, average and marginal revenue for a loaf of white sliced bread costing 50 pence a loaf

Number of loaves sold	Price	Total revenue	Average revenue (per loaf)	Marginal revenue
1	50p	50p	50p	50p
2	50p	£1	50p	50p
3	50p	£1.50	50p	50p
10	50p	£5	50p	50p
50	50p	£25	50p	50p
100	50p	£50	50p	50p

Figure 5.2   Costs under perfect competition.

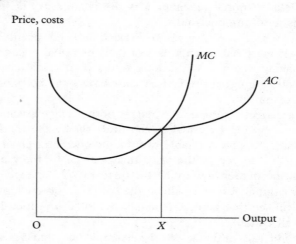

You will see that the marginal cost curve passes through the average cost curve at the lowest point on the average cost curve and is sloping upward as it does so. Think back to the cost curves in chapter 4. The marginal cost curve is the rate at which total costs are changing as output increases; it is the change in total cost divided by the change in output. Similarly, average costs are total costs divided by the level of output. In other words, marginal cost is also the rate at which average costs are changing.

So it follows that if marginal cost is less than average cost, then average cost is falling; if marginal and average costs are equal, then average costs are at their minimum point (i.e. the rate of change is zero);

and if marginal costs are greater than average costs, then average costs are rising. The relationship between the two therefore demonstrates how economies of scale are gained. In order for the company to be operating efficiently, marginal costs and average costs must be equal and the marginal cost curve must cut the average cost curve at the minimum point.

Equilibrium

In order to predict the equilibrium position of a firm operating in a perfectly competitive market structure we put all of these curves on one diagram. We do this simply so that we can see how much control over prices and level of output the company has. In neo-classical economics the concept of equilibrium is important because it shows the level of prices and output consistent with the market clearing (i.e. everything that is produced being sold). For our purposes, the concept of equilibrium is important because it shows us the outcome of a strategy.

The firm needs to make 'normal' profits; that is, it needs to cover all of its costs in the long run and cannot have any surplus profit left over after it has covered its costs, or other firms will enter into the market expecting to make a profit themselves. We develop the concept of 'normal' profits below. For now it is enough that the company has to cover all of its costs and must have nothing left over in the long term. These are the profits of perfect efficiency.

Conditions for normal profits are theoretical although, again, for a company operating in a highly competitive market structure there is a logic behind them. The conditions are:

1   $D = MR = AR = P$. This condition means that the company has accepted the price charged by the market and faces a perfectly elastic demand curve. The company has no control over price movements and so it will not be able to alter price in order to sell more. So average revenue, marginal revenue and price are all equal.
2   $MC = MR$. This is a very important condition for equilibrium. When marginal costs and marginal revenue are equal, the costs of producing an extra unit are equal to the revenue gained from the sale of that unit. For example, it costs 50 pence to produce a loaf of white sliced bread and the revenue gained from selling that loaf of bread is 50 pence.
3   $MC = AC$. Where marginal costs and average costs are equal and marginal costs are rising, all economies of scale are reaped.
4   $SAC = LAC$. In the short and the long term the company has achieved all economies of scale: it is operating at the minimum

Figure 5.3 Equilibrium under perfect competition.

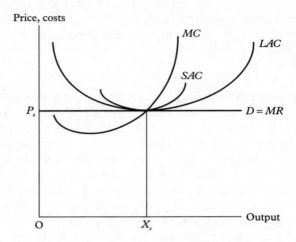

point on the average cost curves for both the short and the long run. It is thus perfectly efficient.

All of these conditions have to be met for the firm to be in equilibrium in the long term. If we draw these conditions, we arrive at a diagram that looks like figure 5.3.

At the level of output X_e all the conditions for making a normal profit are met:

- All costs are covered and there is no surplus profit at price P_e.
- All economies of scale are reaped and costs are as low as they can go in the long run.
- All output is sold; there is no surplus stock.

5.2 The Relationship between the Firm and the Industry

Under a perfectly competitive market the relationship between the firm and the industry is an important one. The firm has to accept the prices set by the forces of supply and demand in the market place because there are so many producers supplying an identical product. Consumers are free to buy the product from any company and will want to pay the lowest prices. Any discrepancies in prices will cause entry and exit of firms until an equilibrium price is reached.

Figure 5.4 The relationship between the firm and the industry under perfect competition.

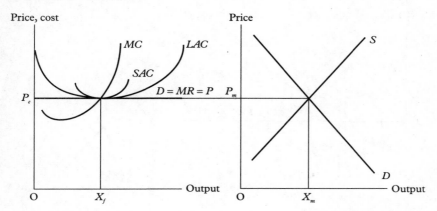

The basic relationship between the firm and the industry is shown in figure 5.4. On the right-and side of this diagram is the market supply and demand model that we have covered in earlier chapters. The equilibrium price is reached where supply and demand cross over one another. At that price everything that is produced in that market is sold; the market 'clears'.

In order to ensure that this happens the firm accepts the price that is set by the interaction of supply and demand, P_e. It has to charge this price and it faces an elastic demand curve about this price. As we saw above, this means that price, marginal revenue, average revenue and demand will all be equal. *Because* it is a price taker, the firm has no choice over the price it charges.

In order to work out the quantity that it must supply to the market at this price, the company looks at its marginal cost curve and produces where marginal cost and marginal revenue are equal. This guarantees for the individual firm that the costs of producing an extra unit are met by the revenue that will be received for the unit. In other words, supply will equal demand for the individual firm. It will produce at the level of output consistent with marginal costs and marginal revenue being equal.

The marginal costs and marginal revenue condition for equilibrium is not sufficient to ensure that the company remains in business in the long run, however. The company will only remain in business if it is covering its average costs in the long run *and* is perfectly efficient. It must therefore be producing at the bottom of the long-run average

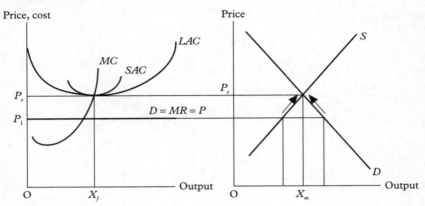

Figure 5.5 The relationship between the firm and the industry under perfect competition: price too low.

cost curve. The level of output, X_f, and the price, P_e, meet all the conditions for equilibrium in the long term.

Look now at figure 5.5. How does it differ from figure 5.4? What do you think will happen to the market if the firm continues to charge the price P_1? Is it covering its costs? What must it do in order to remain in business in the long run?

Figure 5.5 shows the state of the market when the market price is too low at P_1. At this price companies in the industry are not covering their long-run average costs, even though marginal cost and marginal revenue are equal. They cannot afford to operate like this in the long run. Further, there is an imbalance in the market place, where the price which is currently being charged creates excess demand and insufficient supply.

There are two solutions to this problem:

1 Some companies could increase their prices to P_e. This would reduce demand and increase supply, and there would be upward pressure on prices until the equilibrium was reached.
2 Other companies may well go out of business if they continue to be unable to cover their costs. This will also put upward pressure on prices as fewer firms would be producing the product.

Now look at figure 5.6, which shows an imbalance in the market place where prices are too high. What will happen in the market place this

Figure 5.6 The relationship between the firm and the industry under perfect competition: price too high.

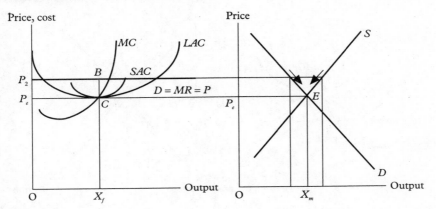

time? Will there be fewer or more producers after a shakeout has taken place?

At price P_2 there is a disequilibrium where more is supplied than is demanded. Individual firms (as shown on the left-hand side of figure 5.6) are making profits because the price is too high: they are more than covering long-run average costs. The amount of profit they make is represented by the rectangle, P_eP_2BC.

Again, there are two solutions to this problem:

1 Individual companies could put prices down. They might have to do this if the cost of unsold stock becomes too high. This has the effect of reducing supply and increasing demand.
2 It is more likely, however, that entrepreneurs will look at the market and see that there is potential for making profits in that line of business. Once they enter the market even more is produced, which makes the good less scarce and, again, puts downward pressure on prices.

6 The Relevance to Business – Examples

A couple of examples will demonstrate why the above analysis is useful. First, take the example of Lucas given in chapters 2 and 4. Here was a company striving hard to reduce its costs and being unable to charge a price other than that set by the market for its product. It

Figure 5.7 The losses of Lucas Diesel Systems when costs were too high and the subsequent improvement.

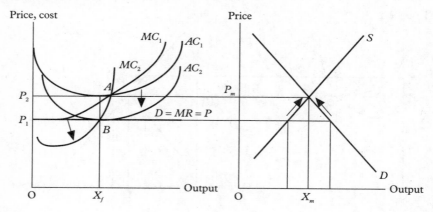

found, however, that in the early days of its reform process, its average costs were very high, say AC_1 on figure 5.7. Although it was efficient at that level of output (i.e. producing at the minimum point on its average cost curve), it argued that it was not *effective* – it was not producing on a low enough average cost curve to survive in the market with its major competitors. Further, it was only able to charge the price P_1, meaning that it incurred losses equal to the area P_1P_2AB in the diagram.

Following the changes represented by the plant rationalization as well as the introduction of quality management programmes and continuous improvement, the plant has seen two things:

1   A fall in its average costs (from AC_1 to AC_2) has meant that it can charge the industry price without sustaining a loss. This is the move from efficiency to effectiveness which the company desired. It has reaped all its economies of scale on both curves but has a lower average cost structure on AC_2.
2   A shift in its marginal costs (from MC_1 to MC_2). The marginal cost curve is, effectively, the supply curve of the company, because it shows the relationship between changes in costs and changes in output which is central to the supply decision. This shift in marginal costs means that the company can afford to supply more at each market price – it has become more efficient and more effective. This shift has been induced by the change in strategic goals of the company.[4]

Figure 5.8 Exit from the magnetic disk drive industry.

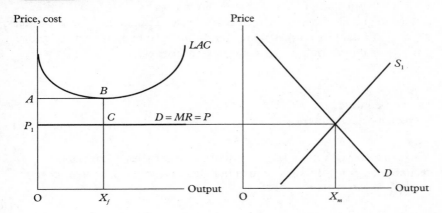

The second example is of the computer hard disk drive industry and is based on a study of the magnetic disk drive industry.[5] This was a rapidly growing market in the 1980s and early 1990s as computer technology developed and enabled the floppy disk market to diminish. It was found that a large number of companies globally entered the market anticipating high profits but that the level of exit from the industry was also high in the early evolution of the product market. It was also found that the exit of firms was accelerated by excessively high costs.

Again this can be illustrated using the models above. Remember, this is a highly competitive industry with technology developing quickly and, therefore, pressures on costs are significant. The equilibrium of a loss-making company is shown in figure 5.8, which shows the equilibrium price set by the market at P_1. At this price a firm with the average cost curve *LAC* is not covering costs. It will exit from the market place because it cannot make a normal profit in the long term.

7 Investigation (2)

Clearly, although the models are highly theoretical, they can be applied to real business situations and used to predict outcomes of competitive forces. The particularly useful conclusion that can be drawn from all this is that although there are many very large firms operating in every industrial sector, these companies have to be very competitive in terms of costs. In other words, the model of perfect competition tells us a lot about competitive pressures in an era of 'lean' production.

You might like to test this on a few other industries. Using Mintel reports to establish market share trends and company reports to gauge costs, you could look at the following industries:

- clothing and textiles;
- semi-conductors;
- personal computers.

What are the common features of these industries (think about new technology, new products, consumer demand and, of course, costs)?

8   Monopoly

We move on now to examine the opposite end of the industrial spectrum, where there is a monopoly supplier of a product. In other words, there is only one firm that produces a product and there are no close substitutes for it. Monopoly power in the UK has traditionally been associated with the 'natural' monopolies of the public utilities, such as water, gas, coal and electricity. We can also see examples of a large amount of market power akin to a monopoly in the provision of railway transportation (British Rail, as was).

Care must be used when looking at monopoly power, however. The public utilities, such as water, electricity and gas, are now in the hands of the private sector and, by 1998, will have been so deregulated that there is the potential for a large number of competitor suppliers of these services. Similarly, British Rail, as the sole supplier of railway transport until plans for its deregulation, was in the position of a monopolist. However, there have always been substitutes for rail travel: cars or coaches, for example. Arguably, competition for the provision of transport services generally has always been fierce and has become more so as increasing numbers of individuals obtain cars.

Once again, then, we have to say that we are studying a theoretical position, but, equally, that it has its applications in the real world. The particular importance of monopoly theory as a predictor of a firm's behaviour lies in the ability of the monopolist to create long-term market power for itself through erecting barriers to entry. These barriers to entry might take the form among others of cost differentials, predatory pricing (low, even loss-making, pricing in order to gain market share) or frequently technological barriers, largely through patenting.

Let's examine this last barrier as a good example of how a company might become a sole supplier of a product and create monopoly power for itself. In 1986 Lotus Development Corporation was an extremely successful software development company leading the development of spreadsheet technology through its revolutionary product, *Lotus 1–2–3*.[6] In a period of five years it had become a company valued at US$400 million, with profits of $38 million a year. It had created a monopoly for itself as the only supplier of a spreadsheet with the power of *Lotus 1–2–3*, and it protected its power by filing a patent on the product which prevented other companies from entering the market.

However, patents on software are short term, lasting for a maximum of five years. During the life of the patent the company had a very effective monopoly position and was cash rich, as the level of profitability showed. However, it was not spending enough money on developing its product in order to withstand the competition once the patent expired. While Lotus was experiencing the excess profit of a monopoly position (which we will explore in a minute), other companies were closely examining the software and 'reverse engineering' it: in other words, dismantling the product, finding out how it operated and then deducing how to manufacture it more cheaply. When the patent ran out, any number of cheap clones were waiting to enter the market.

This process of technological dynamism was termed 'creative destruction' by Joseph Schumpeter, who was the founder of modern thought on technological development. He argued that the excess profit of monopoly was a 'necessary evil' in ensuring that companies had enough resources (or 'slack' or 'synergy') to be able to innovate. There is a fierce debate in the technology literature about the most efficient organizational structure and size for innovation.[7] What is important here is that many companies do use patents as a means for creating monopoly power and the resultant excess profit can, in the short term at least, be against the consumer's interest because of the high prices charged, as we saw in the case of Lotus.

We have already covered the main predictions of the monopoly model: that prices will be higher than under perfect competition, that excess profit will be made and that, cushioned by this excess profit, organizational 'slack', or inefficiencies, will result in the monopolist becoming 'lazy' in terms of innovation and product development. Let us turn to the formal presentation of the model now in order to see how these conclusions are derived.

Figure 5.9 Demand and marginal revenue under monopoly.

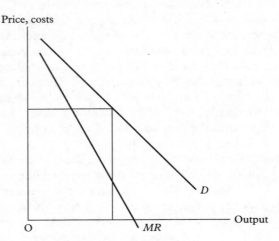

8.1   Demand and Revenue

Figure 5.9 shows the demand curve faced by the monopolist. As you can see, it is a normal downward sloping demand curve. The firm is the only producer of the product and so this is also the market demand.

The relationship between demand and marginal revenue is important for the monopolist. Marginal revenue is downward sloping and it will always be less than demand. The reason for this is common sense: in order to sell more of the product, the monopolist has to reduce the price (this is a basic prediction of the downward sloping demand curve). So, the extra revenue that the monopolist gains from selling an extra unit of the product will be less than the prevailing price of that product.

A numerical example may help to make this point clearer. Marginal revenue is the revenue from the last unit sold minus the net price reduction necessary to sell that unit. Our baker might actually face a downward sloping demand curve – the bread is baked on the premises and is different to anything available in the immediate vicinity.[8] As soon as the demand curve is downward sloping, marginal revenue is less than average revenue, as shown in table 5.3.

For example, as table 5.3 shows, if the baker reduces the price of a loaf from 50 to 49 pence, the total revenue falls from £1 to 99 pence. Average revenue then becomes 49.5 pence and marginal revenue is calculated using the formula:

| Table 5.3 | Illustration of marginal costs |

Number of loaves (Q)	Price (P) = average revenue (AR)	Total revenue (TR = Q × P)	Marginal revenue (MR = $P_x - (P_{x-1} - P_x)$)
1	50p	50p	
2	49p	98p	48p (49 − (50−49))
3	48p	£1.44	47p
4	47p	£1.88	46p
5	46p	£2.30	45p
6	45p	£2.70	44p

$$P_x - (P_{x-1} - P_x)$$

where P_x is the price of the extra unit and P_{x-1} is the price at which the previous unit was sold.

$$= 49 - (50 - 49) = 48$$

Try this calculation now using the price reduction of a penny a loaf, then check your answers against those in table 5.3.

8.2 Marginal Costs and Marginal Revenue

As with the firm in a perfectly competitive market, the monopolist will want to equate marginal revenue and marginal cost in order to establish a market clearing level of output. This is shown in figure 5.10. The monopolist will want to ensure that there is no unsold stock, and so will equate marginal cost and marginal revenue and produce in order to set its level of output. This is represented by X_m in figure 5.10.

You will notice, however, that this level of output does not correspond with demand at the price P_c. This is because the level of output is set by marginal revenue and marginal cost and not by looking at the market demand curve. If you follow the line up from X_m through the point where MC and MR are equal to the demand curve you can find the price that the monopolist will charge. Monopolists are the only suppliers of the product, so they can decide how much to supply and then calculate the price to charge by looking at the demand curve. They are *price makers*.

Figure 5.10   Marginal revenue, marginal cost and demand under monopoly: determination of an equilibrium level of price and output.

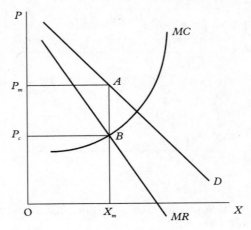

8.3   Equilibrium and Profit under Monopoly

Already we can see that the price charged by the monopolist is higher than that charged by a perfect competitor because the monopolist is a price maker as the only supplier of a product. This makes monopoly unattractive from the consumer's point of view. A further reason for suggesting that monopoly could be against consumers' interest is found in the level of profit that a monopolist makes.

You will recall from the discussion of perfect competition that, under a perfectly competitive market structure, individual firms make 'normal' profits. In other words, they cover all the costs directly and indirectly associated with bringing a finished product to market but do not have any financial 'slack' or money left over. Accountants rather than economists would be able to give exact instructions on budgeting for remuneration to directors and dividends to shareholders, but even these are the types of costs that can be included in the definition of normal profit. The important point is the *efficiency* that making a normal profit implies.

In contrast a monopolist will make an excess profit. We can see why this happens by examining the relationship between the level of output and the costs of production. Remember that the monopolist is the only supplier of the product and thus does not have to be perfectly

Figure 5.11 Equilibrium under monopoly.

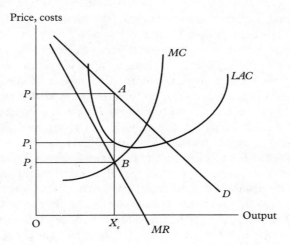

efficient in the long run, as no entrepreneur will be able to enter into the market because of the barriers to entry that exist.

Look carefully at figure 5.11. Where on the average cost curve is the monopolist producing? Can you work out the level of profit that the monopolist is making?

Figure 5.11 shows the long-term equilibrium position of a firm operating as a monopoly. As we have already shown, the monopolist equates marginal revenue and marginal product to establish the level of output it should produce (here, X_e). It then projects this level of output on to the demand curve it faces and calculates the price it should charge given that level of output (here, P_e).

This more than covers the costs of production. The long-run average cost curve is shown by *LAC* in figure 5.11. As you can see, at output X_e, the monopolist is not producing at the minimum point on that curve but is covering the costs of production with the price P_e.

The level of profit, then, is represented by the revenue over and above that which is necessary to cover costs. In figure 5.11 this is the area of the rectangle P_cP_eBA. Excess profit is non-productive money. It is not reinvested and it is not paid out to employees in terms of bonuses. It is the extra money that is associated with monopoly power, i.e. where the company is the sole producer of a particular product, can charge any price and does not need to produce at the minimum point on the average cost curve.

8.4   *Comparison of Monopoly and Perfect Competition*

It is in the predictions about profit that the real differences between monopoly and perfect competition can be established. If you recall from previous chapters and from the beginning of this chapter, economists regard profit as a measure of the efficiency of the organization. Thus, a company that is making a 'normal' profit in a perfectly competitive market is *theoretically* more efficient than a company making an excess profit in a monopoly market because the perfect competitor has to produce at the bottom of the long-run average cost curve.

In either market situation, the equilibrium is set by equating marginal cost and marginal revenue for the industry as a whole. Under a monopoly the firm is a price maker. It equates marginal cost and marginal revenue and produces accordingly. The price that corresponds to that level of output from the demand curve is charged by the monopolist.

For the perfectly competitive market, all the marginal cost curves added together are the supply curve for the industry (simply demonstrating the clear link between costs and quantity supplied). Equating marginal cost and marginal revenue means that the costs of output are covered by the revenue received. You will remember that where supply equals demand (here, where marginal costs equal demand) is the market price; it is also the price that must be accepted by all the producers in the market place. The price will be lower than the price charged by the monopolist. So prices are higher and output lower under monopoly, the monopolist makes an excess profit which is not possible under perfect competition and does not have to produce at the bottom of the long-run average cost curve.

This does not tell us much about which market structure produces the better results for the consumer, however. The perfectly competitive structure is arguably restricted in that it provides economic efficiencies and no slack. While prices are low and output high, the *choice* that individual consumers have could be limited: markets are so competitive in terms of production costs that very little can be put into product development and innovation. This has led some commentators to argue that a degree of monopoly power (at least a downward sloping demand curve) is a good thing. Competition through innovation and product development is fierce, ensuring that any excess profit, or slack, has to be put straight into new areas. Companies have to compete through efficiencies as well as product differentiation and so consumer choice is widened and prices are not significantly higher. The further reading at the end of this chapter allows you to investigate this contention further and we examine different, and less theoretical, types of market structure in more detail in the next chapter.

9   Investigation (3)

Ambitious but a Bit Frightening

Gazprom, Russia's monopoly gas company, plans to sell shares to foreign investors. Robert Corzine, Nicholas Denton and John Thornhill explain why

Soviet-era superlatives may no longer be appropriate to today's recession-ridden Russia. But they still apply to Gazprom, Russia's biggest company and, by at least one definition, the largest hydrocarbon producer in the world, with output greater than that of Saudi Aramco.

Later this year Gazprom, Russia's monopoly gas producer and distributor, plans to sell 9 per cent of its shares to foreign investors.

Some western investors see this as a unique opportunity to get in on the ground floor in a company that could dominate for decades one of Europe's most important and fastest-growing energy markets. Others, however, wonder whether Gazprom can transform itself into a fully competitive, international company, given its bureaucratic culture and the economic and political uncertainties that bedevil Russia.

What is not in dispute is the size and scope of Gazprom's reserves and operations. It controls 34 per cent of the world's known natural gas reserves, supplies nearly a fifth of total west European gas demand and is the country's single largest source of hard currency, earning between $6bn and $7bn a year.

Internationally, bankers regard it as the most creditworthy of Russian companies. At home, Russians joke that Mr Victor Chernomyrdin, its former chairman, took a demotion to become prime minister.

Its plans are ambitious and, to some westerners, a bit frightening. At a presentation in New York last year, Mr Rem Vyakhirev, Gazprom chairman, spoke about the development of yet another giant gas field. 'Our grandchildren will work for Gazprom,' noted one US banker. 'Gazprom 2094: Big Brother,' scribbled another.

Yet it is Gazprom's size and monopoly status that attract many western investors and bankers. Unlike the Russian oil industry, there has been no attempt to split the company into smaller units.

Its influence is such that, last year, 34 per cent of its shares were sold for privatisation vouchers in a closed auction mainly held in gas-producing regions, rather than through the open offer system used for other privatisations. This meant that a large proportion of the shares went to investors in western Siberia, the heart of the company's operations.

Employees hold an additional 15 per cent, while the state retains a 40 per cent stake. Foreign shareholders will be sold the shares now held by the company, a 10 per cent stake.

The company enjoys an independence from government that reflects the country's overwhelming dependence on gas. Russian industry is one of the most gas-intensive in the world, and gas provides the bulk of Russia's heating needs.

The company is not without its domestic critics, however. A group of officials in the Ministry of Fuel and Energy argues that Gazprom should be broken up to introduce greater competition and efficiency in the domestic gas market. They are trying to encourage other companies to develop gas fields independently of Gazprom.

Western experts who have spent time with Gazprom say it makes sense to keep it intact, at least in the medium term. 'Gazprom is among the few Russian organisations that actually works,' says Mr Jonathan Stern, a consultant for the International Energy Agency, the west's energy-monitoring body.

For the moment Gazprom's directors exude confidence. They can be scornful of the reserves and expertise of foreign companies, and have rejected almost all proposals to develop jointly fields in Russia, although they say such co-operation may be possible for particularly remote and technically demanding projects. Gazprom has, however, been busy forging alliances and relationships with western energy groups and suppliers. Last month, it took a 10 per cent stake in the UK–Continent Interconnector, a £440m undersea pipeline being financed by a number of international energy companies to link the British and Continental European gas grids.

It has a 35 per cent stake in Wingas, a joint venture with Winter-shall, the natural gas subsidiary of German chemicals giant BASF. It also has partnership arrangements with companies including Ruhrgas, the German gas company, British Gas, Snam of Italy and Enron of the US. Such companies are among the many mentioned as possible trade investors in Gazprom, although most are non-committal.

But why is Gazprom so keen to see foreign companies on its shareholder register? After all, say industry observers, Gazprom can enter industrial alliances with ease, there is growing western demand for Russian gas, it can raise international loans and it receives preferential treatment from the present government in Moscow.

The main reason is a cash shortage, caused by its need to refurbish much of its network and expand its export capacity at a time when its bad debts are at record levels.

The company's annual sales are thought to be equivalent to $10bn–$11bn. But it is owed about Rbs7,000bn by Russian industrial customers and former Soviet republics. It is politically impossible for it to cut off key industrial users.

The company is pressing ahead with improving the efficiency of its production and pipeline network. Although Gazprom has long been able to buy critical equipment from abroad, parts of the system are less efficient than those of western counterparts. Gazprom's management realises that 'they could make major savings by spending some money now', says Mr Stern.

Gazprom also needs to expand its export capacity and flexibility. At present the main export pipeline to western Europe runs through Ukraine.

That gives Kiev a potential stranglehold over the company, a fact which Gazprom's western customers view with concern.

The company wants to build a multi-billion-dollar pipeline between its vast gas fields in the Yamal Peninsula of Arctic Russia and western Europe via Belarus and Poland. 'Gazprom needs to go ahead with that pipeline even if it doesn't have the long-term contracts to fill it,' says Mr Stern. It will not eliminate Gazprom's dependence on Ukraine, but it at least represents a 'credible alternative' for some customers.

What is the likelihood of Gazprom succeeding in its proposed share offering? Some observers are sceptical that the transaction will take place as planned. One corporate financier recently put the likelihood of the offering coming off at 25 per cent.

Others say that, as long as Gazprom's financial data remain fragmentary and distorted, its advisers and potential institutional investors may not feel able to go ahead. There are also concerns about Gazprom's ability to manage its share register.

It says it will use its powers over the registration process to ensure a ring fence between domestic and foreign shareholdings. But foreign investors have recently complained about the ability of Russian companies to maintain share registers accurately.

Western industrial investors may view a Gazprom shareholding in more strategic terms. They might also be able to use their knowledge of Gazprom's operations to make a more accurate assessment of the true state of the company.

But they too are concerned about the uncertainty in Russia. 'You do not know whether your dividend rise will be greater than the rouble's depreciation,' says an executive with one western company.

In spite of such problems, the prospect of being among the first foreigners to buy into Gazprom, whenever the offering takes place, has excited some investors. But a successful offering is likely to depend less on the company's ability to dazzle investors with its size than on how it impresses them with its mastery over the financial details of its far-flung operations.

You will find the tools of analysis that we have covered in this chapter and previous chapters useful for analysing case 5, which is a study of the Russian monopoly supplier of gas – Gazprom. Read the case and then answer the following questions.

1 What market structure best describes the Russian gas industry? Is this a structure which is replicated in other countries, and if so, why?
2 How would you use economic models to describe the equilibrium operating position of Gazprom? Does this model explain the need for the company to raise cash through issuing shares to foreign companies?

Figure 5.12 A matrix of strategic control.

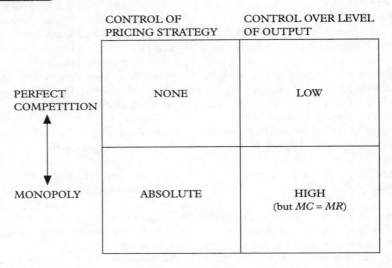

	CONTROL OF PRICING STRATEGY	CONTROL OVER LEVEL OF OUTPUT
PERFECT COMPETITION	NONE	LOW
MONOPOLY	ABSOLUTE	HIGH (but $MC = MR$)

3 How might Gazprom improve its profitability by spending more money? Will this make the company more internationally competitive?

4 Would there be a case for breaking the Russian gas supply market up into smaller competitors? Use examples from the British experience of privatization of its public utilities to inform your answer.

10 Conclusions

This chapter has been highly theoretical and no apology is made for that. But the models have important strategic implications as well. We started off with a definition of strategy which argued that the central thrust of any business strategy was to harness internal capabilities (effectively cost structures and organizational slack) with the external environment. We have looked at one central part of a company's external environment – the competitive structure of the industry – and we have seen that the models of perfect competition and monopoly apply to both small and large companies in the real business world.

We can summarize the strategic implications of the chapter in a matrix (see figure 5.12). The matrix is not meant to be an exhaustive examination of all areas of strategy, but it is a useful starting point. It predicts behaviour given market structure in the strategic areas of pricing and output.

As the market moves from a highly competitive structure to a monopoly structure, so control over pricing and output increases and, as we have seen in the cases covered in this chapter, companies both large and small can be in a highly competitive situation because of the pressure on costs from market forces (Lucas is a large company while the magnetic disk drive companies were not). But equally, any company can create a degree of monopoly power for itself by erecting barriers to entry – particularly through technology, innovation and patenting, which allow it to make excess profits. We return to this in the next chapter.

11 Further Reading

Kay, J. (1996) *The Business of Economics*. Oxford: Oxford University Press, chapter 7.
Lazonick, W. (1991) *Business Organisation and the Myth of the Market Economy*. Cambridge: Cambridge University Press.
Schumpeter, J. (1943) *Capitalism, Socialism and Democracy*. New York: Harper.

Notes

1 See Lazonick, W. (1991) *Business Organisation and the Myth of the Market Economy*. Cambridge: Cambridge University Press; Ormerod, P. (1994) *The Death of Economics*. London: Faber and Faber; Hutton, W. (1995) *The State We're In*. London: Jonathan Cape.

2 We have not studied some of the more complex models within microeconomics, such as indifference curves, revealed preference theory and isocosts and isoquants. If you are interested in these areas or are keen to develop a complete picture of economics as a discipline there are some excellent texts which would provide you with more detail. Sloman, J. (1997) *Economics*, 3rd edn. Hemel Hempstead: Harvester Wheatsheaf; Parkin, M. and King, D. (1992) *Economics*. Wokingham: Addison Wesley; Lipsey, R. G. and Chrystal, K. A. (1995) *An Introduction to Positive Economics*, 8th edn. Oxford: Oxford University Press; and Begg, D., Fischer, S. and Dornbusch, R. (1994) *Economics*, 4th edn. London: McGraw-Hill, all give an introduction to these topics. The topics covered are sufficient, however, to give you a good grounding to understand business, and will lay the foundations for further, business-related study.

3   This analysis does not suggest that lower prices equal lower sales. In fact, the company had *increased* sales by segmenting its market: it would otherwise only have total sales at the full cover price of 65 pence.

4   You will recall that chapter 2 argued that the supply curve had become perfectly elastic at this price. This is not inconsistent with the above argument: at the point where marginal costs and marginal revenue are equal the supply curve for Lucas arguably does become perfectly elastic because the company has to supply any quantity at that price. But it increases the complexity of the diagram and has therefore been omitted from the discussion.

5   Freeman, J. (1995) Technological and economic selection in the evolution of a new product market: an empirical study. Paper to the Science Policy Research Unit, University of Sussex, June 1995.

6   Material for this section is derived from the Harvard Business School case 9–487–036.

7   See Schumpeter, J. (1943) *Capitalism, Socialism and Democracy*. New York: Harper; Galbraith, J. K. (1978) *The New Industrial State*. Harmondsworth: Penguin.

8   We will look more closely at product differentiation in the next chapter. This example is simply to show you how marginal cost is calculated.

Competition and Market Structure 2: Imperfect Competition

Economists prefer, for the most part, to write about firms which always get things right, rather than firms which are fallible. This is not because the typical economist believes that firms do not make mistakes. Rather it is a result of a methodology such an economist employs in order to reduce the possibility that she, herself, will make mistakes or end up with nothing to say.

(Peter Earl, *The Corporate Imagination: How Big Companies Make Mistakes*, Harvester Wheatsheaf, 1984)

I   Introduction

Until now we have been looking largely at hypothetical situations which we have then used as tools for examining (and understanding) the real world. Chapter 5 looked at two highly theoretical models of the behaviour of firms under two different market structures: monopoly and perfect competition. We can use them, as was said, as a benchmark for actual competitive structures in the real economy. More importantly, we need the basic models that we covered in the previous chapter in order to look at two more realistic models of competition in this chapter.

If you recall from chapter 5, we developed a matrix of the power over the key decisions of price and level of output that a company would have under two market structures. We argued that under a perfectly competitive structure it would have very little control over output and no control over price. In a monopoly structure the company has complete control over price (indeed, it can use it as a barrier to entry) and is only constrained in terms of output insofar as marginal cost must equal marginal revenue. As markets become less competitive, the influence over strategy, particularly in terms of price, increases. The market mechanism, then, was a resource allocator and was used to describe how prices were set in a perfectly competitive market.

We are relaxing this assumption slightly in this chapter[1] in order to understand how prices as they are determined by 'the market' translate into company strategy. It is argued that the market mechanism, influenced as it is by the numbers of buyers and sellers operating in the market place, is important in sending a *signal* to companies about the prices that they can legitimately charge. The freedom that the company has to set its own prices without losing competitiveness, then, will be determined by the extent to which the company has to be a price taker. This is, in turn, determined by the slope of the company's demand curve or, more particularly, the extent to which it can command a degree of monopoly power through product differentiation.

We also looked briefly at excess profit and technology. A paradox was beginning to emerge: neo-classical economics regards profit as an efficiency criteria but economists who have specialized in the evolution of technology argue that *excess* profit is necessary for innovation. On the basis of the formal material that we have studied thus far, a company that is making a 'normal' profit will be efficient in that it reaps all possible economies of scale. Conversely, a company that makes excess profits over and above the amount necessary to cover costs is *X-inefficient* (or managerially 'slack') because it has so much power that it does not have to produce at the bottom of its average cost curve. Every day we observe companies that gain from product differentiation, that create barriers to entry through technology *and* that make excess profits. Yet these companies also have to be cost competitive even though they are not operating in a 'perfect' market.

This, then, is where economics comes face to face with reality. In the world which we all recognize, no business has perfect knowledge of the market in which it operates, and there is government intervention. Products, however similar they may seem, are differentiated. Indeed, it becomes very difficult to define 'industries' as distinct from product markets because two apparent substitutes (such as a Rover 100 and a Rolls Royce) serve completely different segments of market demand. As a result, every single company can exert some control over the prices that it charges for its good or service. The result is market imperfections, where consumers send mixed messages to producers about their demand, where consumers are influenced by advertising campaigns, where huge organizational structures override the decisions of single entrepreneurs and where companies innovate in order to create competitive advantage. In short, it is the world where strategy is complex and companies make mistakes.

Of course, this is the world in which we are interested as students of business. It is a world clouded by uncertainty, disequilibrium and asymmetry largely because it is a world controlled by *people*, who do not always act rationally as orthodox economics might have us believe.

Figure 6.1 Market share under a perfectly competitive market.

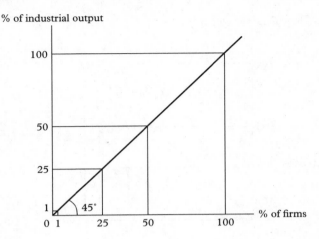

The role of strategy in the operations and competitiveness of the company is central. And this strategy has considerably more strands to it than simply pricing and output.

2 The Theoretical versus the Real World

The model of supply and demand assumes a perfectly competitive economy where there are a large number of buyers and sellers and where no one individual company or consumer can influence the market place. Under this system the market demand curve is normal and downward sloping; the demand curve faced by the individual firm is perfectly elastic. We can represent the market share of each company in this theoretical structure, as shown in figure 6.1.

The 45° line which extends upward to the right is a theoretical 'ideal' where every single company operating in a market has an identical market share. As you can see from the diagram, 1 per cent of firms operating in this ideal industry have 1 per cent of the total market share. Similarly, 25 per cent of firms have a 25 per cent market share, 50 per cent of firms a 50 per cent share and so on to 100 per cent of the firms and 100 per cent of the market.

In reality, markets never look like this. Often you will see a few large firms dominating a high percentage of industrial output at one end of

Figure 6.2 The Lorenz curve showing actual market shares in an industry.

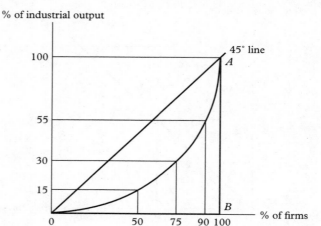

the market, and then a large number of small firms operating in a highly competitive structure but only controlling a small percentage of industrial output. This scenario is illustrated in figure 6.2, which compares the 45° line with an actual industrial structure.

The curved line is called the Lorenz curve. It shows the distribution of market share in an industry. In this hypothetical industry 50 per cent of firms have only 15 per cent of the market, 75 per cent of firms have only 30 per cent of the market and 90 per cent of firms have only 55 per cent of the market. This suggests a highly skewed distribution, where very few firms account for 45 per cent of market share.

This isn't just another theory. A very large number of industries look like this. Examine table 6.1, which shows the distribution of market shares in the first stages of domestic gas deregulation in 1996.[2] From this you can see that it is usual for large firms to dominate the market share, with a large number of smaller competitors fighting it out for a relatively small proportion of the market.

2.1 Investigation (1)

We can use the Lorenz curve as an indicator of the concentration of industrial power and you might like to try this out on some examples of your own. Look at some Mintel reports for industries of your choice. How many firms control 50 per cent of the whole market? How many firms control 75 per cent of the market? Are there a lot of small firms

Table 6.1	Market share of the suppliers to the domestic gas market in the South West of England in phase 1 of deregulation (December 1996)

Company	South West of England market share (%)
British Gas	76.30
Amerada	0.003
Eastern Natural Gas	8.60
South West Electricity Board (SWEB)	6.50
Northern Electric	0.001
Calortex	8.6
Total	100

Source: telephone interviews.

at the bottom of the market controlling a relatively small proportion of industrial output? You could roughly plot this on a diagram (preferably using squared paper). Work out the area of the triangle made between the horizontal axis and the 45° line by counting the squares. Then draw in your example. Count the triangles in the segment between the 45° line and the Lorenz curve. Subtract the second from the first and you have what is called the Gini coefficient of industrial power. If its value is high, the market is highly competitive: the Lorenz curve is close to the 45° line. If its value is low, market power is concentrated in the hands of a few companies: the Lorenz curve is a long way from the 45° line.

3 Competition in Practice

Let's look now at the way in which companies compete at each end of the market as described in the Lorenz curve. There are theories for the small companies at the bottom of the market (called monopolistic competitors) and for the few, large, companies at the top of the market (called oligopolistic competitors). This area of economic theory is one of the most dynamic areas of economic thinking – constantly being interpreted and reinterpreted using models and empirical studies. The models presented here are the simplest ones that allow you to interpret some of the decision-making problems that companies under these structures might face. As such, they are still limited to decisions over pricing and output.

The important point to remember throughout this chapter is this. In contested markets (i.e. highly competitive markets) the role of strategy is central to ensuring that a company remains in business: monitoring demand fluctuations and price responsiveness, keeping costs low and communication channels effective, forecasting macroeconomic trends and their impact on the business and, critically, evaluating the behaviour of competitors in the market place. Collecting together all this information, making sense of it and then turning it into a *strategy* which is appropriate to the company's own internal structures and priorities is a complex process. It is also one fraught with potential for errors, not least because information that comes back from the market, from competitors and even from within the organization is not always reliable or consistent – it is asymmetric.

Coming to terms with asymmetric information and formulating policies accordingly is a central part of strategy but falls outside the remit of a text like this. However, many of the tools that we have already covered in the introductory chapters of this book provide an underpinning to strategy. For example, is demand price responsive or unresponsive? Does the company rely on low costs to achieve low prices? How important are economies of scale in the long term and so on. Ultimately, of course, the importance of each depends on the number of competitors. More specifically, the market structure determines the freedom that the company has over pricing and output decisions. This is the central pillar of the so-called 'structure-conduct-performance' debate which has dominated industrial economics since the 1930s.[3] We have come back to economics again, and it is to more detail on this that the discussion now turns.

4 Monopolistic Competition

Monopolistic competition is often called 'competition among the many'. What this means is that a large number of small companies are competing fiercely for a highly contested but relatively small proportion of the total market share. All these companies differentiate their product so that no two companies are identical. The following conditions apply to a monopolistically competitive market:

1 *Product differentiation.* This is an important distinguishing characteristic between this model and the model of perfect competition. The companies all produce close substitutes for one another (for example, different types of personal computers), but all are slightly

Figure 6.3 Pricing and output in the short run in a monopolistically competitive market.

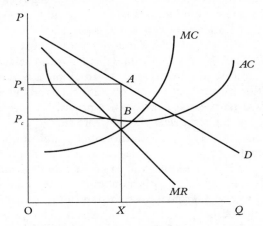

different (different memories, different software, modems, compatibility with other systems etc.). This product differentiation allows it to command some 'brand loyalty'. In order to sustain this loyalty, the company engages in advertising and product development.

2 *Profit maximization.* For simplicity we can still assume that maximizing profits is the overriding objective of the firm. It will pursue strategies such as cost minimization in order to do this.

3 *Cost minimization.* Because of the highly competitive market, with all companies producing close substitutes for similar prices, the monopolistically competitive firm will have to keep costs low – in the long run it will have to produce at the minimum point on its average cost curve. If it does not, it will be pushed out of business by more efficient competitors.

4 *Freedom of entry and exit.* As with the perfectly competitive market structure, we will assume that companies can enter into and exit from the market freely.

4.1 Monopolistic Competition in Pictures

A diagram of the decisions over pricing and output that the company faces under a monopolistically competitive market in the short term is given in figure 6.3. Neo-classical economics usually distinguishes between the short run and the long run in this type of market. Arguably, the monopolistic competitor will not make excess profit in the long run because other firms will enter the market.

Concentrating on the short term for the time being, however, you will notice that figure 6.3 looks very similar to the model of monopoly equilibrium covered in chapter 5. Because there is product differentiation the company commands a small amount of monopoly power. Its share of the total market is very small and its product is only slightly differentiated from those of its close competitors. This means that the demand curve faced by the individual firm is more elastic than that in the market as a whole, but is downward sloping nevertheless.

In practice this means that a firm operating under this type of market structure will have some control over prices. Some customers will be willing to pay higher prices for the product than others simply because they 'like' it. So, as with a monopoly, the monopolistic competitor's marginal revenue curve is less than the demand (and average revenue) curve: it has to reduce the price in order to sell extra units of the product. And, again as with monopoly, the company will equate marginal revenue and marginal cost to determine its level of output. It will look to the demand curve for the price to charge to ensure that that level of output is sold. The result is excess profit in the short run equal to the area of the rectangle $P_c P_\pi AB$.

Neo-classical economics predicts that this position, with a company making excess profits in this type of market structure, will not be sustainable in the long run. There is freedom of entry and exit, so if entrepreneurs see excess profits being made in a given market they will start to operate in that market in anticipation of likewise making a large profit. This scenario is given in figure 6.4.

The main difference between the short and the long run is in the position of the demand and marginal revenue curves. As more competitors enter the market, the demand curve for the individual firm shifts to the left (because there are more firms taking up the, already small, market share). As it shifts, so too does the marginal revenue curve, similarly inwards towards the left. The cost curves do not change because the scale of the company has not changed, but the company may produce less, meaning that it is further away from the minimum point of the average cost curve and experiencing increasing returns to scale. At price P_n the company is not making an excess profit and there is no incentive for further firms to enter the market place.

4.2   Relevance to Business: Two Examples

Again, the models seem very theoretical for an explanation of what happens in the real world, not least because we are still concentrating

Figure 6.4 Pricing and output in a monopolistically competitive market in the long run.

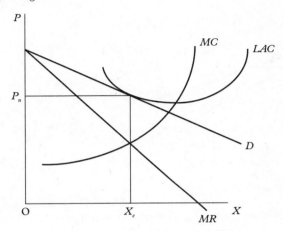

on price, output and profit as the pivots of economic behaviour. We return first to our example of the hard disk drive industry.

One company's disk drive is not the same as the next. There are always small differences in the power and capability of the drives which allow companies producing them to invest in research and development (R&D) (particularly product development) in order to sustain their market share or to formulate strategies for competitive advantage in the market place.

It has already been seen that there was a high degree of entry and exit to and from the hard disk drive industry. We expressed this in chapter 5 in terms of costs, suggesting that if costs were high then companies would be more likely to exit from the market. If we examine this more closely, however, we can see that forces of product differentiation, or more particularly new product development, were extremely important too. The market is highly competitive, with a large number of producers, but it is a monopolistic market because of the importance of product differentiation in the operation of competitive forces.

This product differentiation was extremely important in allowing new entrants to the market to gain a market niche and achieve high profitability quickly. Companies from Far Eastern countries quickly learned to segment the total market so that while they were competing in one area of the market they could develop a new, more sophisticated, product for another segment which then superseded the first.

Figure 6.5   Monopolistic competition through product differentiation and market segmentation in the hard disk drive industry.

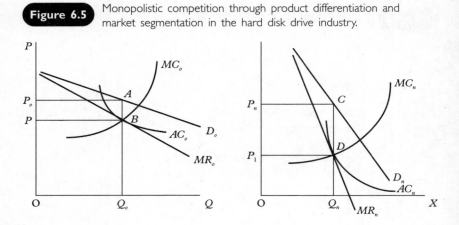

In doing this they created a downward sloping demand curve with a high degree of monopolistic power. The comparison of the two market segments is shown in figure 6.5.

The graph on the left-hand side shows a company that has entered into a market when the technology is relatively old and demand is more elastic (because of the number of competitors producing a similar product). All companies have to be efficient and produce at the minimum point on their average cost curve, as the industry is highly competitive in the long run. However, a degree of excess profit equal to the area of the rectangle PP_oAB is possible because products are differentiated slightly.

The graph on the right shows market segmentation behaviour of the Far Eastern companies. These companies have experienced the level of profits in the old technology as discussed above, but have used this profit to fund extra research and development in order to establish new products for new segments of the market. In these new segments the degree of monopoly power is significant because at the beginning of the product's life there are no close substitutes. As we saw with the case of *Lotus 1–2–3*, the duration of such a monopoly is particularly short in the electronics industry. However, while it lasts, the companies face an inelastic demand curve (D_n) and profits represented by the rectangle P_1P_nCD.

Research has demonstrated that the behaviour of American firms who originally dominated this market has been remarkable. Instead of remaining in the industry and seeking to put large sums of money into R&D they have instead exited from the market and concentrated on alternative areas of production to which their cost structures and capabilities are better suited.[4]

So, in addition to prices, outputs and costs as conditions for competitiveness, we are beginning to see the central importance of new product technology in monopolistically competitive markets. This is further illustrated by the case of small biotechnology companies. 'Biotechnology' as a discrete industry is in its infancy, although it is expanding rapidly as the importance of this area of research has increased in the diagnosis and treatment of serious illnesses such as cancer.[5]

The development of the drug and diagnosis technology which we are witnessing now is a direct result of the R&D conducted by very small companies (called dedicated biotechnology companies or DBFs). As is consistent with a monopolistically competitive market, there were a large number of them founded between 1975 and 1987: 400 in the United States and over 80 in Europe. And in the infancy of the industry the large drugs companies did not enter the biotechnology market at all, choosing instead to concentrate on their existing strength in the traditional areas of chemistry and biology.

The reason why the large companies watched from the sidelines lies in the nature of the technology that was being developed. Biotechnology is an entirely new way of approaching health problems. It represented a revolution in the *process* by which these problems could be approached. While there was always the potential for significant price and cost advantages to be reaped by companies who developed and marketed products from biotechnology, these products could not be developed until enough basic research had taken place on the process of manufacturing these products. So, the small DBFs were developing a process technology for the larger companies to exploit at a later stage.

Small, highly competitive and research-based companies had an advantage in the development of the technology over the large pharmaceutical companies for two very important reasons. First, the development of a path-breaking technology is a risky business. Large companies may be more risk-averse than smaller ones because they will only want to invest in something once they can be sure that they will not lose market share from the investment. The losses of small companies are, by definition, smaller, and from a large company's point of view it is worth waiting until the technology has developed significantly before any major investment takes place. By the early 1990s the large drugs companies were beginning to invest in a large way in the technology in order to develop products. As a result smaller

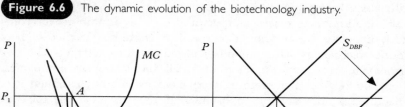

Figure 6.6   The dynamic evolution of the biotechnology industry.

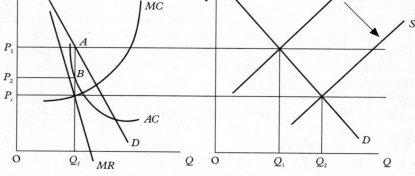

companies have left the market or been taken over by larger companies. This is illustrated in figure 6.6.

The left-hand graph shows a company with costs AC charging a price P_1 for the biotechnology research that it is conducting. It makes a profit represented by the area of the rectangle P_2P_1AB. Once the technology develops and processes become established, more firms enter the market, anticipating profits. In particular, large firms with lower cost structures and more scope for scale economies and new product development start to operate in the market, shifting supply from S_{DBF} to S_1. Prices fall to P_c. At this price a small company with costs AC can no longer compete. It will not necessarily go out of business, however, if its 'differentiated product' (i.e. the research it conducts) is of value to a large company. Instead, it is likely that the company will be merged with a larger company.

The second reason why small companies were responsible for developing biotechnology in its infancy is an organizational one. The technology was new, with the potential profoundly to alter existing managerial and operational structures.[6] A small company, as we saw from the model of perfect competition, has to be efficient and adapt swiftly to changes in the market in order to remain competitive, particularly in terms of prices and output. In a monopolistically competitive market the 'product differentiation' is all important to competitiveness. Thus a small company wanting to remain competitive must not only be efficient in terms of costs, but also adapt rapidly to changes in the scientific and market environment, such as technological advances made elsewhere. A large company, because of its organizational slack (or managerial inefficiencies), is less able to adapt this rapidly.

4.3 Investigation (2)

The above examples show us how dynamic the evolution of technology is in an industry. This is a point worth investigating further in the context of a focused study of technological development generally. You might like to examine the development of the microelectronic industry. Was it large or small companies that were responsible for the development of the technology in its early stages? Here are three books that might help you:

Bessant, J. (1991) *Managing Advanced Manufacturing Technology: the Challenge of the Fifth Wave.* Oxford: Basil Blackwell.

Freeman, C. (1982) *The Economics of Industrial Innovation,* 2nd edn. London: Pinter (although there are more recent editions, this edition contains valuable information about the development of microelectronic technology).

Coombs, R., Saviotti, P. and Walsh, V. (1987) *Economics and Technical Change.* Basingstoke: Macmillan.

5 Oligopoly: Competition among the Few

The case of biotechnology illustrates powerfully how market power shifts as technology in an industry develops. Small companies dominated the market while the emphasis was on process development. Once market share was to be gained through product development, large companies entered the industry.

These are oligopolies, or large companies competing for a large share of the market. The products they produce can be substitutes and highly differentiated (like cars or newspapers) or very similar (like oil or petro-chemicals). Competition between the companies will be very fierce because each has a lot to gain by winning customer loyalty and a lot to lose in terms of profits if it loses that loyalty and, hence, market share. In this type of market structure firms will be able to build up strong technological and pricing barriers to entry, so it is extremely difficult for new firms to enter the market.

Oligopolies are hard to model within the framework of neo-classical economics because of their complexity. They are huge organizational structures with complex decision-making processes that concern all aspects of the good or service being produced – not just the manufacturing. And every large industry is different: different numbers of companies, different regulatory environments (i.e. freedom to set prices), different technologies and, for theoretical purposes at least, different methods of setting prices across the industry as a whole.[7]

The strategies of the individual company are central to its functioning and, for this reason, we will not dwell too much on equilibrium models of the firm under oligopolistic structures, as it makes us concentrate unreliably on pricing and output. As students of business we will find many other disciplines, such as sociology, psychology, human resource management, strategy and even accounting, which can explain extremely well the complexity of modern business. We will instead look at the one area of oligopoly theory which is both simple and extremely powerful in explaining the nature of pricing and competition in oligopolistic markets.

5.1　The Nature of Oligopoly and the Kinked Demand Curve

Large companies, all competing with one another for ever bigger shares of the total market, have three distinguishing features. First, they will not compete in the long run through prices; second, they are strategically interdependent on one another; third, they will erect barriers to entry to prevent other businesses from competing in the market place.

You will be able to think of many examples of large companies which have competed through price: the broadsheet newspaper price war discussed in earlier chapters was a good example of one company in particular trying to gain an ever larger market share. But the price war was very damaging to the newspapers that embarked on it: News International (the owner of *The Times*) lost profitability and the *Daily Telegraph* and *The Independent* lost market share because of it. As a result, *The Times* had put up its price to 35 pence by November 1995.

So, because of an action to gain market share, the pricing strategy of *The Times* had had an impact on its own profitability and reduced the market share of two other newspapers. And, in order to keep their markets at all, both of these newspapers had to follow the types of strategy which were being pursued by *The Times*. Two newspapers, the *Financial Times* and the *Guardian*, were not unduly affected by the price war, but followed alternative strategies to create longer-term customer loyalty. But even these companies had to think seriously about how they were marketing and branding their product as they felt the

Figure 6.7 The kinked oligopoly demand curve.

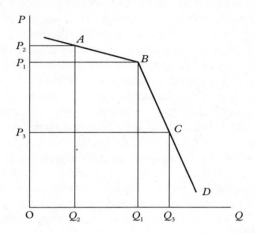

knock-on effect of the price war. This shows how the elasticity of the demand for newspapers generally and the finite size of the total newspaper market makes all the companies strategically interdependent on one another.

One model used to explain the rigidity of prices in an oligopolistic market is that of the 'kinked' demand curve, as illustrated in figure 6.7. You will notice that it is not a straight line but is 'kinked' at the price P_1. This 'kink' implies that a severe price cutting strategy cannot be sustained by an oligopolist in the long run.

The kinked oligopoly demand curve illustrates the 'worst case scenario' of a price war. You will see that the curve is highly elastic above the point B on the curve (for example, price P_2, quantity Q_2). Below the point B (say at price P_3 and quantity Q_3) the curve becomes highly inelastic. Why does the company face a curve with that shape?

The reason lies in the interdependency of oligopolistic firms. Any decision-maker formulating any strategy, especially pricing strategy, will have to examine the effects of the decision made for the company. That is always the case for any decision-maker in any company. But in an oligopolistic market the stakes are high: the sales and market share gains are large and, hence, the potential for profit is also large. Further, other companies producing substitute products will also have sufficient slack or capacity to reduce prices if our company puts prices down; if it puts prices up other companies will sit tight with their prices at lower levels.

5.2   Pricing and the Theory of Games

This dilemma is central to the decision-making process in oligopolies. Using this demand curve we can predict that aggressive pricing strategies can only be followed by a company in the short term, and only if it is making a significant amount of excess profit to be able to support the interim losses it might make. In fact, we can go further and suggest that an oligopolistic company will be reluctant to embark on a price war because of the damaging impact it might have on its market share and profitability. As a result, oligopolists will not compete in terms of prices but will embark on non-price forms of competition.

Examining figure 6.7 more carefully we can see how this works. Remember that all the companies in the market are producing substitutes for one another, which means that consumers can switch their demand to another product if the price goes too high. If a firm increases its prices from P_1 to P_2 and decides to operate at point A on the curve, it will reduce its market share considerably, by the distance OQ_1 to OQ_2. It will lose market share, and, hence sales revenue. But, more importantly, the curve has become more elastic at the higher price because none of the other companies in the market has followed suit and similarly put up prices. The firm is on its own, charging higher prices for a product for which there are close substitutes at a lower price.

The company may decide to put prices down, say from P_1 to P_3, and to operate at point C on the curve. It will gain market share from doing this, as demand has risen from Q_1 to Q_3. But the demand curve has become inelastic because companies producing substitutes have also put down their prices, anticipating that they will also be able to gain market share. The company has to put prices down by a large amount in order to generate a significant increase in demand. This of course results in a loss of revenue equal to the difference between the two rectangles OQ_1AP_1 and OQ_2BP_2.

This is the 'worst case scenario'[8] referred to above. If a company puts up its prices, no one follows suit and so considerable market share is lost. If a company puts its prices down everyone follows suit, so that while there might be a gain in market share there will also be a loss in revenue as the demand curve becomes inelastic. As a result companies will not compete in terms of price in the long term.

An example of how rigid prices in the market translate into non-price competition at a strategic level can be found in the domestic gas market example given at the outset of the chapter. There were, as of January 1997, 12 companies seeking to supply gas to the deregulated domestic market in the South West and the South East of England – still relatively few, and hence an oligopoly structure. One of these companies, British Gas, had previously had a monopoly of the market and thus dominated supply. Further, it was restricted by the regulator, OFGAS, from embarking on anti-competitive behaviour such as price cutting strategies in order to allow competition to develop. We return to the role of the regulator in chapter 7.

As a result, any company seeking to supply to the domestic market could price cut. However, as we saw in chapter 2, demand was fairly inelastic at 0.85 per cent and, again as we saw in chapter 2, this gave an individual company very little scope to cut prices below 30 per cent of the British Gas price. From a marketing perspective, the companies had to offer the consumer significant savings but the potential for gaining significant market share by reducing prices was limited.

The result of this dilemma was for all the companies to offer similar price reduction packages of between 17 and 21 per cent and to create loyalty by some other means. Some offered cash inducements, others offered benefits according to payment method and others still varied the standing charge. But in reality, the price variance between the companies was quite small. Instead, companies sought to attract customers through non-price methods: boiler servicing, transferability of accounts, ease of payment, product branding and niche marketing. The companies competed to differentiate their products to the customer in order to ensure loyalty over a period of time.

Product differentiation, particularly in an industry with a homogeneous product such as gas, is a complex business. It relies heavily on anticipating the advertising and sales techniques of competitors, obtaining information about their strategies, anticipating the behaviour of potential entrants, watching closely consumer behaviour in the market place and, equally importantly, reviewing previous strategies and their effectiveness. Strategy formulation is a dynamic process and an outcome of the 'game' of watching others and yourself in the market.

5.3 Price as Strategic Advantage in an Oligopolistic Market

How, then, will the price P_1 in figure 6.7 be determined? As we have seen, the usual forces of supply and demand will not operate under oligopoly. We have also seen that any aggressive pricing strategy which seeks to win one company greater market share over its competitors is, in the long term, unsustainable. Recent price wars in the newspaper industry, the car industry and the supermarket sector of the retail industry have demonstrated this.

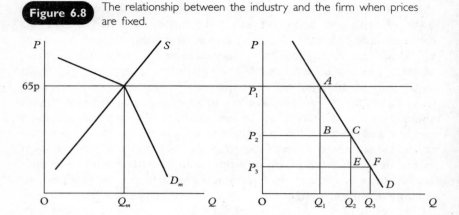

Figure 6.8 The relationship between the industry and the firm when prices are fixed.

Oligopolies may collude, or form agreements to set prices. These can be open agreements, like the recently dismantled Net Book Agreement, which set recommended prices below which companies that signed up to the agreement could not go. Alternatively, the companies can form 'tacit' agreements to allow one company to set prices which the others then follow. This is called *price leadership*. Often the dominant firm which sets prices is the market leader and the 'tacit' agreement is formed by the knowledge that unless other companies follow suit, they are likely to go out of business!

Even under a 'collusive' agreement, companies will be able to follow pricing strategies – it is important to distinguish between interdependency in the industry and pricing as a means of marketing in the individual company. By charging different prices to different segments of the market, a company can gain in terms of both market share and market penetration. We covered this *price discrimination* in chapter 2 in the context of the *Financial Times'* overall marketing strategy. Let's look now at how a company can gain revenue and long-term brand loyalty from this strategy.

Figure 6.8 illustrates the price established by the kinked oligopoly demand curve of 65p for a newspaper (pre-price war) on the left-hand side. On the right-hand side it shows how the individual company can then gain extra revenue through market segmentation and price discrimination.

The FT, shown on the right-hand side of the diagram, charges the price set by the market, say 65p for a newspaper. You should now feel comfortable with the analysis of the demand curve that this diagram represents. What is important here is that the company has gained its market share on the basis of the price set by the market. Without then embarking on the damaging price war which is shown on the inelastic part of the kinked demand curve, the company can increase its market penetration by charging different prices to different markets where there will be no resale between markets.

So, for example, at P_1, the company gains the rectangle OP_1AQ_1 in revenue. However, the company can increase its revenue by dividing its market up into mutually exclusive segments. The segments of the market – for example, students and city fund-managers – cannot sell the newspaper on, as they do not come into contact with one another. Clearly a student is not going to be able to afford the full price of the paper and so a decision is made to sell it at a lower price to this group. This does not prevent the full cover price revenue from being received, but instead, ensures total sales of Q_3. Similarly, an intermediate group, charged the price P_2, increases demand to Q_2. As a result, revenue is increased by the rectangle Q_1BCQ_2 at price P_2 and Q_2EFQ_3 at price P_3. The company has not had to embark on a price war, but has increased its revenue and sales.

Price discrimination such as this (and derivative forms of it) is very common in oligopolistic industries. Theatres charge different prices for different seats; electricity companies charge different prices depending on the time of day that you are using the electricity (this is called peak load pricing); trains charge different prices for different seats and different prices for travelling at various times throughout the day. Car companies combine price discrimination with product differentiation: a company such as Ford has one basic system (or 'power train' – the engine and exhaust system) and then adds different bodies to it. The Ford Sierra and Escort, for example, had the same power train but different bodies. The costs of producing the two models were very similar, but the company charged a different price for each, thereby segmenting the market.

So, at an industry level, prices might well be fixed. An individual company can use prices to develop its market share, however, as some of the examples above have shown. However, economics will predict that oligopolistic companies will tend not to compete in terms of prices but instead will use forms of non-price competition (particularly product differentiation and efficiency) to ensure market share.

5.4 Technology as Non-price Competition?

Look back at the example of biotechnology earlier in the chapter. If you remember, large firms did not enter the market until the product development stage, when real market share advantages could be reaped. By this time all the pricing and cost (process) efficiencies had been developed by the small companies. It would not have been fruitful for the larger companies to enter the market while prices were falling, as this would have been too risky. Instead, they waited until they could gain from the actual products that could be developed on the basis of the research of the small companies. In other words, they entered the market when they could compete in terms of products rather than in terms of prices.

New product development is a vital means by which companies compete, as this ensures market share and a degree of monopoly power while the other companies catch up. Once a new product is established, competition might take the form of advertising, differentiation, distribution, after-sales service and so on. But it is essential that the company invests in R&D in the first instance in order to ensure that it can gain its own competitive advantage.

The role of new product development cannot be overstated, particularly in hi-tech industries like the car industry. Chapters 2, 4 and 5 demonstrated how cost competitive a company like Lucas had to be in seeking to achieve competitiveness. But, by the company's own admission, this was not enough.[9]

Lucas's principal European rival in the car braking market was Bosch. Car component development during the late 1980s and into the 1990s was becoming increasingly complex, with automotive assemblers and components suppliers working together to develop complete 'systems' that would operate to make the car run more smoothly and fuel-efficiently. Accordingly, Bosch worked with the German car company, BMW, to produce the then revolutionary anti-lock braking systems (or ABS), which were electronically controlled braking systems for the car. The product was patented and Bosch enjoyed the resultant increased share of the braking systems market and profitability. It was competing in the industry by means of product development and gained considerable market advantage because of it. Lucas, in conjunction with Ford UK, developed a mechanical ABS for the Sierra which was considerably cheaper than its electronic counterpart. However, the product was never as successful as Bosch's version because competitiveness was determined by the product itself and not by its price.

6   Investigation (3)

Read the article on the Net Book Agreement (case 6).

CASE 6

Final Chapter for Book Agreement

Alice Rawsthorn explains what the death of the pact would mean for the UK publishing industry

At 8.30am today a group of men and women will gather at the elegant Georgian headquarters of the Publishers' Association in Bedford Square, London, to discuss the ending of the net book agreement.

The agreement, the 95-year-old pact whereby publishers can set book prices for six months after publication, has been under attack for months. Several publishers have either opted out of the agreement, or published particular titles outside it, with great success.

HarperCollins, Random House and Penguin, three of the UK's biggest book publishers, and W. H. Smith, the largest retailer, delivered the fatal blow yesterday by announcing plans to withdraw from the pact.

The consensus among publishers is that the net book agreement is now dead. This morning's meeting of representatives of leading publishers is expected to instruct the Publishers' Association council to dismantle the arrangement when it meets tomorrow. The book trade, which has been bitterly divided over the pros and cons of the agreement, will have to adjust to life without it.

The pro-agreement lobby argues that it has fostered diversity in UK publishing by saving independent publishers and booksellers from a price war. Its critics see it as an anachronism that prevents publishers and booksellers from cutting prices to increase

book sales as their counterparts do in the US.

'We've gone to and fro over the agreement for years and we've looked at everything that's happened when they've de-netted in other countries, like the US,' says Mr Roy Davey, a managing director of HarperCollins, 'We can't draw any sensible conclusions because the circumstances are never the same.'

Over the years, several publishers and booksellers have decided it would be to their advantage to opt out of the agreement. They include Reed, which owns the Methuen and Heinemann imprints, and Dillons, a large book chain.

Other leading publishers and retailers continued to abide by the agreement until Hodder Headline announced its withdrawal last winter. Hodder has since published three best-selling novels – John Le Carre's *Our Game*, Rosamunde Pilcher's *Coming Home* and Stephen King's *Rose Madder* – which have gone on sale at deeply discounted prices. All three were sold by the Asda and Safeway supermarket chains for £8.49 ($13.34) against a full price of £16.99, Mr Tim Hely Hutchinson, chairman of Hodder, says that sales of the three are 78 per cent higher than those of the previous works by the same authors.

Other publishers were furious, particularly when W. H. Smith, hitherto a staunch supporter of the agreement, ran a special promotion for *Coming Home*. 'What were we expected to do?' says one. 'Sit back and ignore the fact that Hodder was all over the best-seller lists?'

The pressure intensified when Penguin Books (a subsidiary of Pearson, which also owns the Financial Times) launched its successful Penguin 60s series of short stories and book extracts outside the net book agreement. BBC Childrens Books then announced its withdrawal.

The situation was aggravated by the publishers' financial difficulties. Consumer demand has been weak and costs have risen. Authors have demanded higher advances since Martin Amis signed a £500,000 deal with HarperCollins for three novels. Paper prices have also increased.

Penguin and HarperCollins both announced redundancies this summer. Hodder this week issued a profits warning – and Mr Hely Hutchinson said the situation would have been worse without its successful discounting.

Publishers were also coming under pressure from retailers, particularly from W. H. Smith, which has faced falling sales at its eponymous newsagency chain. 'We're doing everything we can to increase sales,' says Mr Peter Bamford, managing director. 'That involves price promotions of all our other products. Obviously we wanted to be able to do the same thing for books, as we sell more of them than anything else.'

HarperCollins, Random House, Penguin and the other large publishers began formulating plans to opt out of the agreement. 'We always said we'd support it for as long as it was sustainable,' says Ms Gail Rebuck,

chief executive of Random House. 'It doesn't give me any pleasure to say so but the events of this summer have proved that it wasn't.'

If, as the industry expects, the Publishers' Association council decides tomorrow to dismantle the agreement, retailers will be free to decide the price at which they sell books, just as they are for other products.

The impact on the book market will be determined by the scale and depth of discounting. It is highly unlikely that the prices of all books will fall; the industry expects to see selective reductions of particular titles, such as best-selling fiction and popular non-fiction.

'There's no point in cutting the price of a book if you're not going to sell more copies,' says Mr Alan Giles, managing director of Waterstone's, the specialist bookseller owned by W. H. Smith. 'We wouldn't discount a physics textbook, because the demand for that is inelastic. But I'm sure we'd be able to sell more copies of the new Salman Rushdie at a lower price.'

Even selective discounting will have a big impact on publishers. Retailers will demand reductions in the wholesale prices at which publishers sell books to them. In return, the publishers will probably insist that booksellers agree to place firm orders, rather than buying books on sale-or-return. Even if they agree to accept returns, they may require the retailers to sell a proportion of their books.

The pro-net book agreement lobby argues that large publishing groups will be able to adapt to the more competitive environment, but the pressure on smaller publishers will be intolerable. 'If retailers ask us for deep discounts the answer has to be no, because we can't afford it,' says Mr Matthew Evans, chairman of Faber & Faber, a leading independent publisher. 'But I doubt if they will. We don't publish those sorts of books. Who's going to discount Milan Kundera or Seamus Heaney?'

Similarly, small booksellers will find it impossible to negotiate the same discounts as large chains.

Some independents may be able to counter this by buying through wholesalers, which already handle an increasing share of sales. But Mr Tim Godfray, chief executive of the Booksellers' Association, fears other small shops will 'go to the wall'.

The most vulnerable retailers are likely to be independents which face direct competition from big branches of W. H. Smith, Waterstone's or Dillons. 'They'll be the ones that suffer,' says Mr Stephen Dunn, marketing director of Dillons. 'The specialists that sell every travel book ever published will be fine, as will the good independents in small places where chains like ours can't afford to open.'

However, book retailing chains such as W. H. Smith and John Menzies are likely to face stronger competition from supermarkets, such as Asda and Sainsbury. So far the supermarkets have been restricted to stocking non-net books and special batches of remaindered titles, but they are keen to sell more books if they can cut prices. They will now have a wider selection to choose from and are likely to take a larger share of bestseller sales.

The discount bookshops, which have expanded rapidly in the 1990s by selling returns and remaindered stock from publishers at bargain prices, will also come under pressure. They could be the first casualties of the net book agreement's demise if the supply of returns diminishes, and they will find it far harder to compete once mainstream retailers start cutting prices.

'Life in the book trade will never be the same,' says Mr Godfray of the Booksellers' Association. 'We can't turn the clock back.'

Which models from the material we have covered so far in the book are most useful in analysing this case? What market structure is likely to emerge from the demise of the Net Book Agreement and why? What would be the most effective strategies for small companies seeking to succeed in the market place? What would be the most effective strategies for large companies seeking to succeed in the market place?

7 Strategy, Non-price Competition and the Company

This chapter has taken the simple, neo-classical assumption that firms will profit-maximize and related this to how companies in highly

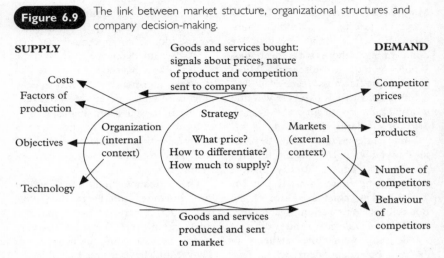

Figure 6.9 The link between market structure, organizational structures and company decision-making.

competitive market structures actually formulate their decisions.[10] It has been shown that even in highly concentrated market structures, like oligopoly, the pressure on companies to be efficient in order to charge similar prices to their competitors is absolute. Companies big and small differentiate their products in order to create customer loyalty and increased market share; they ensure that their organizational structures are efficient in order to keep costs as low as possible.

We can represent this in a simple model of strategy, similar to that found in the introduction to many strategy texts.[11] Figure 6.9 illustrates the relationship between company strategy and the internal (or organizational) and external (or market) contexts with which it has to deal.

Figure 6.9 illustrates the complex relationship between the forces of supply (here, costs, factors of production, goals of the company and technology) and the forces of demand (here, the prices of other, substitute products, the nature and availability of substitute products, the number of competitors in the market place and the behaviour of those competitors).[12] It shows how firmly rooted strategy is in the analytical tools of economics. Put simply, this is the interaction of supply and demand that we covered in chapter 2. However, in this model, we are developing the market mechanism to make it relevant to a strategic context. The internal environment of the company is its costs and efficiencies: how it uses technology and combines its factors of production. The external context of the company is the market place: the behaviour of consumers and the behaviour of competitors.

Strategy is the coordination mechanism that a company employs between the internal environments. Put simply, in an environment where products are differentiated, this centres on the prices to charge, how much to supply and how to differentiate further the product supplied. The latter (largely 'non-price competition'), is arguably the most important because it determines the extent to which the company creates a degree of monopoly power and, hence, excess profit (or slack) for itself.

8 Investigation (4)

Read the article on the French hypermarket industry (case 7) and then answer the following questions.

1 What economic models can be used to describe (a) the small French shops and (b) the large hypermarkets?
2 Why are the large hypermarkets so powerful?
3 What strategies are open to the hypermarkets in order to circumvent the planning restrictions imposed by the French government?
4 What strategic and competitive advantages do these large companies have over the small retailers? In the light of this, is it inevitable that French shopping centres will ultimately move to out-of-town shopping malls?

9 Conclusions

Imperfect competition theory as it is commonly covered still concentrates on the pricing and output decisions of companies under those market structures. Thus, for example, under a monopolistically competitive market we have seen that the company might have less control over pricing and output decisions than a pure monopoly, but will have more influence than a perfectly competitive company. For an oligopoly the role of pricing is less clear cut and depends to a large extent on the nature of pricing arrangements in the industry as a whole. Where there is a collusive agreement, the company will have to accept market prices, but will still be able to increase its market penetration by segmenting its individual market demand (or price discriminating).

In any event, pricing is less important in imperfect markets in the long term because companies can product differentiate and therefore

CASE 7

France's New Foreign Legion

Restrictions on hypermarket developments are encouraging French retailers to shop around overseas, say Neil Buckley and Andrew Jack

The battle is on to save the patisseries, boulangeries and charcuteries of France from the giant hypermarkets and shopping centres that have marched across the French countryside over the past three decades.

Mr Alain Juppé, the French prime minister, will today announce the government's latest policy on the retailing sector. He is expected to unveil tight restrictions on hypermarket developments, while allowing some renovation and the opening of other types of large-scale retail project.

Such an announcement would disappoint big French retailers and encourage them to accelerate international expansion.

'Today, in France, it is impossible for us to open new hypermarkets,' says Mr Christophe Dubrulle, chief executive of Auchan hypermarkets, one of the country's largest chains. 'But, paradoxically, perhaps that is an opportunity. It means we are forced to go international.'

A moratorium would be particularly galling for large retailers, since they had been hoping for a more liberal line on out-of-town projects from the new government.

Many initially expected Mr Juppé to end the temporary freeze on large retail planning consents imposed by Mr Edouard Balladur, the former prime minister, in April 1993. The freeze has already slowed to a trickle the once explosive growth in large stores. This saw 3.9m sq m of hypermarket space alone built between 1975 and 1993. The severity of the freeze makes planning restrictions on out-of-town development imposed across the Channel by the UK government look half-hearted.

While the debate over out-of-town development in the UK and countries such as Germany with tight planning constraints has centred on preserving town centres, in France the debate ranges more widely.

French hypermarket operators are accused not just of destroying high streets. They are attacked for blotting the landscape with large concrete and steel boxes – and indeed, the proliferation of retail parks complete with neon signs and drive-in McDonald's restaurants has left parts of the Gallic countryside resembling the US Midwest.

At the same time, big grocery groups are charged with creating unemployment by killing off small shops, farmers and manufacturers through cut-throat terms of trade.

Mr Pierre Seassari, president of Assemblée Permanente des Chambres de Métiers, a body representing artisans and small business, says large retailers have 'destabilised' small traders by creating huge purchasing centres which allow them to charge very low prices.

'The power is no longer with producers but with retailers,' he says. He calls for an even tougher clampdown on new large-scale retail development, plus firmer policing of prices, to prevent them being set at unrealistically low levels.

An added twist to the debate is that some French grocery retailers have been under investigation for alleged corruption. Directors of three big French retailers were recently questioned by police over allegations that companies made political contributions in the 1980s in return for planning consents.

In their defence, hypermarket and supermarket operators say they support farmers and manufacturers, and that curtailing retail development will damage the economy.

Mr Daniel Bernard, chief executive of Carrefour, France's biggest grocery retailer, says his group is 'partner' to industry, agriculture, and 2,500 small and medium-sized businesses. He says it sells many local specialities that would otherwise have died out.

'Modern retailers are a big engine for the total chain of consumer goods,' he says. 'We are very competitive, we take only a small profit on the goods, so we can distribute more buying power to the nation – which means there is more [demand] for products.'

Mr Bernard argues that his company cannot be held responsible for the trend towards urbanisation that has been apparent in France since the second world war. This has resulted in the depopulation of rural areas and the inevitable closure of services, including shops, as their customer base has declined.

He believes many of the small shops that were forced to close when hypermarket development began in the 1960s provided poor service. Those remaining, he says, are stronger and more efficient.

Some observers feel that large French retail groups, many of them until recently family-owned, need to brush up on their public relations. According to Mrs Denise Larking Coste, executive vice-president of CIES, the Paris-based 'Food Business Forum' whose members include retailers and food manufacturers: 'One problem for the retail industry is that it has not got its message across about how much [large] retailers have done for the economy,' she says.

Property developers, meanwhile, argue that shopping centres should not be lumped together with hypermarkets in the present debate. 'When we build a regional [shopping] centre we always give some priority to local retailers,' says Mr Léon Bressler, chairman of Unibail, one of France's largest shopping centre developers. 'We are not destroying them but creating opportunities for them.'

The most obvious way for French retail groups to respond to a moratorium on out-of-town hypermarkets would be to make older stores work harder by improving product ranges and store environments to attract more customers. Some may also consider extending these existing outlets, although that would require planning permission.

Another option would be to acquire competing stores or chains. Indeed, a series of takeovers has already altered the structure of the industry. Carrefour acquired two chains in financial difficulties – Montlaur and Euromarché – in 1991, while Casino, another large grocery retailer, bought the ailing Rallye group the following year.

Analysts now suggest that Casino could itself become a takeover target. So could Cora, a medium-sized grocery retailer. Many believe the big chains might also target the 40 per cent of French supermarkets and hypermarkets that are independently-owned. This is an unusually high proportion by western European standards.

'We will buy more stores from other people than we do now,' says Mr Christian Toulouse, chief executive of Docks de France, operator of Mammouth hypermarkets and Atac supermarkets. 'It will be expensive, but we will do it.'

The final, and potentially most exciting, avenue for the large retail groups is international expansion.

French grocery groups are already among the most international in the world – three of the top five retailers in neighbouring Spain are French-owned – and they plan to spread their tentacles further. Carrefour, after 20 years of international development, passed a landmark in August, for the first time operating more hypermarkets outside France (117) than in its home country (116).

Carrefour has not been successful in every overseas market: its attempts to branch out into the US and UK in the 1980s ended in failure. However, its Pryca subsidiary is Spain's second-biggest retailer. The group also has stores in Italy, Portugal, Turkey, Argentina, Brazil, Mexico, Malaysia, Thailand, Taiwan, and, since last month, in China. It expects to increase the proportion of turnover coming from outside France from 40 per cent to well over half by 2000.

Promodès, France's second-biggest grocery retailer, is Spain's third-largest retailer, through its Continental subsidiary. It also has stores in Germany, Greece, Italy, Turkey, Morocco and Mauritius. Auchan is the number four retailer in Spain, with 21 Alcampo hypermarkets. It has stores in Italy and Portugal and plans to open in Poland, Hungary and Mexico.

Even a medium-sized retailer like Comptoirs Modernes, a supermarket group, talks confidently of moving into Brazil and Argentina.

French grocery groups believe they have created flexible store formats that can easily be adapted to overseas markets and filled with locally-produced goods. Such an approach would contrast with that adopted by UK retailers, such as Marks and Spencer, J. Sainsbury and Tesco, whose stores rely heavily on own-label products.

Although still interested in acquisitions in established markets, French retailers believe the biggest opportunities may lie in less mature markets such as eastern Europe, South America and Asia. 'We can start with a developing country at the bottom of the [economic] curve, and grow with the country to the top of the curve,' says Mr Bernard.

Carrefour, he adds, will open stores in 'any country where people like good food – especially fresh food, as the French do'.

While hypermarkets may be accused of killing off high streets, Mr Bernard would claim to be exporting the spirit of the patisserie and boulangerie to the rest of the world.

Figure 6.10 Strategic matrix of companies in imperfectly competitive markets.

	Pricing/output	Product development and technology	Competitor analysis
Monopolistic competition	Depends on number of competitors and elasticity of demand	Centrally important: creating market share and creating innovation base to new industries	Vital: especially costs and new products
Oligopolistic competition	Price interdependency at industry level, but pricing to increase market penetration	NON-PRICE COMPETITION Essential, although large companies will hold back from new industries	Strategic interdependency: firms depend on each other's behaviour for market share and R&D strategy

compete through non-price means. As we saw from the case of both the magnetic hard disk drive industry and the new biotechnology industry, the particular relevance of this is in the development of new product and process technologies. We could not draw any conclusions at all about company size and innovativeness: in the disk drive industry it was small, low-cost Far Eastern companies creating new product markets; in the case of biotechnology it was small companies pushing forward the innovation process in order to establish the industry.

We ended chapter 5 with a matrix highlighting the key aspects of strategy under a perfectly competitive market structure and a monopoly. We can now refine this somewhat to include the importance of technology – both products and processes (figure 6.10).

The matrix shows that pricing, output, product differentiation and technology and strategic interdependency are high among companies that are operating in imperfect markets. Strategic interdependency means that all companies have to look at what their competitors are doing not just in terms of prices but also in terms of products. Failure to anticipate effectively the strategies that competitors might be following, particularly if it involves new product development, can be very costly, as the case of anti-lock braking showed.

It is this vulnerability and uncertainty in the relationship between the firm and its industry that makes strategy central to achieving competitiveness. But any strategy has to be based on an analysis of trends in the external environment – demand, costs, and, critically into the twenty-first century, technology. Any mistakes in that analysis mean mistakes in strategy and, hence, loss of competitiveness. Under imperfect structures it is impossible to predict definitively how companies are actually going to behave – the real world is more complex than our models!

Notes

1   Relaxing this assumption is an unorthodox use of the market mechanism. Usually, the market mechanism is used only to explain how prices are set in perfectly competitive markets. Other models, such as those covering monopoly, monopolistic competition and oligopoly, are used to explain pricing under other market structures. However, the market mechanism can be used as a method of understanding the means by which prices are determined through the signals that buyers and sellers send to one another. As such, it becomes a powerful tool for understanding the basis of company pricing decisions.

2   The data presented in this table are derived from consultancy work undertaken during 1996 and 1997. There were more companies than presented here competing in the market place, but these were the companies who provided information. The point about market share and number of competitors still stands.

3   This debate is central to an understanding of contested markets and underpins much of the strategy literature that is covered elsewhere on business studies courses. There is not scope to enter into this debate in great detail, not least because, even after all this time, economists disagree over it. For further reference, however, see Vickers, J. (1996) Strategic competition among the few – some recent developments in the economics of industry. In T. Jenkinson (ed.), *Readings in Microeconomics*. Oxford: Oxford University Press.

4   Again, research for this section is taken from Jonathan Freeman's work at the University of Warwick.

5   Information for this section is taken from research into small biotechnology companies carried out at the Science Policy Research Unit between 1989 and 1993 by Mark Dodgson, now Director of the Managing Business in Asia Programme, Australian National University, Canberra.

6   See Dodgson, M. (1990) Technology and organisational learning: an interdisciplinary microstudy. University of Sussex, SPRU discussion paper.

7   The pricing behaviour of oligopolies is complex and depends to a large extent on the degree of agreement (or 'collusion') between competitors. For example, until 1996, all book producers and retailers agreed recommended prices at which to sell books. This price agreement kept prices in the market steady and focused company strategy on non-price competition, such as product development. With its demise a price war broke

out, particularly from supermarkets undercutting the prices of popular books. Non-collusive and collusive oligopoly is a whole area of theory in its own right. For further reference, see Rees, R. (1996) Tacit collusion. In T. Jenkinson (ed.), *Readings in Microeconomics*. Oxford: Oxford University Press.

8   You will sometimes see this referred to as the prisoner's dilemma.

9   Information for this section is taken from research carried out by the author between 1989 and 1992 and carried on since then. It has now been published: Harding, R. (1995) *Technology and Human Resources in Their National Context: a Study in Strategic Contrasts*. Aldershot: Avebury.

10 The assumption that firms will always try to maximize profits in an economic sense (i.e. maximize the difference between revenue and costs) can also be relaxed to provide an even more realistic view of how companies make decisions and the goals they pursue. For example, writers such as W. J. Baumol argued that companies *empirically* aim to maximize sales rather than profit as this is an easier target to achieve. Other writers, such as Penrose, Marris and Downie, found that companies would seek to maximize growth as a response to the uncertainty caused by asymmetric information in the market place. (Baumol, W. J. (1959) *Business Behaviour, Value and Growth*. London: Macmillan. Penrose, E. T. (1959) *The Theory of the Growth of the Firm*, 2nd edn 1980. Oxford: Blackwell. Marris, R. L. (1964) *The Economic Theory of 'Managerial' Capitalism*. London: Macmillan. Downie, J. (1958) *The Competitive Process*. London: Duckworth.) A full discussion of these would fall outside the remit of an introductory text like this, but for further information, see Earl, P. (1984) *The Corporate Imagination: Why Big Companies Make Mistakes*. Brighton: Harvester.

11 See, for example, Johnson, G. and Scholes, P. (1995) *Exploring Corporate Strategy*, 3rd edn. Englewood Cliffs, NJ: Prentice Hall.

12 Their advertising, branding, product development, pricing and efficiencies, for example.

7 Imperfect Markets and the Need for Policy

I will intervene before breakfast, before lunch, before tea and before dinner.
(Rt Hon. Michael Heseltine MP, Conservative Party conference,
October 1993)

The market mechanism serves as an intellectual barrier to perceiving the
changing institutional reality of successful capitalist development; for, as history shows, this changing institutional reality is characterised by the growing
importance of planned co-ordination within the business organisation over the
determination of economic outcomes.
(William Lazonick, *Business Organisation and the Myth of the Market
Economy.* Cambridge: Cambridge University Press, 1991)

In the United States around $60 billion a year is spent on personal beauty
care. In the United Kingdom, over £1 billion is spent on pet food. Yet in both
countries the public has been told repeatedly that there is no money available for the provision of better public health care or better public education.
(Paul Ormerod, *The Death of Economics.* London: Faber & Faber, 1994)

1 Introduction

We concluded chapter 6 with a brief discussion of the relationship
between industries, markets and firms. It was argued that, under the
neo-classical economics that we have covered, the market mechanism
is seen as the way in which resources are allocated in the economy
through the interaction of supply and demand. As we saw in chapter
6, however, in imperfect markets such as those represented by monopolistic competition and oligopoly, firms have considerable control over
the way in which they differentiate their products and thus have some
degree of monopoly power and excess profits in the long run. The
market mechanism is not something that will operate efficiently under
an oligopolistic market structure. Because of the market power that
all companies have, neo-classical economics has been criticized for

placing too heavy a reliance on markets and ignoring the fact that businesses (and particularly large businesses) determine the allocation of resources in the interests of their profitability and not in the interests of consumer welfare.[1]

Neo-classical economics does not, indeed cannot, claim to provide the answers for the macro economy unless it operates under a structure more closely resembling perfect competition than monopoly. Under a highly competitive market structure, where there are a large number of firms and no one individual firm has dominant market power, the model of perfect competition will work: markets will clear, prices will be stable, costs will be low (therefore companies will be internationally competitive) and any person who wants to work will be able to find work. The market mechanism can be relied upon to allocate resources.

But companies producing a differentiated product in imperfect markets spoil this mechanism because they can price fix and then can control markets. Critiques of *theoretical* economics generally do not allow for the fact that many of the predictions and models of the economy (micro and macro alike) are just that – models and theories – and will not work when some of the critical assumptions are dropped, particularly the assumption that the market mechanism can be relied upon to allocate resources effectively.

The problem lies not with economics as a theoretical discipline, but rather in the interface between economics and the real world, and in particular politics.[2] Governments intervene in order to relieve the imperfections and inequalities in the market place which occur because the models of economics will not work in the real world. As students of business we are interested in the impact of this intervention *and* in the impact of non-intervention for the operations of industry.

2   Aims and Objectives

It is the purpose of this chapter to look at the interface between the micro and the macro economy. We examine the relationship between the theories of the first six chapters of this book and the practice of government intervention and government macroeconomic policy. Ultimately we will arrive at an understanding of the interdependence of the industrial and the macro economy; we will realize that the actions of individuals affect the economic health of the nation, but similarly that the macroeconomic actions of government can affect the competitive health of industry. This interrelationship is critical to the effective running of an economy; where it breaks down, structural problems begin to arise.

Economists and political economists have been struggling with the issue of the link between the macro and micro economy since the origins of the discipline. It would not be appropriate to suggest that, in the context of introducing the subject, we could come up with a definitive answer to these problems. The aim of this chapter, then, is a modest one: to work towards an understanding of the link between the micro and the macro economy in order that we can understand the basic tools of macroeconomics covered in the next four chapters and realize the implications of macroeconomic policy for business.

At the end of the chapter, however, you should have a grasp of the following:

- the case for leaving the market to operate freely with no government intervention;
- the case for regulation and control of the market to eliminate welfare problems caused by market imperfections;
- some of the mechanisms by which the government might seek to intervene to ameliorate market imperfections;
- the types of regulatory policy in key 'social' areas such as the environment, technology and, of course, monopolies and mergers.

3   Investigation

All governments intervene to a greater or lesser extent. You may find it interesting to compare government spending in a number of different countries with different attitudes towards government intervention, such as the USA, Japan, Germany, Sweden, Britain and France. You will find OECD[3] and Eurostat publications useful sources of information for this exercise. You might like to look at the following areas:

- health;
- education and training;
- transport;
- welfare.

You will need to make sure your data are comparable – an index is a useful tool for doing this. How reliable do you think a cross-country comparison such as this is?

4   Why Does a Government Intervene?

Clean air is a public good — nobody can be excluded from using it — nobody has any incentives to pay to use it. (Frances Cairncross, *Costing the Earth*, London: Business Books, 1991, p. 1)

The market mechanism does not simply determine the price and quantity of goods and services sold in an economy. In order for goods to be sold, they need to be produced. In order to produce, entrepreneurs need factories, employees, raw materials and machinery, all of which have to be bought at a price. In the process of setting up production and then producing, a company might destroy the natural habit of a species of wildlife, pollute local rivers with toxic emissions and increase income inequality in the country as a whole by locating in one region rather than another. Equally, in setting up production, it might be providing jobs, and therefore income, to more people locally, providing training in the state-of-the-art technology used on the shopfloor and modernizing a whole degenerated area of the country.

These are some of the *externalities* of the market mechanism, the hidden consequences of the operation of the market. Every day we hear, for example, about the costs of environmental pollution and global warming, the costs of road building and the costs of monopoly power. Not all externalities are bad — no one could argue that bringing employment to an area of poverty is against the public interest, particularly if those jobs encourage skills training and education. But the really noticeable externalities are usually negative and the example of pollution is a highly topical one.

Before we go any further, we should take care to distinguish between the *economic* costs and the *social* costs of the operation of the market. An example of economic costs might be the cleaning up programme after toxic waste has gone into a river. Here it is quite clear that the 'polluter' should pay for clearing up the mess caused. Social costs are less clear cut, however. These are the externalities that affect all of us: the effect on the world's climate of global warming, the increased incidence of asthma caused by vehicle emissions or the greater occurrence of childhood leukaemia around some nuclear power stations. We are not all equal in the impact of these externalities on us — we all have a right to clean air and an unpolluted environment, but we do not all have access to it because of where we live.

The central purpose of government economic, and social, policy is to ameliorate the inequalities as they arise from the operations of the

Figure 7.1   The Lorenz curve showing income distribution.

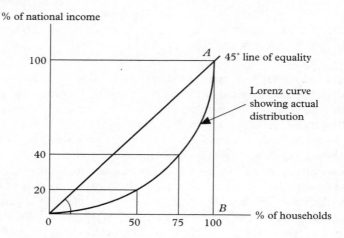

market, or particularly arise from the externalities of the market. A government needs policies towards 'markets' because, as we have seen in the previous chapters, in reality there are large companies that can price set and create barriers to entry. These large companies have their own control over resource allocation and do not rely solely on the market mechanism for the allocation of their resources. As a result, they employ individuals on differential wages (giving their employees unequal market power), they employ suppliers on medium- and long-term contracts (overriding the market mechanism for supply) and they decide where and how to sell their products.

So, we do not all have equal access to clean air, good housing, schooling, health and transport. Some, because they are wealthier, have better access to housing, schooling, healthcare, transport and even fresh air. Others are relatively disadvantaged because they are on lower incomes. Governments, then, have to intervene to set minimum standards and to ensure that, where possible, these externalities and inequalities can be reduced.

We represented market power on the side of suppliers in terms of the Lorenz curve and the Gini coefficient. The curve showed us how market power was distributed unevenly in a market between large and small companies. We can construct a similar curve for income distribution in an economy, as shown in figure 7.1.

As with the Lorenz curve showing the distribution of market power, this Lorenz curve shows the distribution of income in terms of

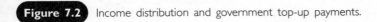

Figure 7.2 Income distribution and government top-up payments.

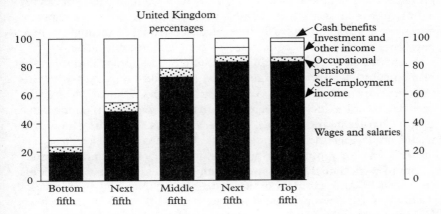

Source: CSO (1995) *Social Trends.* London: HMSO.

percentages of households in the country. This curve illustrates an economy where 50 per cent of households in the economy account for only 20 per cent of national income[4] and 75 per cent of households account for only 40 per cent of national income.

The distribution of income in an economy very often looks similar to this – with a few very wealthy people dominating income at the top of the scale (top directors and national lottery winners, for example). At the bottom of the scale will be a large number of people with very little money.

Figure 7.2 divides the population into 'quintiles' or fifths and looks at the income sources of each section. The bottom fifth derive only 20 per cent of their income from paid earnings: the rest comes from government payments such as income support and child allowance. Government reallocative expenditure to provide 'top-up' income to the lowest paid households is important as a means of reducing income inequality.

Income distribution data are always emotive. Analysts and politicians of all political persuasions feel strongly about the welfare of people in a country, particularly if the distribution tends to demonstrate big inequalities. The reason why the data provoke such strong feelings is because inequality suggests a misallocation of resources somewhere in the economy – a failure of the 'market'. Of course, any misallocation represents an economic cost. Individuals in the lowest income quintile are not able to spend as much money as they would like, so demand in the economy as a whole is sub-optimal. This means that producers are unable to sell as much as they want to, do not employ as many people and so on. More direct economic costs are those of government expenditure to reduce income inequality through welfare payments or to provide equal access to education or health.

There are two opposing schools of thought in approaching this type of inequality. Some would argue that it is a good thing. As with competitive industrial structures, covered in chapters 5 and 6, it encourages fierce competition between individuals and gives them an incentive to work harder in anticipation of higher earnings. So, some economists would argue that the six-figure pay settlements to top executives are justified on two grounds: as a reward for their efforts and to induce others to work harder. Economic growth is created and competitiveness enhanced because all are working harder to achieve higher earnings.

Others argue the opposite. Since the Second World War it has been UK government policy to provide a safety net for all those who are out of work or unable to work, and to provide a 'socially desirable' level of healthcare and education in order to ensure that the workforce is well educated and healthy. In return for this basic provision individuals pay an amount out of their salaries in 'national insurance' and taxation while they are working. The service is not free – we all pay for it. Those on higher incomes pay more out of their salaries and those on lower incomes less. This ensures that the overall level of provision is 'fair'. Reducing inequality is the cornerstone of the ideology of 'welfare' approaches to intervention. By reducing inequality, it is argued, people have more to spend on the goods and services that are produced in the economy. This, accordingly, stimulates economic growth and competitiveness.

The critical relationship here is that between inequality and economic stability and growth. Those who favour intervention argue that inequality means that some are not spending enough money on consumption of goods and services – demand is at a lower level than it could be, and therefore companies within an economy are not supplying as many people as they could otherwise do. The premise of the welfare system has always been that small injections of money will level out some forms of inequality and, hence, provide greater opportunities for economic growth (for example, by increasing general educational standards or spending money on ensuring the health of the nation). In contrast, the non-interventionists argue that, if the economy is allowed to operate with no form of interference (as with the perfectly competitive market structure, for example), the price mechanism will work to ensure that all are equal in the market place in the long run. In the short run, people will work harder to enable themselves to earn more and, hence, be equal in the long run.

In any event, even the most market-driven governments of the world do intervene, as shown in figure 7.2. But welfare budgets around the world are strained as governments come under pressure to reduce taxes (the source of their income) and as technology develops, making key areas like healthcare both more effective and more expensive. The French, for example, spend an average of £250 per year on prescriptions,[5] an amount which is likely to increase as drugs increase in price. This amount is funded largely by the government but cannot be sustained indefinitely. And even the 'ideal' German model of the social market economy has come under serious pressure to reform in the mid-1990s, with increased welfare payments and high unemployment. Similar problems occur elsewhere around the world, where a general pressure to review intervention is taking place.

This, of course, impacts on business. There are two main ways in which it does:

1 If individuals are not trained to a basic level, not given some form of 'free' healthcare and not provided with some form of 'social' care should they be unable to work for any reason, then they may be less skilled, less healthy and less motivated. This is a *general* cost to industry: it is one faced by all companies and one which directly affects their international competitiveness.
2 Some companies may feel that they need to provide some form of training, some form of health insurance and some form of social insurance in lieu of the general (or transferable) services provided by the government. They do this in the interests of creating a well trained, healthy and motivated workforce. These costs are *company-specific*, i.e. if the individual employee changed his or her place of work they would not be carried on to the next employer.

We will return to this when we are evaluating the case for social and industrial policy. For now it is enough to realize that if the government does not provide these basic services the onus falls on private companies and private individuals to pay them, which, obviously, puts up the costs to industry. The answers to the dilemma have already been outlined and we will look at these in some detail now.

Figure 7.3   The model of supply and demand.

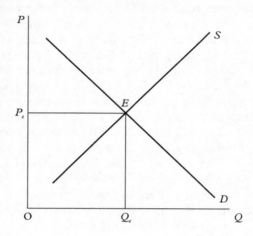

5   Answer I: No Intervention at All – *Laissez-faire* Policies

The case for leaving the economy to operate with no government intervention rests on the 'beautifully simple' model of supply and demand covered in previous chapters. If you recall the model, we arrived at a perfect equilibrium under a competitive market structure where supply equalled demand, and markets cleared and were stable in the long term. To remind you, the model is redrawn in figure 7.3.

The equilibrium price of P_e and quantity of Q_e is socially desirable as well as economically desirable. At the equilibrium point, E, all the consumers who wish to buy the good at that price are satisfied and the producers who supply the product at that price are selling all of their produce. All are equal and all have had an equal part to play in the process of defining the equilibrium price for the product.

The point E is consistent with the socially desirable *Pareto optimality*.[6] This is the position in the economy where changes have been made to benefit individuals (for example, by improving their welfare) without harming the interests of others in the economy (for example, by increasing taxation). At a Pareto optimum point all resources are efficiently allocated through the price mechanism, and no further changes can be made without harming individual groups of people.

It will already be becoming clear to you that this condition for Pareto optimality is highly theoretical and will only work under conditions of perfect competition, where there are none of the externalities discussed above and where markets can be relied upon to allocate resources effectively. That is, no one gains or loses in non-financial terms from the operation of the market, and the large number of buyers and sellers means that all are made equal through the price mechanism. For this reason Enoch Powell once called the operation of free markets the 'counterpart of democracy', and argued that all governments should inject competition into markets where possible in order to ensure that this type of social welfare could be achieved.

This *laissez-faire*[7] thinking lay behind the monetary economics of the Conservative government that came to power in 1979 and has underpinned policy ever since. To paraphrase, if the frontiers of the state are 'rolled back' then individuals take responsibility for their own lives. Everyone acting in his or her own self-interest will create the greatest welfare for the greatest number of people.[8] There are incentives to work hard in anticipation of high earnings. Public and private services compete with one another in the same market place and consumers are free to choose between, for example, schools, methods of transport and hospitals. The state reduces taxation so that there are greater incentives to work (less is taken away in tax) and funding of public services comes from efficiency gains. Many gain from reductions in taxation, and public services are provided at the same level but more cheaply and efficiently; many have gained and no one has lost out, so a Pareto-optimal solution has been reached.

There are circumstances under which even a *laissez-faire* government will intervene. One is where monopoly power is great, is seen to be against the interests of consumers and is preventing a Pareto-optimal solution from being reached. With this scenario the policy solution is to provide incentives to entrepreneurs to enter into otherwise barred markets. For this reason it is often called 'deregulation' rather than intervention.

Again this was a central part of Conservative government policy after 1979 as successive attempts were made to reduce the monopoly power of state monopolies such as electricity, gas and water. We can demonstrate the case that underpins this deregulation using the tools of earlier chapters. Look at figure 7.4, which illustrates the equilibrium position for a monopoly company. For the sake of simplicity the diagram does not include the average cost curve.

This was also covered in chapter 5, but to refresh your memory we will briefly go through the monopoly position. In order to ensure that

Figure 7.4   Comparing monopoly and perfectly competitive prices.

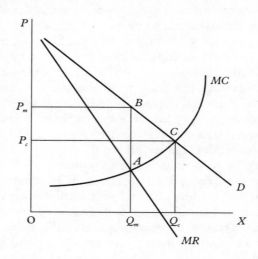

costs are covered by revenue the monopolist produces at the level where marginal cost and marginal revenue are equal. This is point A on the curve and relates to the quantity, Q_m. In order to find the price that should be charged for this level of output the monopolist goes up vertically from this point to the demand curve and charges the price, P_m. Monopolists can do this because they are price makers – they dictate prices of a product because they are the sole suppliers of that product.

Figure 7.4 also shows the position for a perfectly competitive firm. You will remember that under perfect competition a firm is a price taker: it has to accept the price set by the market because there are so many other companies supplying the same product. The demand curve is the same as that for the monopolist because the monopolist's demand curve is the market demand curve. In order to establish the level of output, the firm equates marginal revenue (which is equal to demand) and marginal cost. This means it produces at level Q_c. Remember, though, that the company has to charge the market price for the product: at point C, demand and marginal revenue are equal because the individual demand curve for the firm is perfectly elastic (the line P_cC) and are equal to marginal cost. The price set is P_c.

You will see from figure 7.4 and remember from chapter 5 that P_c is considerably below the price P_m charged by a monopolist. Further, output is higher under a perfectly competitive market. We called this the *dead-weight loss* of monopoly. It is said to be against consumers' interest and, hence, attempts are made to inject competition, with the end objective of increasing competition and output and reducing prices.

6   Answer 2: Intervene

We turn now to the case which has traditionally been argued by the political left. The case for non-intervention is simplicity itself – positive economics at its best. The market operates and everything else falls into line. The alternative approach to welfare and government intervention is, largely, more normative. It is based on the fact that imperfections in the operations of the market are observed – in disparate income distributions, in large numbers of unemployed people, in skills shortages and, above all, in the very existence of large-scale companies. Their critique of the market mechanism and Pareto optimality rests on the fact that we never witness a perfectly competitive market: products are differentiated and knowledge of the market is incomplete (particularly on behalf of buyers). In short, it is not possible to reach a Pareto-optimal solution where markets do not operate perfectly and, as this never happens, governments have to intervene to protect the interests of those who might experience the negative externalities of the system, and to provide minimum standards for 'public goods' like clean air, education and healthcare.

Much of the discussion on intervention here will be based on the fact that, in reality, governments around the world do intervene. The British and the American governments are perhaps the least interventionist in the world but they nevertheless do have significant public expenditure budgets. The Anglo-American policy maxim is to allow the market to operate and to allow the private sector to take responsibility for its own actions, but to provide a safety net for those who suffer disproportionately from the operations of the market.

In Germany and Sweden (and to some extent Japan), in contrast, there is a much more carefully delineated relationship between the provisions of the state and the provisions of the market. The model of the 'social market economy' is based on a tripartite responsibility for the social costs of running an advanced industrialized nation. The three groups within this triad of responsibility are government, business and employees (or their representatives). Thus, for example, in provision of post-school vocational training in Germany, unions, employers and representatives of government meet to discuss the content of courses and the balance between on-the-job and off-the-job training. This ensures that all courses offer the same basic (or general) level of training, with companies bearing responsibility for the company-specific training. Similarly, in healthcare the government has a scheme of national insurance which ensures a basic (general) provision, but companies top up this national scheme through private insurance to guarantee the adequate healthcare of their employees.

Germany and Japan also have striking similarities, not only in the provision of education and training, but in terms of the degree of government funding for basic R&D. American and British governments have traditionally provided significant proportions of their R&D budgets to defence technologies. This was on the assumption that eventually the scientific research from defence projects would filter through supply chains into the civilian sector. Germany and Japan, constrained by the post-war treaties, spent their budgets predominantly on developing an R&D infrastructure in the civilian sector.[9]

7   Is There a Link with Performance?

The superior performance in terms of inflation, unemployment and innovation of the Japanese and German economies in the post-war period has caused commentators and politicians to vaunt the virtues of some degree of government intervention. The 'German model' has excited particular interest among the 'new' left, based as it is on a mutual cooperation between government, industry and employees,[10] which, it is argued, allows decisions to be taken on a uniform and harmonious basis in the interests of the economic and social welfare of the population.

Similarly, studies on education and training and industrial productivity have pointed to the superiority of the systems in Sweden, Germany and Japan.[11] In these countries levels of mathematical ability and language skills are higher on leaving compulsory education and the vocational training systems provide dedicated skills training to meet the needs of industry. Correspondingly, it is argued, productivity levels are also higher.

But it would be wrong simply to equate the structure of government intervention with economic performance and draw out any 'positive' conclusions without further analysis which extends beyond the scope of a text like this. The opposing view is that the Germans and Japanese have not responded to the challenges of the 1990s (particularly reunification and globalization) as well as might have been expected.

Figure 7.5 The model of strategy including the role of government.

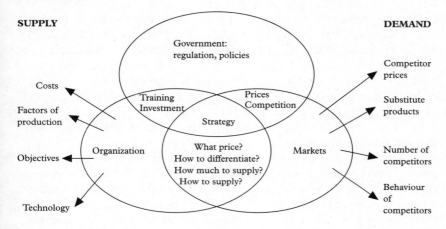

They cite rising inflation and unemployment in the two countries and increasing industrial unrest as evidence that the models do not provide swift and ideal answers. Indeed, many Germans themselves subscribe to this view, arguing that their system needs profound changes in order to make it more competitive.[12]

8 What Can Business Learn from This Discussion?

We have talked a lot in previous chapters about strategy as a coordinating mechanism between a firm's internal, organizational, environment and external, or operating, environment. It is also a means of ensuring that companies anticipate and accommodate trends in their national economic and infrastructural environments. We have covered many areas in this chapter, but the strategic implications of the discussion are clear and illustrated in figure 7.5, which is a development of the strategic model put forward in chapter 6.

Figure 7.5 is best explained in terms of an example. Return to the domestic gas market in the UK covered in previous chapters. The market is in the process of being deregulated, which means it is being opened up to competitive (or market) forces. A company wishing to enter the market clearly has to think about its own supply conditions (costs and technology, for example). It also has to think about the behaviour of other companies entering the market and how customers

will make their choices. But it also has to think of how the deregulated market will itself operate. This is represented by the circle in
figure 7.5 containing 'government'.

The gas industry generally, and the domestic gas market in particular, is regulated by a government appointed body called OFGAS. Its
job is to ensure that British Gas is not embarking on uncompetitive
behaviour (for example, by price cutting) and to ensure that any company wishing to enter the market complies with safety standards and
codes of practice. It grants licences to companies to supply gas and
monitors complaints accordingly.

For a company wishing to enter the market, then, there is not only
the competitive environment to take into account, but also the regulatory environment. This means that companies have to comply with
government standards both in the product they are selling and in how
they sell it. Their strategy has to take account both of competitor
behaviour *and* regulator behaviour.[13] Governments (and their representatives such as the regulator) impose constraints on, for example,
pricing, output, training, employment conditions and R&D. They
hence represent a real cost to the company which has to be dealt with
through the coordinating mechanism of strategy.

Perhaps paradoxically, however, businesses tend to be in favour of
government intervention in areas where they consider that they should
not bear the full cost: in provision of education and training to ensure
basic literacy and numeracy, in funding of 'blue sky' (or basic) scientific research, in the definition of standards of cleanliness and in the
provision of fiscal (tax) incentives to encourage businesses to be environmentally conscious.

From a company's point of view there is a lot to be argued in favour
of spending money on the areas that the government does not provide. Specific training courses improve motivation and, of course,
increase the skills and productivity of employees. Investment in R&D,
as we saw in chapters 5 and 6, can provide market share advantage
to companies and even a degree of monopoly power, and thus is logically also funded by the company itself. And, if only in the interests
of a 'clean' corporate image, it is appropriate for companies to clean
up any environmental pollution they cause.

In order to formulate strategies for these areas, companies will often
undertake *cost–benefit analyses* on their proposals. Very broadly these
involve weighing up both the tangible (monetary) and intangible (non-
monetary) costs of a particular strategy and setting against them its
possible benefits. Where the benefits outweigh the costs it will pay the
company to go ahead.

9 Investigation and Further Reading

Antagonists Clear the Air

David Lascelles was present when two sides of the ecology divide met to find some common ground

Business and the environment are fundamentally at odds with each other – that seems to be a fact of life. Business makes money by exploiting the environment, the environment fights back by curbing business.

Much of the environmental debate is about trying to find some common ground: a point in the middle where the motivations that drive business can be harnessed to minimise environmental damage and even do some good.

Several dozen senior representatives of business, government and environmental groups made their way to Madingley Hall, Cambridge, last week to explore that common ground. They came at the initiative of Prince Charles who has been trying to promote dialogue between the conflicting parties.

With the row over Brent Spar still ringing in their ears, the businessmen were, not surprisingly, in an anxious mood. The incident had told them that environmentalists were more interested in headlines than the facts; it also showed the depth of popular mistrust of business, and how far business is from scoring Greenpeace-type points in the environmental debate.

But the purpose of the gathering was to inspire rather than depress the assembled delegates, and they were treated over four days to a parade of reasons why some of the world's largest companies take the environment seriously.

National Westminster Bank thinks an understanding of environmental issues helps it to reduce losses on bad loans. Munich Re, the large German insurance company, sees a 'healthy' environment as a way of controlling claims from pollution and changing weather patterns.

Procter & Gamble of the US uses environmental concerns to push through tighter management controls on waste: 'more from less' is the watchword.

National Power, Britain's largest power generator, has little choice: unless it cleans up it could lose its operating licence. Thorn EMI admitted that one reason it started publishing an environmental audit was pressure from its pop artists who wanted to be sure they were signing up with a 'clean' company.

Are these shining examples enough to move the sceptics – cynics even – who make up the vast bulk of the business community? As one delegate commented: 'You're looking at less than 1 per cent here.' Of the world's thousands of multinational companies, only 110 have published environmental reports.

Fear of loss is probably the biggest motivator: loss of business, customers or licences. But even these potential losses have to outweigh the considerable costs associated with cleaning up a company and implanting genuinely green attitudes, which is why many of those who were pomoting the green message at Madingley strove to couch the benefits in business terms.

In one sense, environmentalism is only another word for better waste management. Reduce waste or, better still, stop producing it in the first place. Dow Chemical plans to halve its incinerator capacity over the next five years by eliminating waste. Procter & Gamble's 'more from less' drive has cut waste by 300,000 tonnes.

The environment is also a good way, companies have found, to strengthen line management and motivate staff. A well-managed environmental programme can do a lot more than simply clean a company up: it boosts morale and profits. Environmental audits are probably little read, but the process that goes into their preparation provides a further incentive to good housekeeping.

Cynicism is not all-pervasive, though. Some business people do act out of personal commitment to the environment: they don't like to see nature spoilt or resources squandered.

But an executive who sets out on this road will not find it easy. He has to defend himself in terms that he may not, as a businessman, feel comfortable with. And he will not enjoy many victories. 'It's a treadmill for life,' was how one company chairman at Madingley described it.

So much, though, for companies' internal affairs. The external situation is something else. The prevailing view at Madingley is that business is beset – unfairly of course – by unsympathetic regulators and public opinion, and by a financial system that wants quick results. Even customers are fickle: they demand 'green' products and then refuse to pay for them.

What can business do to improve its lot? The delegates set about identifying 'stakeholders': those people with a legitimate interest in a company's behaviour, and with whom companies should seek to co-operate.

Shareholders are the most obvious, but others are employees, customers, suppliers, government regulators, non-government organisations and even the media. The purpose of contact should be to raise understanding and find areas where companies can do something to satisfy demands that they make their operations more sustainable.

The difficulty lies in the fact that, eventually, environmental commitments on the part of profit-driven organisations require a leap of faith: a belief that measurable benefits will result, even if the process makes an easy target for the cynic.

Having an heir to the throne present at Madingley meant that people treated these issues with due solemnity – and probably emerged more inspired from their four-day immersion in the subject than they would otherwise have been.

But few would have disputed Prince Charles's parting comment that 'there must be something sacred about the environment. If there wasn't, we would have ripped the place apart years ago'.

UK Treasury perspective

Andrew Turnbull is uniquely placed to see how the environment fits into Britain's political agenda. A former official in the UK Treasury, he became permanent secretary at the Department of the Environment last year, so he sees things from two conflicting perspectives.

Treasury people are not instinctive environmentalists, he told the Madingley meeting. They are rational, logical, not easily carried away. Quite the opposite from environmentalists who are moved by feelings and beliefs.

The Treasury role is to control public spending and spread taxes as widely as possible: environmentalists want to boost public spending, and fund it with special taxes. And, at the end of the day, Treasury people have far bigger fish to fry than the environment, which consumes less than 0.5 per cent of the total budget.

But Turnbull sees signs of change. The Treasury is beginning to take more notice of environmental issues, he thinks, and has even found common ground with its environmental colleagues. He gave some examples:

- Treasury economists understand the concept of externalities, which is central to the environmental debate. So the doctrine that companies should pay for the environmental costs they inflict on others (such as dirty air and water) finds acceptance.
- The growing interest in economic instruments to advance environmental objectives, such as taxes on resource use and pollution, and tradeable permits.
- Green accounting: redrawing the national accounts to measure depletion and depreciation of national assets.

Turnbull is particularly heartened by the fact that the Treasury is setting up a cross-departmental team to work on environmental issues, which will be headed by a senior economist from the Department of the Environment.

Turnbull did not mention what cynics might say was the main reason behind the Treasury's growing green interest – a potential tax growth area. But perhaps that should be taken for granted.

Read the green audit case (case 8) and then try to answer the following questions.

1　Are business and the environment really at odds with one another?
2　How can a good 'green' image add to a company's competitiveness?
3　What does a company have to lose from 'going green'?
4　How might a company formulate a 'green' strategy in which the interests of government, environmentalists and competitiveness are best served?

In addition, you might like to look at some of the following texts, which provide some international examples of government intervention.

The Economist (1996) Restoring Germany's shine? 5 May. Lead article and several relevant articles contained in this issue.

Foray, C. and Freeman, C. (1993) *Technology and the Wealth of Nations: the Dynamics of Constructed Advantage*. London: Pinter.

Freeman, C. (ed.) (1992) *National Systems of Innovation*. London: Pinter.

Harding, R. (1995) *Technology and Human Resources in their National Context: a Study of Strategic Contrasts*. Aldershot: Avebury.

Porter, M. E. (1990) *The Competitive Advantage of Nations*. London: Macmillan.

Prais, S. (1981) *Productivity and Industrial Structure: a Statistical Study of Manufacturing in Britain, Germany and the US*. Cambridge: Cambridge University Press.

10 Conclusions: a Cost–Benefit Analysis of Government Intervention

We have looked at the case for government intervention and against it, but have concluded that, as governments intervene to a greater or lesser extent anyway, there will always be a case to be argued for some form of intervention. Government intervention can be divided roughly into two separate areas and we can look at these separately: to reduce inequalities and to ameliorate externalities caused by the operation of the market.

The first, to reduce inequalities, is the most controversial area of government intervention. As we saw, some argue that inequality is, in fact, a good thing in stimulating economic activity. But governments around the world do intervene to provide some level of basic service, particularly in education, health, housing and the environment, in order to guarantee a minimum acceptable access to public goods. This type of intervention takes the form of welfare payments as well as the form of actual provision of services. In the area of the environment it might also include legislation to control toxic emissions or adequate waste disposal systems, for example.

The second area is to reduce the effects of negative externalities. This is less controversial because even *laissez-faire* economists argue in favour of reducing monopoly power, through monopolies and mergers legislation, and creating a cleaner environment. Here, governments tend to be less interventionist in the UK and the USA than perhaps businesses would like – in a *laissez-faire* market economy the exact

Figure 7.6 The strategic matrix including the regulatory environment.

	Pricing/output	Product development and technology	Competitor analysis	Impact of regulatory environment
Monopolistic competition	Depends on number of competitors and elasticity of demand	Centrally important: creating market share and creating innovation base to new industries	Vital: especially costs and new products	High – impact on costs
Oligopolistic competition	Price interdependency at industry level, but pricing to increase market penetration	NON-PRICE COMPETITION Essential, although large companies will hold back from new industries	Strategic interdependency: firms depend on each other's behaviour for market share and R&D strategy	Low – can be taken up within slack and turned to competitive advantage

demarcation between the responsibilities of the government and those of business are less clear than they are in the social market economies of Sweden and Germany.

It is in the regulatory legislative framework that the real costs to business arise from government intervention and, conversely, where the social benefits might be derived. Environment, minimum wages, training schemes, national insurance schemes and so on all represent costs to business which need to be minimized or accommodated if the company is not to be unduly burdened. During 1995, UK Government promises on reducing 'red tape' were testimony to how expensive these types of legislation can be, particularly for small businesses that do not have the slack in their structures or profits to take on extra administrative or regulatory procedures.

For these reasons we could add an extra column to our strategic matrix that we developed over the previous two chapters – that of the regulatory environment (see figure 7.6). This affects small businesses disproportionately, as arguably they do not have the extent of excess profit to be able to fund environmental projects or training programmes.

What we have seen in this chapter is that government, through regulation and intervention, has a profound impact on the operations of business, adding both costs and potential benefits. It is hoped that you now realize the full extent of the interdependency between the micro and the macro economy through government policy and the market mechanism.

Notes

1   Lazonick, W. (1991) *Business Organisation and the Myth of the Market Economy*. Cambridge: Cambridge University Press, pp. 10–11.

2   See Kay, J. (1996) *The Business of Economics*. Oxford: Oxford University Press.

3   Organisation for Economic Co-operation and Development.

4   It is not appropriate to have a debate about national income as a measure of equality or as a measure of social welfare in this chapter. This is saved for the next chapter, where national income is discussed more fully.

5   *PM*, BBC Radio 4, 6 November 1995.

6   After the Italian Economist Vilfredo Pareto (1848–1923), who developed this condition of social welfare.

7   *Laissez-faire* or 'let it be' – a policy of non-intervention.

8   Smith, A. (1776) *An Enquiry into the Causes and Nature of the Wealth of Nations*.

9   See Freeman, C. (ed.) (1992) *National Systems of Innovation*. London: Pinter.

10   See Hutton, W. (1995) *The State We're In*. London: Jonathan Cape.

11   Work conducted by the National Institute for Economic and Social Research since 1978 has consistently produced the same result. Authors such as Professor Sigmund Prais, Karin Wagner, Hilary Steedman and Geoff Mason write regularly in the *National Institute Economic Review*, which is an excellent source of current applied economic data.

12   Marsh, D. (1996) Paper to the 25th Annual Conference of the Association for the Study of German Politics.

13   Other layers of regulation stem from European and international law with which companies have to comply. There is not scope to discuss these in any great depth here, but you may find Dickens, P. (1992) *Global Shift: the Internationalization of Economic Activity*, 2nd edn. London: Paul Chapman Publishing, of interest. Similarly, part IV of Jenkinson, R. (ed.) *Readings in Microeconomics*. Oxford: Oxford University Press, provides some good insights into European regulation and its effects on the market place.

Introduction to Macroeconomics: the Circular Flow and National Income

8

Seasonally adjusted, this is the biggest rise in optimism that we have seen for the last four years.
(Norman Lamont MP, then Chancellor of the Exchequer, 29 October 1991)

If it were up to me, I would do without economic forecasts altogether. After all, Gladstone managed perfectly well without them.
(Norman Lamont MP, *UK PLC*, BBC Radio 4, September 1995)

I Introduction

We turn now to macroeconomics, or the economics of the whole economy. It would be a mistake to regard this as a completely separate subject area. The economic health of a country is generated through the operation of its industry. Competitiveness in individual markets is important; added together all these individual markets will contribute to the economic health of the nation. Chapter 7 demonstrated that governments formulate policies in order to create an environment where companies can expand and compete on 'a level playing field'[1] with their overseas counterparts through micro policies. The subsequent chapters look at how governments do this through policies which affect all businesses and not just those in one sector.

The key factor here is the creation of a stable economic environment for industry. This is a central function of any government, as the following sequence shows.

- Increased social welfare stems, at least in part, from increased national income.
- National income is generated by the country's companies producing goods and services.
- Similarly, individuals spend money on these goods and services and if their level of personal wealth is higher then they will, other things being equal, spend more.

- They will feel better off if their employers (generally the companies) pay them higher salaries.
- Firms can pay higher salaries if they are performing well, i.e. profitably selling their product.
- Firms will sell more of their products, other things being equal, if individuals either perceive themselves to be, or are, better off.

The role of government in this sequence is clear. If companies are dependent on the level of total (or aggregate) demand for their revenue, and hence their profitability, then it follows that governments should create a social and economic environment in which that demand is allowed to flourish. Generally it is believed that low inflation (i.e. prices increasing at only a slow rate, if at all) and low unemployment should be central goals of government policy.

The mechanism by which a government might seek to reach these goals is less clear, however. We saw in the previous chapter that policies towards government intervention are profoundly affected by the political persuasions of the people responsible for those policies. Unfortunately, there is similarly no agreed method of achieving a stable macro environment with low inflation and low unemployment. Indeed, economists disagree on the definition of a stable economic environment. Some, called monetarists, argue that the primary target must be low inflation, because that keeps prices low and enables people even on low incomes to carry on consuming. Others, called Keynesians,[2] have argued that low unemployment is the only goal to work towards, because this gives individual households higher average earnings and greater earnings stability. Yet others argue that a 'dream' balance between the two can and should be achieved.

As this is a textbook you will be relieved to know that we are not going to enter into the minefield of political economy. Instead we will cover the respective policies towards each area and look at other possible goals of government policy so that, by the end of the book, you will understand the importance of government policy for business *and* have formulated, or confirmed, your own opinions using the appropriate economic models.

2   The Macro Economy and Business

Until now we have covered models in a way that looks directly at the implications for company strategy. With macroeconomics this is more difficult to do: unemployment and inflation are *environmental* factors with which companies have to deal. They may alter the impact of strategy (for example, a marketing strategy might be less effective in an area that has high unemployment compared to an area with low unemployment), and, as we saw at the end of chapter 7, may also be factors which influence strategy. Government policy itself is not a direct input into strategy in the way that costs, demand analysis and competitor analysis are. However, the *effects* of government policy can have a profound effect on the freedom that a company has to follow its strategies through. For example, high interest rates will make borrowing expensive, which may in turn affect the freedom that a company has to expand or invest. This further emphasizes the role that strategy has in coordinating the forces in the external and internal environment.

Companies do take account of economic trends both domestically and worldwide. Most companies and consultancies employ economists to forecast what will happen in the economic environment. Economic forecasts are not always 100 per cent reliable: no one adequately predicted the depth of the worldwide recession at the beginning of the 1990s, for example.[3] But had there been no forecasts at all, many companies would have continued to produce at the levels they did in the mid-1980s. This would perhaps have worsened the problems of adjustment that many companies experienced and exacerbated the recession generally.

So, companies need to know about the economic environment in order to gauge the likely effectiveness of their strategies. Companies cannot sell as much when unemployment is high because large numbers of people do not have enough income to buy. Similarly, when prices are rising markets become volatile and fickle. Consumers become uncertain about how much their income will purchase and may hold back in order to ensure that they can consume in the future; alternatively they might buy immediately in order to protect themselves against rising prices in the future. This is exactly what happened in the UK housing market after 1987. Consumer expenditure is affected by the macro economy. As consumers, obviously, buy the products of companies, the impact of the macro economy is a vital input into company strategy.

3 Aims and Objectives

The aim of this chapter is to introduce macroeconomics to you in a way that makes it both understandable and relevant to you as students of business. The learning objectives are as follows.

- To ensure that you understand income flows within the economy.
- To ensure that you understand at a basic level the components of national income.
- To enable you to be aware of the difference between income and money and to realize the role of money in the economic mechanism.
- To ensure that you have understood the difference between micro- and macroeconomics by looking at aggregate demand and aggregate supply.
- To introduce you to the role of governments in macroeconomic policy through the manipulation of aggregate demand and aggregate supply.

4   Investigation (1)

It is being asserted here that the health of the macro economy has a major impact on business. In order to establish this for yourself it would be useful to find out about recessionary trends and their impact on companies. There have been three major recessions in the past 20 years: one in the early to mid-1970s, one at the beginning of the 1980s and one at the beginning of the 1990s. All had different causes and all had different effects on business. Some of the following texts will help you to develop an understanding of the link between the macro economy and business.

- Andrea Boltho (ed.) (1982) *The European Economy – Growth and Crisis*. Oxford: Oxford University Press. This is historical and covers the main European economies in the post-war period up to the monetarist 'revolution' in Britain after 1979. It also provides documentation from different political perspectives.
- Carlo M. Cipolla (ed.) (1978) *The Fontana Economic History of Europe*. London: Fontana. There are six volumes to this economic history of all the major economies in Europe. It is dated, but provides excellent background to the analysis of contemporary European economy.
- Will Hutton (1995) *The State We're In*. London: Jonathan Cape. This is an excellent and readable coverage of the socio-economic and infrastructural implications of 16 years of monetarist government.
- Jonathan Michie (ed.) (1993) *The Economic Legacy 1979–1992*. Harlow: Harcourt Brace Jovanovitch. This provides an excellent analysis of the 'monetarist experiment' of the Conservative government

between 1979 and 1992. It looks at the macro economy and business, and puts the analysis in a global context.

5 The Circular Flow of Income

In order to understand how consumers and producers interact with one another we need to examine the simple model of income flow in the macro economy. This is, of course, theoretical, but it gives us a framework for looking at the relationship between the two groups. Ultimately, then, it will allow us to see how one group's behaviour can affect the other's.

When we were looking at microeconomics we divided the economy up into two groups – buyers and sellers. We carry on with this division in macroeconomics and call the two groups 'households' and 'firms'. Households are defined as those individuals, or groups of individuals, who have ownership of the factors of production (if you remember, these are land, labour, capital, raw materials and entrepreneurial skills). Firms are those individuals, or groups of individuals, who take these raw materials and turn them into goods and services.

Of course, the two are not mutually exclusive. If you were a company director then you would be an entrepreneur converting inputs (factors of production) into outputs (goods and services). But you would also be an employee of your firm so you would yourself be one of the factor inputs: here, entrepreneurial skills. Further, if you owned the company, then you would be its capital as well. There would be a transfer of resources from yourself as an employer to yourself as an employee. This transfer of income is called the circular flow of income. It is the macroeconomic counterpart of the model of supply and demand in that it shows the interrelationship between firms and households in the whole economy.

That relationship can be seen as a *flow* of income. When you go out to work you are paid money (i.e. given income) by your employer. You are working to produce goods or services which your employer produces and then sells. Your employer generates income from the sale of goods or services; you and others like you buy them and so, effectively, you give your income back!

We can represent this very simply as in figure 8.1. You will see immediately that there is no government intervention in the model. This is for simplicity – so that you can see how income flows between households and firms.

Figure 8.1 The circular flow of income in the closed economy.

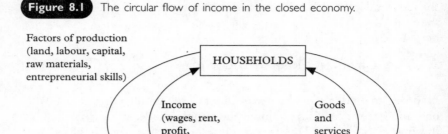

The arrows in the diagram show the direction in which income and resources are flowing. Look at the left-hand side of the diagram first. Households 'own' the factors of production and so provide the firms with their inputs. In return, firms pay the households a monetary value for the use of these factor services. Hours worked receive a wage, land accrues rent, capital accrues interest and raw materials and entrepreneurial skills receive profit. These payments represent *income* to the households.

On the right-hand side we can see what happens to the goods and services once they are produced. The firm takes them into the 'market' and sells them to households. Households then spend the income they have received from providing the factors of production on the goods and services that are being produced. This represents income to the firm in the form of sales revenue, which is then spent on buying the factor services.

The whole process is circular and is a flow of *value* between households and firms. There is no need for the income to be in monetary terms – if the unit of exchange in the economy were bananas, then households would be paid in bananas and firms would receive sales revenue in bananas. However, as money is generally less perishable and, more critically, more homogeneous than bananas, the unit of exchange in modern economies is money. Money is a tool by which the value of goods and services can be measured. Money passing from one person to another in exchange for goods, services or factors of production represents a movement of income from the first person to the second. We will examine this in more detail later.

Let's start now to make this model look like a real economy. We shall start by looking at the households and the firms themselves. As the model stands at present it only shows us how income is changing hands at one point in time. It does not show us how individual firms and households plan their expenditure over a period of time. In order to be able to look at this we need to include savings and investment.

A saving is an amount of money which is taken out of current expenditure in order to be able to spend tomorrow. All of us can remember the pocket money days when we were given £1 to spend on toys or sweets. Our instinct was to run out and spend it all at once. But at the back of our minds we all knew that if we saved, say, 50 pence from that £1 we would be able to buy a bigger toy or more sweets next week.

Investment, on the other hand, is money spent now by firms to ensure production in the future. If a company buys a new, best practice, machine then it might be better able to cope with increased demand or changed demand in the next time period – next month or next year. Investment is expenditure over and above the replacement of machines – it is the expenditure that allows the company to grow and compete in the long term.

As they are described above, savings represent money taken out of the circular flow of income. We call these *leakages*, as they are resources which are not used in the circular flow of income at any one given point in time. Investment expenditure is money being injected into the circular flow from a previous time period – we call these *injections*. Injections and leakages can be represented as shown in figure 8.2.

As you can see from figure 8.2, savings are income taken out of sales revenue to firms: saved money is money that is not spent on goods and services, so it is 'lost' revenue (income) to companies. Investment is expenditure that adds value, however, and, as such, increases income to firms. The arrows represent the direction in which income is flowing.

You will be wondering about the role of government in all of this. Much of the text so far has discussed the role of government in both the micro and the macro economy, yet here is a model of the macro economy which appears to ignore government altogether. Is this another unrealistic assumption?

The answer, of course, is no. We can drop all our assumptions about no governments now and look at the role of government in the circular flow of income. The government can affect the circular flow in two ways: through spending money on stimulating the economy and through raising revenue from taxation. These interventions are called

Figure 8.2   The circular flow of income showing savings and investment.

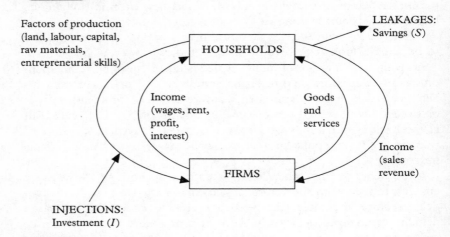

Figure 8.3   The circular flow of income showing government activities.

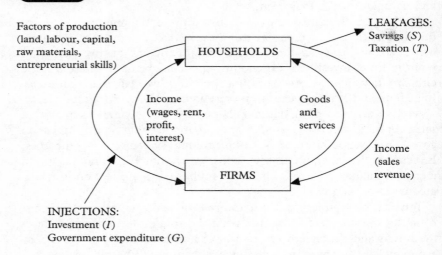

fiscal policy, and we will look at the actual mechanisms by which they work and the effects they have in the next chapter.

Figure 8.3 draws the circular flow diagram again, and this time includes government activities in the model. The government takes money out of the circular flow in the form of taxation, represented by the symbol T. This affects the income of individual households if a proportion of income is taken away in taxation. It thus affects company sales revenue because individuals with less income will, other things being equal, spend less money. It also affects companies in two further ways: through taxation on profits and indirect taxation on intermediate goods (i.e. supplies in the production process), which make these goods more expensive.

The revenue that is raised through taxation is used by the government to inject money into the circular flow. The type of expenditure that adds to the circular flow is expenditure that generates income for companies; for example, government-funded road building plans or other government investments in the economic infrastructure that create work. We would include expenditure on schools, housing and healthcare in this. But we do not include expenditure which redistributes income from higher to lower paid members of the community. This is because such expenditure does not add to income – it merely reallocates it.

The final area to introduce is the open economy. No model of the macro economy would be accurate without allowing for the influence of overseas markets and competitors. Indeed, as businesses throughout the world become more 'global' in their operations, the impact of overseas consumers and overseas companies as well as of other countries becomes more important.

The open economy is slightly more difficult to grasp, although quite logical on reflection. Our economic activities with other countries have two general components: imports and exports. Imports are the goods that we bring in from overseas and sell in the domestic economy for our consumers to buy. If we as consumers spend money on these goods, i.e. those produced by companies with their domestic operations in other countries, then we are effectively taking money out of our circular flow of income and adding it to the circular flow of other countries. Similarly, consumers from abroad buying the goods and services of this country are, effectively, injecting money into our circular flow of income.[4]

The activities of all companies in an economy (i.e. the amount they produce in goods and services) create the sum of the nation's income. This is the goods and services produced on the right-hand side of the circular flow diagram. At issue here is how that income moves between households and companies and the areas from which income flows into and out of the economy.

For example, Siemens is one of the largest companies in Germany and, as such, contributes significantly to the country's national income. But a company like Siemens has around 80 per cent of its sales

Figure 8.4   The circular flow of income including the open economy.

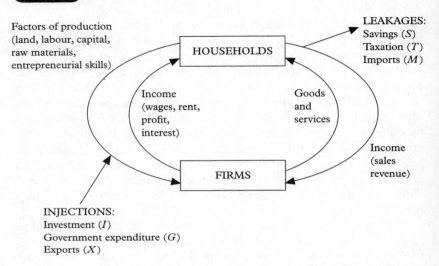

turnover accounted for by sales outside Germany. The contribution of Siemens to the national income of Germany is measured by the total *value added* of its products – put very simply, the amount that customers pay for the end product of that company. It is immaterial whether this revenue comes from Germany or from abroad – it still contributes to the profits of Siemens and the national income of Germany. The amount of money that flows into Siemens (and, hence, the German economy) from its overseas activities (i.e. its exports) represents an injection into the circular flow of income.

It should by now be clear that exports represent injections into the circular flow and imports represent leakages from the circular flow. Let us now look at how this affects the circular flow of income diagram. In figure 8.4, exports (represented by the symbol X) are shown with the injections into the circular flow. Imports (represented by the symbol M) are shown as leakages from the circular flow.

6   Why Is All This Important? Introducing National Income

National income is important because it is the total income in an economy that is generated by economic activity. As such, it is the nation's wealth. Adding up the added value of everything that is produced will give us a measure of how much the nation's companies are generating. Similarly, adding up everything that is spent in an economy and taking away the amount that is spent on imports will also give us an idea of how much income is generated.

It is not the intention to go into great detail of how national income is calculated. But companies do need to know about aggregate demand because this obviously tells them something about how their products will sell. Aggregate demand is a 'real' measure of expenditure on goods and services, in other words national income, so we at least need to be aware of its importance. Before we move on to this, two points in calculating national income need to be borne in mind.

1 We would not get an accurate measure of national income if we added together everything that was produced in the economy. Some goods are produced as inputs into another company's production process, so we would end up with a much bigger value than would be accurate. Instead we add together the *added value* at each stage – or the difference between the price for which the component is bought and the price the final product is sold for. This eliminates the problem of *double counting*.

2 *Double counting* would also occur if we added together all the value added of all the goods and services produced in the economy to all the consumer expenditure in the economy. For this reason we add together either consumer expenditure or production, but not both.

With these points in mind, let's turn now to some elementary facts about national income. The circular flow of income shows us how income moves about in an economy from households (the owners of the factors of production) and firms (the country's businesses). It also shows us how income flows in in the form of injections (investment (I), government expenditure (G) and exports (X)) and how income flows out in the form of leakages (savings (S), taxation (T) and imports (M)). It does not tell us anything about how that income is generated or its value. It is simply a descriptive tool which allows us to understand how income allocates and reallocates itself in the macro economy.

In order to look at how income is generated and the value of that income we need to look at national income statistics. We have used the term 'national income' very loosely thus far without really pondering on what it means. However, if we understand national income we can understand the true link between the micro and macro economies.

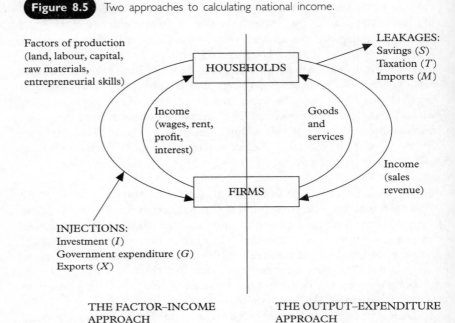

Figure 8.5 Two approaches to calculating national income.

THE FACTOR–INCOME
APPROACH

THE OUTPUT–EXPENDITURE
APPROACH

This is because national income is the nation's wealth. It is the income that is generated from a given allocation of resources in the economic activity of all actors in the economy. You will have heard terms like GNP and GDP or per capita GNP and per capita GDP in economic news bulletins; indeed, these terms have been used earlier in this book. Very broadly these are ways of calculating the value of the nation's income, and we look at these more closely now.

We can calculate national income in two ways: either by adding up all the expenditure on end (tertiary) goods and services in the economy or by adding up all the incomes of factors of production used to produce all the end products in an economy. The first approach is called the 'output–expenditure' approach, the second, the 'factor–income' approach. The two arrive at very similar figures for national income because households cannot spend more than they receive in payment for their services on the output of the country's industry. In both methods of calculating national income the role of injections and leakages remains the same.

Using the circular flow diagram we can illustrate each of the approaches to calculating national income (figure 8.5). We need to look at how the data for national income are derived because this allows us to see the link between the operations of industry and the macro economy. As students of business we need to know about trends in national income and we need to know about trends in aggregate demand because these give an indication of the competitiveness and the health (or otherwise) of the national economy.

The two most commonly used measures of national income are gross domestic product (GDP) and gross national product (GNP). As these are indicators used by governments and companies alike we will look at their components.

GDP, very simply, is the income of the closed economy (as implied by the word domestic). We construct it using the five following steps.

All household income is either consumed or saved. If you are given any money you either put it on one side for the future or you spend it on goods and services. We can illustrate this in shorthand as symbols:

$$Y = S + C$$

where Y is income; S is saving; C is consumption.

Similarly, all expenditure is on consumption or investment. One person's expenditure is income to another. Effectively, then, total expenditure is also total income and can be represented by the symbol Y. Again we can illustrate this using symbols:

$$Y = C + I$$

where Y is expenditure; C is consumption; I is investment.

Rearrange the equations. National income accountants and economists reorganized these two equations as follows:

$$Y = C + I$$

Firms receive income from consumption expenditure by households and investment expenditure.

$$Y = S + C$$

All household income is saved or consumed.

Taking away consumption from each equation gives:

$$Y - C = I$$

$$Y - C = S$$

Therefore

$$S = I$$

The equality of savings and investment is a vital national income equilibrium. (a) If investment is greater than saving, aggregate demand will exceed aggregate supply (or output); in the short term this will create inflation until output increases (inflationary gap). (b) If investment is less than saving, demand will be less than output and companies will have unsold stock; pressure will be on prices to fall (the deflationary gap). (c) Where savings and investment are equal prices are stable.

National income is therefore made up of consumption expenditure, investment expenditure and government expenditure.

$$Y = C + I + G$$

where G is government expenditure.

Add in any income from exports sold abroad, and subtract expenditure on imports, to arrive at the calculation for GDP:

$$GDP = C + I + G + (X - M)$$

where X is income from exports; M is expenditure on imports.

GDP, then, is defined as *all the expenditure on the goods and services produced in an economy*. It is all domestic expenditure plus the net balance of trade, i.e. the expenditure of oversesas consumers on exports minus the amount that domestic consumers spend on imports.

You will often also see GNP, or gross national product, referred to in tables and articles about the economy. GNP is the same as GDP but adds in the net property incomes accrued from abroad.

7 Investigation (2): Which Measure of National Income Best Reflects National Wealth and National Competitiveness?

Politicians in any country will often quote national income statistics and claim that they provide conclusive evidence of the state of economic health of the nation. Often they will divide GDP or GNP by the number of people in the country and give a figure for income per person, or per capita. The *International Marketing Year Book* provides comparative and simple data and economic statistics. Look in this and find some comparative GDP and GNP figures. You may also find the following articles of interest.

Eisener, R. (1996) The point of using GDP. *New Economy*, 3(1).
Oswald, A. (1996) GDP can't make you happy. *New Economy*, 3(1).
Hawkins, R., Webb, J. and Corry, D. (1996) Sense of well-being. *New Economy*, 3(1).

1 Which measure do you think is the best indicator of national wealth for a government to use?
2 Which measure of national income provides the best indicator of (a) aggregate demand and (b) international competitiveness for companies to use in their forecasting?
3 Do aggregate data like this present an adequate picture of economic *and* social well-being in an economy?
4 On the basis of your research for the first investigation of this chapter, why do you think Britain had rapidly increasing GDP during the mid-1980s.

8 The Importance of National Income Calculations: Aggregate Demand and Aggregate Supply

As was mentioned above, it is not the intention to enter into a long debate about national income or the merits and demerits of either system. What is important about what we have covered so far, however, is that it gives us a method for looking at demand and supply in the whole economy and, therefore, to move on to examine inflation and unemployment.

We have used a number of shorthand symbols in this chapter to represent the major components of national income:

C, consumption
I, investment
G, government expenditure
X, exports
M, imports

These five components represent all expenditure in the economy. All income is spent on consumption, investment, government projects, exports or imports. So, when we are measuring national income in

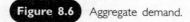 Aggregate demand.

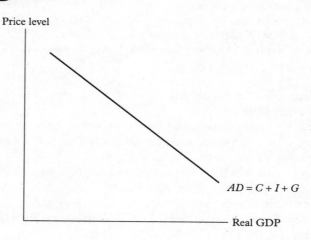

terms of what is spent on the goods and services in an economy, we are actually measuring aggregate demand.

Aggregate demand is all the demand in an economy (i.e. all consumption, all investment, all government projects as well as the external trade balance). Think back to microeconomics for a moment. When we looked at market demand it was the sum of all individual demand curves for a particular product. Similarly, if we want to calculate all demand for everything produced in an economy, we are adding together the demand curves in every single market. We are looking at all the expenditure on the goods and services in the economy – in other words, national income.

We can write the equation for aggregate demand using the same shorthand symbols that we use for national income:

$$NY = C + I + G + (X - M)$$

and

$$AD = C + I + G + (X - M)$$

As with market demand, we can represent aggregate demand graphically, as shown in figure 8.6.

We turn now to aggregate supply. National income can also be calculated in terms of the value of output in the economy, as we saw

Figure 8.7 The aggregate supply schedule.

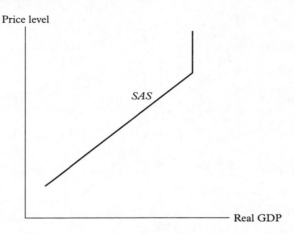

Price level

SAS

Real GDP

above. Effectively this is the sum of all that is supplied in the economy: all the goods and services of all the markets in the economy. As we discussed above, it is important to be wary about calculating national income like this because of the problem of double counting, so we look only at the value that is added at each stage in the value chain. If we add up the value at each stage we again arrive at the figure for national income. So we can similarly argue that aggregate supply is the sum of all final goods and services produced in the economy and is the same as real gross domestic product. It can be represented as in figure 8.7.

We should pause for a minute to look at the importance of aggregate supply for business and distinguish between the short term and the long term as we have done in our discussion of costs earlier in the book. Aggregate supply is the productive potential of the economy. In the 'short term' this is variable and upward sloping to the right, as shown in figure 8.7. In the long term, however, the total productive capacity of the economy is fixed: put simply, there is a finite supply of labour, only a given supply of land and so on.

Thus, in the long run, the aggregate supply curve will be a vertical straight line. Long-run equilibrium in the economy as a whole (where, if you recall from the above equations, savings will equal investment) will be at the intersection with the aggregate demand curve, as shown in figure 8.8. At the level of national income, NY_e, prices will be stable at P_e because savings equal investment (i.e. demand equals supply).

Figure 8.8 Aggregate demand and long-run aggregate supply: equilibrium national income.

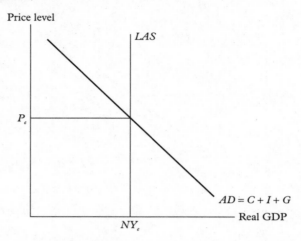

From our discussion of national income you will understand that aggregate supply and aggregate demand are very similar. Aggregate demand is the total amount that is spent on goods and service in the economy. Aggregate supply is the value of goods and services produced in the economy (i.e. the real worth of the nation's output).

You will note that the shape of the short-run aggregate supply curve is different from the shape of supply curves used in microeconomics. This is because the economy reaches a point (a level of income) where resources are utilized to their full capacity, i.e. every industry is performing at its full potential in the short term. The economy can experience short-term supply shocks that affect aggregate supply in the same way that shocks affect supply in microeconomic analysis. For example, a rise in oil prices affects every company in the same way by increasing input costs.

Prices can, and do, fluctuate in the short term, causing imbalances in the economy. These 'imbalances' or disequilbria can cause unemployment or inflation. National income can, and does, vary. In fact the debate about the importance of the shape of the long-run aggregate supply curve is central to the analysis of policy: if, like monetarists,[5] we stick rigidly to the idea that the output capacity of the economy is fixed, then we cannot increase national income through policy measures except by injecting inflation (or higher prices) into the economy. Conversely, if, like Keynesians, we believe that an economy can settle at a level of national income which is not at full capacity, then we can increase aggregate demand and, hence, national income. Much of the policy debate in the post-war period has attempted to pull these two poles together.

9 Conclusions: Why Is This Relevant to Business?

While it might seem that most of the material covered here is highly technical and complex, the essence of it is very simple. Demand and supply in all the separate markets of the economy added together make the total economic activity, or national income, of a country. This total economic activity, and, hence, economic health, is determined at a very basic level by the behaviour of producers and consumers. Once they are added together we can see how behaviour in one market, say housing, can affect that in another, say construction, and have a ripple effect through the economy as a whole.

This shows the interdependency between the micro and the macro economy. The macro economy would not exist without its individual markets – in short, business. Similarly, the behaviour of companies, which is manifested through its strategies, is fundamentally determined by the economic health of the nation. But the health or otherwise of an economy is affected by policies of governments. Although these might seem small, a rise in interest rates of 0.5 per cent or a reduction in taxation of 1p in the pound, they make ripples throughout all areas of economic activity and can affect the behaviour of companies and consumers in individual markets. They can create either vicious or virtuous circles.

If we revisit the strategic model of previous chapters, we can see that the influence of government on strategy is more complex than regulation. Think again of the components of national income: consumption, investment, government expenditure and exports minus imports. These, of course, are the principle concerns of business: consumer demand, investment, incentives (for example, for training, location or R&D) and the international economy, which we return to in chapter 10. So, if a government follows policies which expand the economy (i.e. boost national income growth) by spending money, companies operate in an environment of rising demand and, potentially, rising prices. Conversely, if a government follows policies which contract the economy (to bring down inflation), companies will operate in a climate where demand is falling, prices are falling and the cost of borrowing and expansion is high.

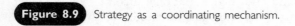

Figure 8.9 Strategy as a coordinating mechanism.

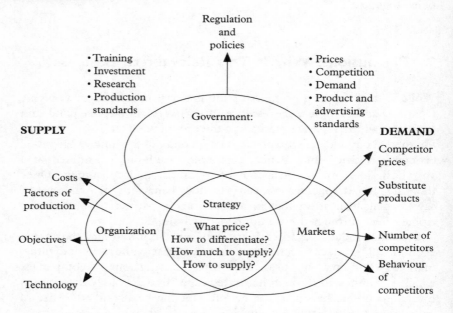

The coordinating role for strategy is made more complex by the impact of goverment policy. This is illustrated in figure 8.9, which is a development of the strategic model of previous chapters. Regulation and policies are put at the top of the diagram because they affect both demand and supply conditions: for example, anti-inflationary policy creates stable prices but may also make borrowing relatively expensive through high interest rates.

9.1 Investigation (3)

The areas of influence on company strategy illustrated in figure 8.9 are by no means exhaustive. How many areas can you add to the list? Categorize your answers into 'supply' effects and 'demand' effects. What might a company do to minimize the effects of government policy on the effective operation of its strategy?

9.2 Summary

We need to add yet another column to our strategic matrix – that of the macro economy and government policy. As with government

Figure 8.10   Aggregate demand, forecasting the macro economy and strategy.

	Pricing/output	Product development and technology	Competitor analysis	Impact of regulatory environment	National income and macro economy
Monopolistic competition	Depends on number of competitors and elasticity of demand	Centrally important: creating market share and creating innovation base to new industries	Vital: especially costs and new products	High – impact on costs	High impact: forecasting expensive but severely affected by swings in macro environment
Oligopolistic competition	Price inter-dependency at industry level, but pricing to increase market penetration	NON-PRICE COMPETITION

Essential, although large companies will hold back from new industries | Strategic inter-dependency: firms depend on each other's behaviour for market share and R&D strategy | Low – can be taken up within slack and turned to competitive advantage | Potential high impact which can be reduced through economic forecasting. |

intervention and the regulatory environment, the matrix in figure 8.10 shows a sharp distinction between small companies and large companies, with small business feeling the effects of government policies perhaps more greatly than large companies.

To summarize, then, the following points can be drawn out of the material in this chapter:

1 The micro and macro economies are interdependent on one another through the operations of companies and behaviour of consumers. Individual markets can be added together to create aggregate demand and aggregate supply for the economy as a whole. Income flows between households and companies.
2 The health of the macro economy will affect individual businesses through costs and through consumer demand.
3 Companies can formulate strategies to deal with fluctuations in the macro economy based on forecasts of those fluctuations. But forecasting is expensive and small companies will be less able to insure against macroeconomic environmental fluctuations than large ones.

10 Further Reading

Jenkinson, T. (1996) *Readings in Macroeconomics*. Oxford: Oxford University Press.

Notes

1   A phrase coined during the 1980s referring to the difficulties of diverse competitive conditions in members of the European Community in the run up to European Union.
2   After the economist John Maynard Keynes, who formulated policies to resolve the problem of unemployment in the 1930s in Britain.
3   See Kay, J. (1996) *The Business of Economics*. Oxford: Oxford University Press.
4   The open economy is complex and is dealt with in this text only insofar as it is necessary to understand the contemporary operations of business. A more substantial discussion is contained in chapters 10 and 11, with particular reference to the impact on company strategy.
5   This is a cursory discussion and is intended only as a means of explaining why aggregate supply is important and how it is rooted in politics. The issues are explored in more depth in the next chapter, but you may find Stewart, M. (1993) *Keynes in the 1990s: a Return to Economic Sanity*. Harmondsworth: Penguin, interesting.

9 Unemployment and Fiscal Policy

I know what unemployment is. I grew up in the 1930s. When my father didn't have a job, he didn't riot, he got on his bike and looked for work.

(Rt Hon. Norman Tebbit MP, 1981)

Technology and the structure of the economy are changing so fast that unless we train our labour force adequately there will be no long term return to full employment.

(Labour Party, 1992)

The main cause of unemployment today is the determination of monopolistic trade unions to insist on levels of pay that price men out of work altogether.

(Rt Hon. Nigel Lawson, then Chancellor of the Exchequer, 1985)

1 Introduction

We come now to the first of two chapters on specific areas of the macro economy which have a profound impact on the way in which companies operate and which have dominated the debate over macro-economic management in the post-war period throughout the indus-trialized world. As has been repeatedly stressed in earlier chapters, company strategy cannot directly include a component which caters for 'government policy'. Policies change, as do macroeconomic conditions. To minimize the effects of these changes companies can undertake eco-nomic forecasts, but many commentators are dubious about the accu-racy of these and the role they should play.[1] Management theory itself recommends a PEST analysis – a breakdown of trends in the polit-ical, economic, social and technological environment – in order to assess the efficacy of particular strategies. However, these tools can at best only give a probable indication of trends in the macro economy.

Yet the whole purpose of government economic policy is to create a stable environment for the operations of business. One method of doing this is by manipulating the components of national income,

which, if you recall, are consumption (C), investment (I) and government expenditure (G).[2] It can inject money into the economy through
spending and take it out and redistribute it through taxation, thereby
affecting both the level and the components of national income. These
are the instruments of so-called 'fiscal policy' which affect the real
economy and, hence, employment. But clearly these fiscal instruments
affect both the macroeconomic environment in which companies operate, particularly aggregate demand, *and* the investment environment;
for example, through tax incentives.[3]

Policies have an impact on business, but so too do the problems
that they attempt to resolve. For example, inflation, or persistently rising prices, causes problems for companies because of the uncertainty
it creates in markets. These uncertainties manifest themselves as fluctu-
ating demand in individual markets and in aggregate demand. This is
dealt with in more detail in chapter 10. Similarly, unemployment has
an impact on business. If people are either unable to find work or
uncertain as to how long they will remain in work, then their consumption is depressed. Companies are uncertain as to how much they
will sell and may also be reluctant to invest. The remainder of this
chapter focuses on the problem of unemployment.

The phrase 'on your bike' has become such an integral part of the
English language that few would recall its origins and even fewer
recollect that it was intended as a statement about the problem of
unemployment. Yet while the phrase 'on your bike' has been swallowed
into our phraseology, unemployment has far from disappeared off the
economic, social and political agenda.

Apart from the social and psychological damage caused by unemployment,[4] it is a problem for good economic reasons. It represents a
misallocation of resources – resources standing idle when they could
be usefully employed in creating national income. Thus unemployed
workers lose income and companies lose profit. The government loses
tax and national insurance revenue but spends more in income support
to those who are unemployed. Both in terms of this misallocation and
in terms of welfare expenditure, unemployment is a cost to the nation.
It represents a cost to business as well: graduate engineers unemployed
in the South East of England might be extremely useful to a company in the North, yet labour is relatively immobile – it does not get
'on its bike'. The pressure on firms to become 'leaner' and 'fitter' has
inevitably involved redundancies, with high costs in terms of severance
payments irrespective of any potential increases in productivity.

For all these reasons, government policy has to be directed at achieving, at the very least, an 'acceptable' level of unemployment. Since

John Maynard Keynes's great work in the 1930s[5] British governments have wrestled with the objective of achieving 'full' employment. During the 1980s we saw a change in policy to one directed at reducing inflation to zero. The objective was to create an economic environment in which prices were stable so that companies could be certain of how much they would sell and, hence, be certain about the numbers of people they should employ. By the mid-1990s we were seeing a return to the view that policies towards unemployment were vital to sustain an acceptable level of economic and social well-being.[6]

Some basic information will give you an idea of why unemployment is a problem in this country.

1 In 1978, 5.1 per cent of the population was out of work and claiming unemployment benefit. This rose to 11.6 per cent in 1986. After a fall in the late 1980s, unemployment rose again to 10.3 per cent of the workforce in 1993.

2 Unemployment varies significantly between regions in the economy. For example, in 1993, it stood at 12.1 per cent in the North East and 10.2 per cent in the South East. In East Anglia it was 8.5 per cent. Unemployment is felt most greatly in those areas most affected by changing patterns of employment (for example, the move from manufacturing to service sector employment, and more latterly, the reduction in employment in the service sector itself).

3 The largest proportion of people who are unemployed falls into the category of up to 26 weeks. In 1992 this was 46 per cent of the total unemployed and had fallen to 42.9 per cent of the total by 1993. However, more worryingly for policy-makers, long-term unemployment (i.e. out of work for more than 52 weeks) had risen from 34 to 38.4 per cent during the same period despite concerted efforts to reduce it.

It is not just Britain that experiences problems with unemployment. As table 9.1 shows, unemployment has risen alarmingly in the economies of some of our major competitor nations, with traditionally low-unemployment countries, like Germany and Sweden, experiencing comparatively high (and increasing) levels.

1.1 The Business Context of Unemployment

Unemployment is important to business for good strategic reasons. First, already mentioned is the fact that unemployment is a misallocation of resources. While people are unemployed they are not adding

Table 9.1   Comparative European unemployment levels, 1990–1994

Year	France	Germany (W)	Germany (E)	Japan	Sweden	UK	USA
1990	8.9	7.2	–	2.1	1.9	5.9	5.5
1991	9.4	6.3	10.3	2.1	3.2	8.1	6.7
1992	10.3	6.6	14.8	2.2	5.9	9.9	7.4
1993	11.6	8.2	15.8	2.5	8.7	10.4	6.8
1994	12.5	9.2	16.0	2.9	8.8	9.5	6.1

Source: Economic Review, Data Supplement, 1996.[7]

to the productive capacity, or national income, of the economy. They may rely on government support and, equally, may also be forced to deplete their savings. Thus national income is at a lower level: aggregate demand is below its full employment level, and thus companies produce less. Further, as savings are depleted and demand falls, investment becomes unattractive, even if interest rates are low because companies are uncertain as to the future profitability of their markets, so investment reduces, which may affect the long-term competitiveness of the company. We return to this last point soon but, as we saw in chapter 8, companies have to insure against the loss of potential demand by forecasting economic trends.

The impact of unemployment on businesses is felt most acutely if savings fall (as indeed, they will if individuals are reliant on them for finance during a period of unemployment). This comes about through the components of national income detailed in chapter 8. You will recall that savings must equal investment and therefore *ceteris paribus* the rate of interest will correct any imbalance in this equilibrium. The 'price' of investment is clearly the interest rate, i.e. what it costs to pay back the amount that has been borrowed. The return from savings is also the interest rate – the reward that is paid to individuals now for putting aside money for use in the future. Money that is saved in the economy represents 'loanable' funds, from which money is borrowed to fund investment. The interest rate is, according to this model, the means by which the market for loanable funds reaches an equilibrium where savings equals investment.

However, as Keynes argued in the 1930s, 'savers' and 'investors' are not usually the same group of people. Those who save are individuals, while large-scale investors are businesses. Thus, although for accounting reasons savings and investment must be equal, there is no reason why this should produce full employment: it is not the interest rate that is important, but the level of *income*: people may save a fixed amount of money a month, say, but if their income falls – for example, through unemployment – this fixed amount becomes a proportionately higher amount of their total income. GDP, through something called the *multiplier*,[8] itself is the correcting mechanism. This means that unemployment, which creates falling expenditure, can have real effects on output and investment in the economy generally and by companies in particular.

Finally, and just as significantly, there is a paradox that has begun to emerge with the prevalence of 'new' microelectronics-based technologies. These technologies require operative skills such as knowledge of computers. While millions were unemployed in the 1980s, companies complained of skills shortages and being unable to fill job vacancies because applicants are not adequately trained.[9] For many companies this was not only a chronic waste of resources, it also represented a loss of competitiveness because their overseas counterparts had access to the skilled labour force that they needed to operate the new machinery that technological progress required.

These points bring us back to the whole issue of government intervention. First, the government is obviously in a position to alter its spending and consumer spending using monetary tools (such as interest rate manipulation) and fiscal measures (such as taxation). Either approach to macroeconomic management will have very real effects on the levels of investment by companies. Second, the delineation of responsibilities between the state and industry for areas, such as training, that we covered first in chapter 7 is also central to the discussion of the impact of policies on business. Based on our analysis of the social market economies of Germany and Sweden we drew the conclusion that, arguably, governments have a role in the provision of basic skills, while companies should fund the skills that are specific to their productive needs. In any event, the skills shortages faced by many British companies during the 1980s caused a major review of their personnel strategies in order to cope with the perceived inadequacies of the national infrastructure.[10]

2 Aims and Objectives of the Chapter

As with previous chapters, the aim here is simply to give you an overview of the problem of unemployment, some possible ways in which governments might seek to solve it and, of course, why it represents an important issue for business. There are, of course, specific objectives which will also be achieved by the end of the chapter.

1   That you will understand the nature of unemployment and the different ways in which it might be caused.
2   That you will understand that the solution to unemployment depends on how it is perceived that unemployment is caused.
3   That you will understand the fiscal policy tools used by governments to create employment and reduce unemployment.
4   That you will understand the approach of *laissez-faire* governments towards unemployment.
5   That you will understand the links with industrial policy through the provision of training, for example, and therefore realize that business itself has an important part to play in the solution to the problem of long-term structural unemployment.
6   That you will understand the impact of unemployment itself and of policies to cure unemployment on business.

3   Investigation (1)

In order that you can understand the extent and depth of unemployment, you will find it useful to examine the following:

- comparative wage data (see table 4.1);
- the unemployment data given in this chapter (regional, comparative, structural change).

Look briefly at tables 4.1, 9.1 and 9.2 and figure 9.5 before you read the chapter, and see if you can draw any conclusions on the nature of unemployment. Think carefully about your own perspective on unemployment, again before you read the chapter. Do the data support your preconceptions?

4   What Causes Unemployment and How Can We Cure It?

Unemployment is the number of people who are in the labour force minus the number of people from that labour force at any one point in time who are working.

This is a straightforward and non-political definition of unemployment but one which extends beyond the definition currently used by the government.[11] We use a broad definition like this in order to include all possible types of unemployment in our discussion, which, after all, is of economics and not of politics.

4.1 'Wages Are Too High'

This first cause of unemployment is that taken by the classical economists after Adam Smith and the monetarist economists that dominated policy in Britain and the USA in the 1970s and 1980s. Look again at the brief discussion of the components of national income and, particularly, the link between savings and investment above. The classical economists believed that savings and investment would automatically fall into equilibrium with one another through the market for loans, and hence the interest rate.[12] If savings fell, interest rates would also fall. There was no need for a government to intervene in this mechanism as companies would be induced by low interest rates to invest more. This would bring up the level of saving, and hence the level of national income. The restored level of national income would be at a full employment rate because of the buoyancy of investment.

The logical extension of this, then, is that any unemployment is short term and caused not by imbalances in spending and output, but by workers charging too much for their services, as suggested by the quote at the top of the chapter. The theoretical rationale behind this statement lies in the very simple models of demand and supply that we have covered in earlier chapters. Very simply, the argument runs that, if workers charge high prices for their services, companies will be able to afford fewer of them. Hence, a smaller number of people will be able to find work than would otherwise be the case.

This perspective is represented in figure 9.1. On the vertical axis is the 'price' of labour – i.e. its wage – and on the horizontal axis is the quantity of labour that is demanded. The model shows the equilibrium of the 'labour market', where labour is a product with a price much like any other product – potatoes or bananas, for example. In other words, this model is assuming that labour is a 'normal' good: demand will be downward sloping to the right and supply will be upward sloping to the right. The work of one person for one hour will be much the same as another's – labour is homogeneous.[13] If the 'price' is high, more will be supplied and less will be demanded, creating a disequilibrium and downward pressure on prices.[14]

Figure 9.1   The market for labour.

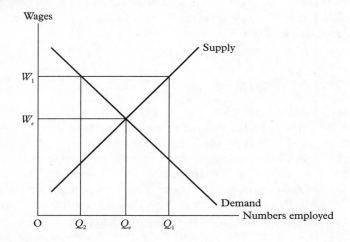

In figure 9.1, wages are set high at W_1. At this price, the quantity Q_2 is demanded but Q_1 is supplied. The 'unsold' surplus (i.e. the labour services that are not bought) represents individuals who are unable to find work – the unemployed. Because labour is a normal product, 'full' employment will be reached when demand and supply are equal. In other words, when the wage has fallen to W_e.

Under this model, unemployment is caused by the imperfect operation of the labour market that causes labour to be priced too high; for example, at W_1 above. A number of factors can set wages at a level which 'prices' people out of work: these include trade unions with strong collective bargaining powers and, most topically, a national minimum wage which would ensure that no individual was paid less than a basic rate for an hour's work. If that basic rate is above the level that is determined by the operation of the market (W_e) then the result is a permanent surplus of labour over the quantity of labour demanded.

The policy implications
The implications for policy of this, essentially micro, view of the labour market are clear. If labour is a normal product much like any other, then the market left to its own devices will arrive at an equilibrium wage in a relatively short space of time. Individuals will realize that they cannot charge an unrealistically high price for an hour's work if they wish to be employed, so they will reduce the wage they are

Table 9.2   Regional unemployment in the UK, 1980–1993

Region	1980	1985	1988	1989	1990	1991	1992	1993
North	7.7	15.4	12.1	10.1	8.7	10.1	11.2	12.1
Yorks.	5.0	12.0	9.5	7.5	6.7	8.6	9.8	10.4
E. Mids	4.2	9.8	7.3	5.5	5.1	7.1	9.0	9.6
East Anglia	3.6	8.1	5.4	3.6	3.6	5.7	7.7	8.5
S. East	2.9	8.0	5.5	4.0	3.9	6.7	9.2	10.2
S. West	4.3	9.3	6.4	4.6	4.3	6.9	9.2	9.9
W. Mids	5.2	12.8	9.1	6.7	5.8	8.3	10.4	11.1
North West	6.2	13.7	10.6	8.7	7.7	9.2	10.7	10.9
Wales	6.5	13.6	10.0	7.5	6.6	8.7	9.9	10.3
Scotland	6.8	12.9	11.3	9.4	8.2	8.6	9.3	9.7
N. Ireland	9.1	15.9	15.7	14.7	13.3	13.4	13.9	14.0
UK	4.8	10.9	8.2	6.4	5.8	7.9	9.7	10.4

Source: Economic Review, Data Supplement, 1995.

demanding to a level which is acceptable to employers. Indeed, any intervention into the market place for labour will create false expectations of potential earnings which cannot be realized because in the long run the market will prevail and the equilibrium will be restored.

Unemployment of this type is often called short-term unemployment.[15] It is a limited problem which can only be resolved by non-intervention; people out of work will quickly find work because they will be willing to reduce the amount they are demanding for their labour services.

4.2 'On Your Bike' Unemployment: a Special Case of Short-term Unemployment

During recessionary periods some areas of the country are affected more severely than others. Table 9.2 gives an indication of this problem for Great Britain during the recessions of the early 1980s and the early 1990s.

This table demonstrates an interesting difference between the two recessionary periods. In the early 1980s it was the North of England that suffered most severely, with large numbers of jobs going in the traditional employers in heavy manufacturing industries. In the late 1980s and early 1990s the recession was felt equally as strongly in the

Figure 9.2 The regional mobility of labour.

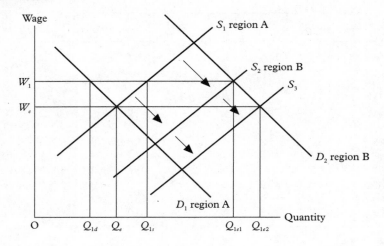

South. This was because this major employers were service sector companies which were particularly badly hit by the high interest rates between 1988 and 1990.

The problem of regional unemployment like this was the one that Norman Tebbit was seeking to address in his statement referred to above. If, he argued, people are unemployed in one area, then all they need to do is look for work elsewhere in the country where there is employment at a wage for which they are willing to work.

This is a specific example of the short-term type of unemployment we have looked at already. It again assumes that labour is a 'normal' product and that the market will function perfectly. But there is an assumption that labour is also perfectly mobile – that if there is no work in one area then people will move around in order to find work elsewhere.

The model can be represented as in figure 9.2. Look carefully at the diagram, which shows two separate labour markets for region A and region B. First examine the demand curve D_1 and the supply curve S_1 for region A. An equilibrium price for the labour in this market is W_e. Currently, however, there is unemployment caused, in this case, by the high wage expectations of potential workers. The wage currently being demanded is W_1 which results in unemployment of $Q_1s - Q_1d$. These individuals will be unable to find work in region A at that wage.

The model predicts, however, that if these individuals move to region B they will be able to find work. This is because the demand for labour in region B is D_2. There is currently a shortage of labour because only S_1 is being supplied.

If the unemployed individuals in region A move to region B, supply will increase from S_1 to S_2, meaning that a new equilibrium wage in the short term will reached at W_1 where Q_{1e1} of labour is supplied. In the long term, as more workers move to region B in anticipation of higher earnings (S_3), wages will fall to the original equilibrium of W_e, with a new quantity of labour supplied at Q_{1e2}.

The policy

How does a government 'cure' the problem of regional unemployment illustrated above? There are two approaches that have, historically, been taken. The first is simple – leave the market mechanism to operate freely and the problem of unemployment will resolve itself as workers realize that they have to accept the wages that are set by the market. Labour will freely move between areas because it is perfectly mobile and the sovereignty of the price mechanism will ensure that any unemployment is a temporary phenomenon.

Since the Second World War, however, governments of every political persuasion have tended to be more pragmatic about the problem of unemployment. The unfettered *laissez-faire* approach to the market has major limitations in that it assumes that all individuals' labour is identical *and* that labour will move perfectly between areas to restore equilibrium. Clearly this is not the case – if it were, we would not have the vast differences in unemployment levels between regions that you saw in table 9.2.

So the second approach is to provide individuals with incentives to move between areas actively and passively – largely through benefits and training programmes – and to provide incentives to companies to locate in areas that are suffering from particularly high unemployment. The location of the Nissan plant in Sunderland in 1986 was an example of a company that made use of this scheme,[16] with many other multinationals like Siemens and Samsung following suit by 1996.

4.3 The Natural Rate of Unemployment

The models reviewed thus far all point to one policy conclusion for a government: unemployment is caused by imperfections in the market place and not by imbalances in national income. Thus, by allowing the market to operate relatively freely (providing minor stimuli such as investment grants as necessary), an equilibrium level of employment and national income will be reached.

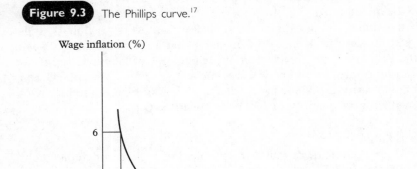

Figure 9.3 The Phillips curve.[17]

Subscribers to this view of unemployment hold that there will always be a degree of 'frictional' unemployment: people between jobs or unemployable (for example, because they will not move to other areas or accept lower wages). This unemployment is 'natural', even voluntary, and there is very little that the government can do about it without creating inflationary pressures. This is illustrated in figure 9.3 which is called the 'Phillips curve'.

The natural rate of unemployment, argue monetarist economists, is where the Phillips curve crosses the horizontal axis, at point N. This point is consistent with zero inflation and will correspond to a level of frictional unemployment of between 5 and 10 per cent.[18] Any attempts to reduce unemployment below that level will create inflation because of the expansionary measures used to boost aggregate demand. And, as we have seen throughout in our analysis of demand and supply, any increase in demand will create rising prices unless supply can adapt quickly. We return to this in chapter 10.

4.4   The Incomes-gap Approach to Unemployment and the Role of Fiscal Policy

The above models of unemployment have always been criticized by economists who argue that demand for labour can settle at a level which does not guarantee full employment. This interpretation was first realized by John Maynard Keynes in 1936 in his book *The General Theory of Employment, Interest and Money*, which sought to arrive at an explanation for the massive levels of unemployment experienced in 1930s Britain, and his insights and analysis have informed both debate about and policy towards unemployment since then. His argument was that the unemployment of the 1930s was caused by slack aggregate demand (or national income). The economy had settled at a level of national income which satisfied existing demand for goods and services but still left a large number of people without work.

This happens because the demand for labour is *derived demand*: in other words, labour will only be demanded if goods and services are demanded in the economy. If aggregate demand for goods and services is slack then companies will not be able to sell their products. In turn, they will start to supply less and, accordingly, demand for labour (to produce the goods and services in the economy) will also fall.

For this reason policy-makers in Britain, in particular since the Second World War, have found convincing the idea that if they could boost aggregate demand then the problem of unemployment would be resolved.

We will look first at the theory which predicts that increasing aggregate demand will reduce unemployment[19] using the simple model of demand and supply in the labour market above for simplicity. Figure 9.4 shows the relationship between the total demand for and supply of labour in the 'market' (here the economy as a whole).

Look first of all at the situation before any form of government intervention (D_1, S_1). Here the economy has reached an 'equilibrium' wage of W_1 and a level of employment at Q_1. Keynes maintained that it was possible for this level of employment to be sub-optimal; in other words, with an unacceptably large number of people unable to find work. The model of the market mechanism leads us to predict that there is nothing we can do about this – if wages are not to rise then we must accept that this level of unemployment is 'natural' and unavoidable. The severe problems that many experienced in both Britain and America in the 1930s, however, led Keynes to suggest that not only was unemployment an economic problem in terms of misallocated resources, it was also a social and political one.

Remember, then, that the demand for labour is derived demand. If we can boost aggregate demand in the economy companies will have to expand production in order to meet the increased demand. And, if production expands, so too, other things being equal, will employment. The government is in a position to manage aggregate demand in a

Figure 9.4   Reducing unemployment by boosting demand.

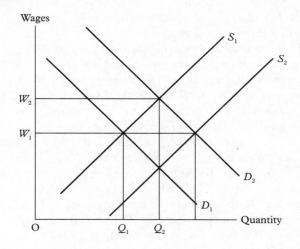

number of ways, which will be discussed shortly. For the time being, it is important to realize that the reason why demand shifts from D_1 to D_2 is that aggregate demand (or national income) has increased (ΔY). This will increase the level of employment from Q_1 to Q_2 at increased wages (W_2). In the long term, as more individuals join the labour market, supply will increase from S_1 to S_2 and, if the market operates effectively, wages will fall to W_1.

Another of Keynes's insights, however, was that wages will tend to be 'sticky' downwards. Potentially, then, there would be a tendency for wages to rise successively and, hence, create wage inflation. This is one of the main criticisms of Keynes's analysis. Keynes, however, argued that the fact that wages are rising is a positive factor in the economy rather than a negative one. As wages rise, people have more money to spend. If they have more money to spend then they buy the goods and services of producers in the economy. In turn, this boosts the income of companies, which allows them to take on more workers to meet the increased demand.

The policy

Keynes's great insight was that an equilibrium level of national income can be reached that is consistent with less than full employment. If the level of *effective* (or real) aggregate demand is low, then savings and investment will also be low, and the level of national income does not produce full employment. The government has therefore to undertake to maintain this effective aggregate demand at a level which will produce full employment, because this will stimulate consumer spending, stimulate investment and, hence, provide jobs.

This results in a prescription for policy-makers to cure the problem of unemployment through fiscal measures to affect the level of consumption and investment in the economy as follows.

1   The government injects a small amount of money into the economy so that people feel 'better off'. This might be through a combination of tax reductions (increasing personal disposable income), increased universal welfare payments (i.e. non-means tested benefits like child benefit, again increasing personal disposable income) or expenditure programmes like investment in the nationalized transport infrastructure (directly increasing employment and, hence, income). These *fiscal* measures have the effect of increasing everyone's income slightly, hence giving all more spending power.
2   The economy has been resting at a slack level of aggregate demand (or national income). So, when income is increased slightly, the effect is to unleash some of the 'latent' demand in the economy. In other words, on aggregate, people will spend the small amount of extra income they receive from government fiscal policy.
3   Added together, the extra expenditure by individuals amounts to a large demand stimulus (and extra income) to companies.
4   Faced with long-term increased demand, companies anticipate greater profitability from increasing their output. In order to achieve this increased output they expand their capacity, taking on more employees in the process.
5   As more people gain employment (and more is produced in the economy), national income and aggregate demand continue to rise without any further prompting by the government. Full employment is restored and aggregate demand settles again at a level where capacity in the economy is fully utilized (i.e. national income has increased).

This process is *the multiplier* referred to above, and it underpinned economic policy-making throughout the post-war period until the first oil crisis of 1973. Even after that crisis, when prices rose substantially, governments continued to believe in the desirability of full employment until the Thatcher government which came to power in 1979.

The multiplier effect has a compelling appeal to policy-makers. Put very simply, it means that a government can inject a small amount of money into the economy using fiscal measures which affect the real level of income in the economy. That relatively small amount of money will 'multiply' in its effect if the economy has started at a sub-optimal level of national income, as expenditure increases and companies realize that the increases are permanent. Thus, in order to ensure that as many people within the working population as possible are able to gain work, and that national income is at as high as possible, all governments need to do is inject a small amount of money into the economy. And a degree of government debt to fund this expansion is a small price to pay for the benefits of full employment.

Further justification for this policy stance comes from the very Phillips curve which monetarists have, more recently, used to justify their approach to unemployment. Using wage inflation as a proxy for actual inflation, the Phillips curve was seized upon in the 1950s by Keynesian policy-makers who saw in it a vindication for the economic policies they were following. It appeared to them that Phillips had demonstrated a clear policy trade-off between inflation and unemployment. They could therefore justify the increases in inflation that were inevitable from Keynesian-style aggregate demand management policies in the interests of reducing the level of unemployment to an acceptable level.

4.5   Structural Unemployment

This approach worked for governments in the immediate post-war period, when, arguably, demand was at a sub-optimal level. But many economists have subsequently argued that the *policy application* of the theory is flawed on two main grounds. First, the monetarist economists who believe strongly in the market model of unemployment criticize the approach because it can lead to spiralling wage inflation. As income rises companies 'catch up' with the corresponding increases in aggregate demand only after a time lag. This time lag, they argue, leads to a vicious economic circle where individuals have too much money while not enough is produced in the economy: demand outstrips supply and, as we learned in the chapters on the market mechanism, this will lead to increased prices in order to restore equilibrium. Even more worryingly, workers will expect their incomes to continue to rise and see prices rising in the shops. This makes them put high wage claims before their employers, thus pushing up producer costs. Extra costs will be passed on to the consumer in terms of higher prices, and so on.

Even more disturbing than this is the second critique of the policies that were followed in the post-war period on the back of Keynes's macroeconomic theories. Companies are producing more to meet increased demand but this does not guarantee that investment is at a high enough level to ensure that international competitiveness is assured. Governments are providing stimuli to aggregate demand but not to investment, which, if you remember from the chapter on the circular flow, represents another way in which income can be injected into the economy. Indeed, if aggregate demand rises too high, then, argue monetarist economists, companies, faced with rising prices domestically, will begin to restrict their investment, anticipating a fall in demand as increased prices reach the market place. If companies do not invest, they will not be able to sustain their market share because better (or cheaper) substitute products will be imported from abroad. Further, they will find their export markets severely damaged by the inferiority of their products compared to those of their overseas competitors. Another source of injections into the circular flow, that of export revenue, is limited.

Corresponding with the declining investment in the level of investment in the British economy in the two decades in question were two further factors which acted to the detriment of domestic-based companies. The first was an increase in investment by other countries overseas, particularly in the area of non-military R&D, which, arguably, increased the technological sophistication of Britain's competitors – most notably Germany and Japan.

Perhaps paradoxically, however, the British economy has historically been strong in the area of services, especially financial services. Industry-funded investment in this area continued apace throughout the decades, while, because of technological and competitive weaknesses in manufacturing, manufacturing industry declined both as a source of investment and technological excellence and as a major employer. The trend was further exacerbated by a worldwide trend away from employment in manufacturing as technology progressed (hence requiring fewer personnel to operate machinery).

This move from manufacturing to service sector employment and the deep-seated changes in the economy that caused it is called *structural* unemployment. The extent of the change is represented in figure 9.5.

There is no direct measure of structurally unemployed individuals, but a good proxy is the number of people who are long-term unemployed. Snapshot data for this were given at the beginning of the chapter and the issue of long-term unemployment has been on the political

Figure 9.5   Structural change in employment in the British economy.

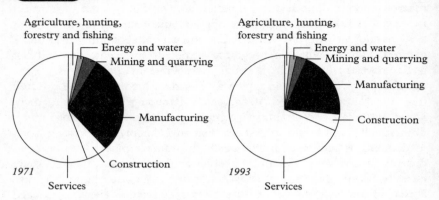

Source: *Economic Review*, November 1995.

agenda for many years now. Clearly, then, this is an important aspect of the overall problem.

The policy

There is no direct 'cure' for structural unemployment. The policy battleground over full employment has been debated long and hard in the post-war period, but particularly for the nearly 20 years since the process of *deindustrialization* (i.e. the move from manufacturing employment to service sector employment) was first recognized. On the one hand are monetarist economists who believe firmly in the power of the market ultimately to bring the economy into equilibrium. For them, as with other types of unemployment, the cure is to leave the market to operate, with free international trade ensuring that domestic companies are made to realize what competitive best practice is and compete with it. In order to ameliorate the hardships of the frictional unemployment caused while people retrain themselves to be able to work in jobs where new technology predominates, companies themselves will set market-based incentives to individuals to undertake such retraining through rewarding technologically skilled workers with higher salaries.

The contrasting view argues that the market cannot be relied upon to provide the incentives to retrain or the ultimate equilibrium that would produce both stable prices and full employment. For these economists, the harsh reality is that in times of recession the first cost to be cut is training by companies and the second is the investment that would make companies internationally competitive. Some argue that the solution is to protect domestic industry against overseas competition by imposing tariffs on imported goods, thus giving them a price disadvantage. Others argue that the only solution is massive and nationwide investments in two main areas: education and training and government-funded R&D.

5 The Relevance to Business: Strategy Revisited

The impact of the whole economy on business is felt in two ways: first, in terms of the macroeconomic health of the country; second in terms of the policies used to 'restore' or sustain its macroeconomic health. Policy, as we have seen in relation to unemployment, is fraught with difficulties of interpretation and politics. Thus the purpose of this section of the chapter has to be to evaluate the effect of unemployment and policies towards unemployment on strategy rather than the policies themselves. The link between the macroeconomic environment and strategy should now be clear. Strategy is a coordinating mechanism between the firm's internal and external environments. In the area of macroeconomics, this means that company strategy has to insure itself against untoward fluctuations in market conditions by anticipating any changes either in those conditions or in policies to lessen them.

In the area of unemployment, the coordinating role of strategy becomes especially important. The 'workforce', after all, represents two things to a company – both an input to the production process and the potential purchaser of end products. So, in terms of our model in chapters 7 and 8, unemployment can affect both supply and demand conditions. Figure 9.6 is a development of this model.

The figure shows how unemployment affects both the supply side and the demand side of a business's operations. If unemployment is viewed as short term then a government will take a *laissez-faire* approach to it and provide market-based incentives to enable individuals to train or move from area to area (for example, by altering the basis of income support to encourage individuals to take training). A company response to this is to ensure that, even if the unemployment lasts for longer than anticipated, it has the technology and incentive and skills structures to enable it to obtain the employees it needs in order to compete. This it might do through training schemes and investment programmes.

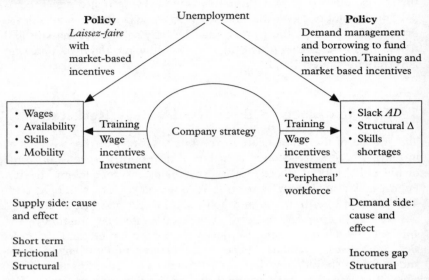

Figure 9.6 Strategy as a coordinating mechanism to ameliorate effects of unemployment policy.

If unemployment is viewed as being caused by deficient demand in the economy, government policy will take a Keynesian perspective to boost aggregate demand. Similarly, if the root of unemployment is seen as being structural change the government will follow policies to boost investment spending, and hence aggregate demand. The response of a company is in all respects except one identical to that for 'supply side' unemployment: greater investment in machinery and training and market-based incentives like higher wages to some groups of employees.

One area is not the same, however. Companies such as IBM during the early 1990s experienced such a downturn in the demand for their products that they changed their employment structure. Analyses of market demand trends were undertaken and a suitably sized 'core' of employees were employed on permanent contracts to ensure that market demand could be met at its lowest point. In order to guarantee that any growth in demand could be met, companies kept a 'periphery' of workers, sometimes on retainer contracts and levels of pay, on whom they could call should demand conditions change for the better.

For companies, however, skill shortages remain a severe problem. While 57 per cent of the workforce had been unemployed for more than six months in 1994, companies were complaining of a skills mismatch between the jobs they had available and the applicants for those jobs. Put simply, applicants were not sufficiently technologically capable to fill the posts that were available. And, while this problem is not as severe as it was in the mid-1980s, it still represents a major misallocation of resources to the companies of the UK.

Competitors from abroad establishing manufacturing sites in the UK have approached the problem constructively by investing in the 'human resources' of their workforce and providing education and training internally. Similarly, some of the British companies that have had most success in achieving competitiveness over the past 10–15 years have also spent vast amounts of money on training their employees to operate the new technologies.

You will remember from chapter 7 that a distinction was made between general and specific skills or investments in relation to government policy. To recap, the argument runs that governments provide the basic skills which are transferable between organizations, but companies provide training for those specific skills which add value to their production processes. A similar argument holds for investment in R&D: governments fund 'basic' research in universities and research institutes upon which all companies can similarly build. But the R&D which is company-specific and provides competitive advantage must be funded by the companies themselves.

6 Investigation (2)

On the basis of the whole discussion of this chapter you will by now be realizing that the cure for unemployment depends very much on the policy-makers' perception of what the *cause* of that unemployment is. Certainly at a macroeconomic level, this deadlock has hindered efforts to find a satisfactory and long-term policy solution to the problem. From a micro point of view, however, individual companies have worked hard to invest in training and their 'human capital' in order to achieve competitiveness. The two cases below are interesting and relatively easy to research, as information is freely given in company reports and newspaper articles as well as in some of the published material already cited in this text:

- Rover Group;
- Lucas.

Figure 9.7 The strategic matrix including human resources and unemployment.

	Pricing/output	Product development and technology	Competitor analysis	Impact of regulatory environment	National income and macro economy	Unemployment and human resource strategies
Small companies	Dependent on competitors and demand	Vital	Vital	High – impact on costs	High impact	High – training expensive and impact of skills shortages significant
Large companies	Price interdependency	NON-PRICE COMPETITION	Strategic interdependency	Low – can be taken up within slack and turned to competitive advantage	Potential high impact	High – loss of revenue and skills shortages. Can be reduced through specific training

7 Conclusions

The jury is still out on what causes unemployment and what the cure for unemployment is, and there is not scope within the context of a textbook to enter fully into that debate. Much of the discussion is laden with politics and value judgements, and these are not areas into which positive economics treads happily.

Clearly, there is a role for company strategy in overcoming the resource misallocation represented by unemployment through skills training. We can add this 'human resource' dimension to our strategy matrix as shown in figure 9.7. For ease of presentation, the strategic implications of previous chapters are abbreviated.

Perhaps as students of business (where, maybe, we can allow ourselves to be normative sometimes!), we can see the dilemma of unemployment for companies across the world, because it presents itself as a cost in terms of wasted resources and extra training. Nor should we regard the problem of unemployment as unique to Britain. Indeed, the overseas competitors whose education and training and system of investment are almost universally praised have not been immune to the pressures of unemployment and increasing domestic labour costs.

8 Further Reading

Lindbeck, A. and Snower, D. (1996) Explanations of unemployment. In T. Jenkinson (ed.), *Readings in Macroeconomics*. Oxford: Oxford University Press.

Notes

1 See, for example, Kay, J. (1996) *The Business of Economics*. Oxford: Oxford University Press; Bootle, R. (1996) *The Death of Inflation: Surviving and Thriving in the Zero Era*. London: Nicholas Brearley Publishing. As the quote at the beginning of chapter 8 demonstrated, even politicians are dubious about their own forecasts!

2 We assume here a 'closed' economy with no international sector at all. The 'open economy' is examined in chapter 11 in some detail, but for the time being, it is a relatively safe assumption to ignore it, not least because governments have relatively little control over the flow of imports and exports in and out of the economy (see Stewart, M. (1993) *Keynes in the 1990s: a Return to Economic Sanity*. Harmondsworth: Penguin).

3   By changing the level or means of corporate taxation, for example, the government can provide a stimulus to R&D. Indeed, this restructuring of corporate taxation was central to the Conservative Budgets of 1993 and 1994.

4   See Jahoda, M. (1982) *Employment and Unemployment: a Social Psychological Analysis.* Cambridge: Cambridge University Press. This is an old study now, but still represents a definitive analysis of the social and psychological problems of unemployment.

5   Keynes, J. M. (1973) *The General Theory of Employment, Interest and Money.* Cambridge: Macmillan/Cambridge University Press for the Royal Economic Society. There are numerous studies of Keynes and his writings, but one of the best, and simplest, is that by Stewart, op. cit., note 2.

6   See, for example, Stewart, op. cit., note 2.

7   The table shows comparative data and thus does not give a completely up-to-date account of the unemployment rates in the countries covered. For example, as of January 1997, unemployment in the UK was around 7.9 per cent. However, this does not undermine the point that unemployment is a problem in all the major economies covered by this table.

8   The multiplier was central to Keynes's analysis of savings and investment. Falling expenditure, for example, through unemployment, leads to falling incomes. Falling incomes clearly lead to falling expenditure, but as the cycles continues, it multiplies. The strength of the multiplier is dependent on tax rates, import expenditure and propensities to save and invest and, as such, is highly complex. As we will see later in the chapter, it can be used to create growth in the economy by policy-makers.

9   Institute of Manpower Studies, University of Sussex, 1987/8.

10 This is covered in some depth in Harding, R. (1995) *Technology and Human Resources in Their National Context: a Study in Strategic Contrasts.* Aldershot: Avebury.

11 The government uses the definition, the number of people out of work *and* claiming benefit.

12 See also Stewart, op. cit., note 2.

13 You will already be beginning to realize that this is a model of the market which assumes that it is perfectly competitive – a homogeneous product and a large number of buyers and sellers with no government intervention and freedom to enter and leave the labour market at will.

14 If you are not comfortable with this model, check back over chapters 2 and 3.

15 A special case of this type of unemployment is called 'frictional' unemployment: where workers are unemployed because they are between jobs or unemployable. This is the level of unemployment consistent with the 'natural' rate discussed elsewhere in the text.

16 The company would, of course, maintain that there were other factors involved in its locational decision. However, regional investment grants have been a significant part of government policy and have been directed at attracting this type of direct foreign investment.

17   In 1958, Professor A. W. Phillips published an article which demonstrated
     a *statistical* link between the level of inflation and the level of unemploy-
     ment. Using data for the period 1861–1957 it showed that there was a
     negative correlation between the level of *wage* inflation (i.e. the rate at
     which wages were rising) and the level of unemployment for the UK eco-
     nomy. In other words, as wage inflation rose, unemployment appeared to
     fall and, as wage inflation fell, unemployment began to rise. During the
     period that he researched, Phillips showed that when unemployment was
     low, say at 3 per cent, wage inflation was high, say at 6 per cent. When
     the unemployment rate was high, say at 10 per cent, then inflation would
     be low, say at 2 per cent. He noted that where wages were stable, i.e.
     there were no real wage increases, or falling, the rate of unemployment
     accelerated rapidly.

18   The level of the natural rate of unemployment is the subject of fierce
     empirical debate between monetarist and Keynesian economists. Original
     estimates of the natural rate for the UK economy of 5 per cent were
     revised upwards by the beginning of the 1980s. In any event, the level of
     'natural' unemployment varies between economies and may be a function
     of infrastructural factors like the collective bargaining system. See also
     Nickell, S. (1996) Inflation and the UK labour market. In T. Jenkinson
     (ed.), *Readings in Macroeconomics*. Oxford: Oxford University Press.

19   It would not be possible to examine Keynes in terms of the analysis he
     used within the context of a text like this. Instead we focus on a simple
     analysis of aggregate demand and aggregate supply in order to ensure
     that the mechanism by which full employment can be restored can be
     understood.

Inflation and Monetary Policy

10

To the ordinary man it is obvious that inflation matters, but the economist would be unwise to take it for granted.

(J. Hicks, 1945)

1 Introduction

Everyone has some perception of what inflation is and everyone can think of an effect that it has had on his or her life. Many of us will have complained about how our money does not seem to buy as much as it used to, and if we haven't yet, we soon will! Over the past 15 years, the British government has been following an anti-inflationary policy, yet many of us remember fondly back to our childhood when we could buy more sweets for our pocket money than children can 'now'. It is for this reason that Hicks argued in the quote above that inflation is obviously important to the ordinary 'man'.

He also argued, however, that it is less obvious that an economist should worry about inflation. Surely this is a paradox, because, after all, economists are concerned with people and how they make their decisions about what to buy and when. If inflation is important to people (in that it affects their demand) then must it not also be important to economists?

As with all areas of macroeconomics, opinions on inflation are divided. Broadly speaking, there is a camp of economists, monetarists, who argue that low, even zero, inflation should be the central macroeconomic policy target of any government in order to ensure that companies can be certain of the prices at which they can sell their products *and* of the prices at which they can buy in their factors of production. In the other corner are those who argue that low inflation is desirable, but the policies that are necessary to achieve that low inflation are so severe that such a policy is not justified on either social or economic grounds. Instead, they suggest that a government tolerates a degree of inflation in the economy and concentrates on achieving an acceptable level of employment and growth instead.

Aside from all this, though, the principle issue, of course, has to be why we are interested in rising prices as students of business. The answer to this is quite unequivocal. Most business-people are concerned about inflation because rising input prices (wages, machinery costs, land costs etc.) mean rising prices in the shops and less being supplied, which, in turn could mean slack demand. Similarly, rising aggregate demand means that in the short term prices go up as producers adjust to the new levels of demand. But, as shop prices rise, consumers find that they need higher income in order to pay those rising prices, so they put higher wage claims in to their employers. This pushes factor prices up and so the vicious cycle begins again.

However, as we did with the area of unemployment, we have to distinguish between inflation itself and the effects of policies intended to cure inflation in order to assess the impact on business. In this area we have to tread carefully because it is highly political. For example, a monetarist economist would argue that increases in prices are a 'monetary' rather than a 'real' phenomenon – a price increase, for example, will be offset by an analogous increase in wages which makes no 'real' difference to the price level. Thus, for a monetarist, the real dangers of inflation are when it spirals out of control and creates uncertainties. For that reason it is best to keep inflation as near to zero as possible. This is done, as we will see later, by preventing aggregate demand from rising too high. In other words, the government, by restricting its own expenditure and borrowing, and by discouraging consumers from spending (through high interest rates to encourage savings) keeps the level of *effective* aggregate demand low.

But the criticisms of this approach stem from the fact that, very frequently, policies to restrict aggregate demand create a recession, and companies then become uncertain of their markets, for the reasons discussed in chapter 9. Indeed, individuals use up their savings and reduce their expenditure despite the inducement of higher interest rates, simply because they are unemployed or uncertain as to their employed future. Worse still, if interest rates are high the cost of borrowing is high and this potentially stifles investment, creating structural problems in the economy.[1]

Clearly for business the issue is a complex one which centres on the importance of the monetary economy and the real economy. Again, economic forecasts are used as a means of predicting the rate of inflation. But, again, the policy impact of attempts to reach zero inflation is more difficult to anticipate and plan for.

However, if we look briefly at inflationary pressures in Britain compared with its major overseas competitors we can see why the impetus

Table 10.1   Comparative inflation data, 1975–1994

Year	Germany	Japan	UK	USA
1975	5.9	11.8	24.2	9.1
1976	4.3	9.4	16.5	5.7
1977	3.7	8.2	15.9	6.5
1978	2.7	4.1	8.2	7.6
1979	4.1	3.8	13.5	10.4
1980	5.4	7.8	18.0	13.5
1981	6.3	4.9	11.9	10.3
1982	5.3	2.7	8.6	6.2
1983	3.3	1.9	4.6	3.2
1984	2.4	2.2	5.0	4.3
1985	2.2	2.0	6.1	3.6
1986	−0.1	0.6	3.4	1.9
1987	0.2	0.1	4.1	3.7
1988	1.3	0.7	4.9	4.0
1989	2.8	2.3	7.8	4.8
1990	2.7	3.1	9.5	5.4
1991	3.5	3.3	5.9	4.2
1992	4.0	1.7	3.7	3.0
1993	4.1	1.3	1.6	3.0
1994	3.0	0.7	2.5	2.6

to cure inflation has been so strong over the past 20 years (see table 10.1).

If rising prices create demand instability and investment uncertainty then we can see that British companies have indeed been at a disadvantage compared to their American, Japanese or German counterparts. Domestic inflation in those countries was lower and, critically, less volatile over the period to 1992 than in the UK. British inflation fell below German inflation in 1992,[2] but by the end of 1996, German inflation stood at 1.2 per cent compared to 2 per cent in Britain.[3] The comparative figures for Japan and the United States were 0.1 and 2.9 per cent respectively.

Empirical evidence that inflation itself causes severe uncertainty for businesses is sadly lacking.[4] Some analysts argue that the expectations of price rises cause inflationary pressures in the economy and these, in turn, create difficulties for producers. Others argue that it is the policies put in place to keep inflation low that cause the problems of uncertainty – for example, high interest rates make borrowing for investment and consumption more expensive and thus stifle aggregate demand. But a *perceived* problem will become an *actual* problem if solutions are not found and if it spreads into popular consciousness. And the fact remains that both the American and the British governments over the past 16 years have followed specifically anti-inflationary policies as their primary policy goal. This, then, is why we, and our counterparts in business, have to be bothered about inflation and the best way to 'cure' it.

2 Investigation (1)

Examine the figures in table 10.1 then re-examine some of the company reports that you may have looked at in previous investigations. How many companies cite inflation as opposed to recession or high interest rates as a factor in their performance?

3 Aims and Objectives

This chapter aims simply to give understanding of three areas: why inflation is an important problem for governments and business; where inflation in an economy comes from; and the policy tools which can be used to cure inflation. And, while matters of policy and interpretation obviously arise, it is not the intention to enter the policy debate. The specific objectives, in this context, are as follows.

1 To give you an understanding of the difference between demand-pull and cost-push inflation and the means of resolving each.
2 To give you a basic understanding of the difference between money and income and the policy implications of this distinction.
3 To allow you to use the tools of this chapter in interpreting policy and forming your own opinions.

4 The Causes of Inflation

Until we have looked at the origins of inflationary pressures it will be impossible to come to any conclusions at all. Again we can look at the causes of inflation very simply in terms of demand and supply.

Figure 10.1   Demand-pull inflationary pressure.

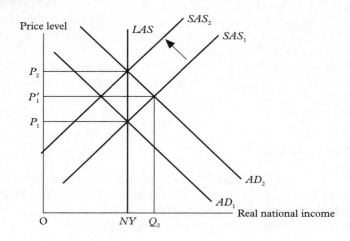

4.1   Demand-pull Inflation

As the name suggests, demand-pull inflation is caused by excessive aggregate demand in the economy. This is represented in figure 10.1.

By now you should be feeling quite comfortable with the analysis of demand and supply that this model represents. The economy is in equilibrium at a price level of P_1 with a national income of NY. An expansion in demand shifts the aggregate demand curve upwards to the right. Such an expansion can come from the fiscal measures to reduce unemployment illustrated in the previous chapter. It can similarly come from other, more indirect policies which give a perception of increased income, like access to credit facilities or short-term stimuli to individual markets (the housing market, for example, has represented a target for such stimuli – the 'Lawson boom' of 1987 and the temporary removal of stamp duty in 1992 were two such attempts to boost the market).

As aggregate demand shifts to AD_2, inflationary pressure in the economy builds up. This is for two reasons. First, we learned when we studied microeconomics that supply cannot shift in the short term: this means that, in the short term, prices will rise from P_1 to P_1'. Quite simply, there is 'too much money chasing too few goods', a popular monetarist phrase to mean that excessive demand is pushing up prices. Microeconomics tells us that there will be a movement along the supply curve, meaning that slightly more will be supplied at this price but

Figure 10.2   Inflationary pressure accumulating in the economy.

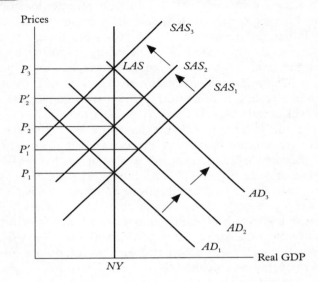

this increase can only be short term due to the fact that in the long run the productive capacity of the economy is fixed.

Second, as we have learned from macroeconomics *and* from our study of imperfect markets, prices will tend to 'stick' at higher levels rather than go down. This was one of Keynes's insights and it is exacerbated by the inelastic nature of aggregate supply, which we covered in chapter 8. It is therefore unlikely that supply will respond in the same way as it did in microeconomics – by shifting downwards to the right (i.e. more being supplied at each prevailing market price). In fact what will happen is that companies' costs increase as a result of having to supply the increased demand, and these costs are passed on to the consumer in the form of higher prices (P_2). So, instead of prompting supply to increase, greater demand only pushes up prices because supply is fixed around the productive capacity of the economy. It is important, however, to stress that the increase in prices due to the shift in short-run aggregate supply from SAS_1 to SAS_2 will only occur after a time lag.

Now look carefully at figure 10.2. Rational workers, seeing prices increase from P_1 to P'_1, anticipate reductions in their real income. They therefore push for higher wages over and above the price level of P'_1. Because of the time lag after which aggregate supply will shift, prices do not rise immediately. The result is that consumers, now earning more than ever, think that their real income has grown: they are suffering from '*money illusion*'. This results in aggregate demand shifting again, this time from AD_2 to AD_3, and while, in the meantime, aggregate supply has shifted back to SAS_2, this is insufficient to meet the still buoyant levels of demand. An inflationary spiral has begun.

Now, argue monetarists, businesses are uncertain as to how much to produce. They know that consumers are suffering from 'money illusion' – the feeling that they have more spending power than the economy will permit. But they also know that this illusion cannot last forever: eventually the 'bubble must burst' (i.e. people will realize that prices are rising faster than their income is rising), at which point aggregate demand will fall again. They cannot predict when this will happen, but also do not want to be caught with unsold stock. This uncertainty can lead to wider structural problems: increased imports to cover aggregate demand and under-investment, for example.

Thus, they argue, it is extremely important for the economy to keep this type of inflation under control. Non-inflationary demand can only rise when it is within the productive capacity of the economy; thus monetarist governments in the UK and the USA have sought to keep aggregate demand firmly under control in order to prevent demand-pull inflation.

4.2   Cost-push Inflation

Cost-push inflation, again as its name suggests, is rising prices caused by increases in supply costs to companies. These might be caused by shortages of raw materials, rising land prices, increased machinery costs and so on. But the common culprit is often cited as labour and, more particularly, the rising wages associated with the inflationary claims of powerful trade unions, particularly in the public sector (i.e. the part of the economy which is controlled by government rather than by private industry). In any event, the 'cost-push' pressures are said to come from the institutions of the economy rather than from the operations of the market.

This distinction between the wage claims of the private and public sectors is important when we are discussing the monetarist approach to the source of cost-push inflation. The issue is illustrated in figure 10.3.

The economy is an initial equilibrium with prices at the level P_1 and national income at NY. A rise in costs from the inflationary wage claims of a large public sector union shifts aggregate supply from SAS_1

Figure 10.3 Cost-push inflation and the public sector.

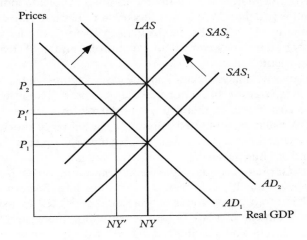

to SAS_2. In the short term, as you will remember from our analysis of labour markets in the preceding chapter, any increase in labour costs means a reduction in employment and, hence, a reduction in national income (from NY to NY').

However, you will remember that a critical part of the equation for GDP is government expenditure (G). If these increased wage costs are in the public sector, then, by definition, they have to be met by the public purse; that is, government expenditure. This increases aggregate demand from AD_1 to AD_2 and, hence, inflation from its original P_1' to P_2. In economies where there is a social security structure for the unemployed, government expenditure has also been directed towards income support for those who are made redundant from the first increase in costs; this may further exacerbate the problem of rising aggregate demand.

Cost-push inflation is not usually associated with monetarism, however. As we will see later in the chapter, monetarists tend to view inflation as essentially a *monetary* phenomenon caused by an increase in the level of aggregate demand and, hence, the demand for money.

Non-monetarists tend to regard this type of inflation as incurable, stemming as it does from the institutions of the economy (i.e. the imperfections in the operations of the market) over which the government has but little control. Assuming that demand-pull inflation can be anticipated (for example through index-linking real incomes), they argue that unanticipated inflation, where prices rise faster in some areas than in others, must be tolerated in the interests of growth: 'an economy starved of money will be unable to grow'. Indeed, some go even further and argue that there is a necessary and 'natural' rate of inflation in an economy which will be determined by its institutional structures, particularly patterns of government expenditure and collective bargaining arrangements.[5]

In one area of analysis there can be few disputes: those cost-push pressures which come from outside the economy. These 'exogenous' shocks are cost increases that are felt uniformly by every sector of the economy. A usual example that is given is the oil price shocks of 1973 and 1979, which caused increases in raw materials prices for all economies and all businesses throughout the world.

For the German economy the reunification in 1990 presented a similar supply 'shock'. Companies expanding into Eastern Germany and supplying to a larger domestic market experienced increased costs quite aside from the increased costs of rebuilding the eastern economy at a macro level. The resultant inflation and unemployment figures for Germany since 1990, shown in this and the previous chapters, are evidence of the profound effects of such an exogenous shock.

4.3 A Definition of Inflation and How It Is Measured

Whatever the source of inflation, its definition remains the same: persistently rising prices in all sectors across an economy. Some sectors, however, will have a greater impact on the reaction of aggregate demand to rising prices generally. For example, a dramatic increase in mortgage prices will have a far greater impact on the average household than an increase, say, in the price of caviar (although a rise in the price of more usual foodstuffs might indeed affect them). As a result the government looks at a selection of 'typical' products that such a household might consume on a week-by-week basis and measures how their prices change over time by use of an index. It then uses this index as a proxy for how prices are rising throughout the economy as a whole.

In the UK the 'Retail Price Index' is the most publicized measure of inflation. It is a 'basket' of representative goods and services that households buy each month, and includes food, clothing and mortgage payments, among other things. As such, it represents a good measure of how a household might allocate its monthly income and, hence, how it is being affected by inflation.

You may also have heard the phrase the 'underlying' rate of inflation. This excludes mortgage interest because this is regarded as distorting the overall inflation figure. If we exclude mortgages, UK inflation figures are more comparable with those abroad, where the private housing sector is not as large.

5 Anti-inflationary Policy[6]

As with unemployment, then, we have a stark divide in policy attitudes towards inflation, with some arguing that the number one economic objective is to achieve zero inflation and others arguing that a degree of inflation is necessary in order to ensure economic growth. The policy chasm has narrowed somewhat into the mid-1990s, with hitherto non-monetarist politicians in Britain realizing that inflation is regarded as an evil by business and, conversely, monetarist politicians realising that zero inflation is a politically and economically difficult goal to achieve. Even so, there still remains considerable debate on the key goals of macroeconomic policy.

5.1 The Fisher Equation and Control of the Money Supply

We can safely assume that a government pursuing primarily antiinflationary policies will be a monetarist one, and it is useful to look at that policy in relation to the economic management of the British and American economies since 1979. To that end, we will also assume for the time being that inflation is essentially caused by demand-pull factors, or, as was said earlier, 'too much money chasing too few goods'. This means that, as policy-makers, we can control inflation if we can control the demand for money in the economy.

This can be put more formally as follows. Monetarists regard inflation as 'in all ways and everywhere a monetary phenomenon'. For example, if the government decided to give every adult in the economy a cash handout that immediately doubled everyone's income, demand would increase. However, the increase in income would be a 'money illusion' (as referred to above) because, if everyone had twice as much income, prices would also double. This is shown graphically in figure 10.4.

As you can see from the diagram, a doubling of income shifts aggregate demand upwards to the right from AD_1 to AD_2. Although in the short term it might be possible for supply to shift, in the long term it is not. The money illusion that people suffer (because their income

Figure 10.4   A doubling of income and its effects on prices.

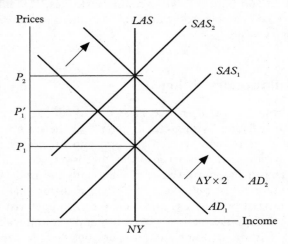

increase is greater than the price increase (P_1 to P_1') is temporary and, eventually, the forces of demand and supply will shift prices up to twice their previous level at P_2.

Milton Friedman, the founder of the 'modern' monetarism on which British and American economic policy has been based since 1979, called this his 'helicopter' thesis: that if money dropped from a helicopter and all of us picked up exactly the same amount, there would only be a *monetary* increase in income and not a *real* one, because prices would increase by the amount that was dropped from the helicopter.

This distinction between the *real* and the *monetary* economy is vital to monetarist economics. Inflation, by this model, is a monetary phenomenon caused by too much aggregate demand. Excessive aggregate demand means excessive demand for money, which, in turn, will mean an increase in the money supply (i.e. the amount of money in the economy). Very simply, if we all realize this and adapt our expectation of price increases accordingly by reducing our wage claims, then inflation will come down without affecting the real economy (i.e. people's real incomes) at all.

Let's look now at how a government might seek to do that. Monetarists propose that there is a straightforward relationship between the money supply (which is derived from the demand for money) and the price level in the economy. This is not 'new' – it in fact comes from a classical economist called Fisher who argued that growth in the money supply was directly related to growth in the level of prices:

$$MV = PY$$

where M is the money supply; V is the rate at which money changes hands (velocity of circulation); P is the price level; Y is people's real income.

This was rearranged to arrive at the 'Cambridge equation':

$$P = 1/kM$$

where $1/k$ is the accelerator: the rate of money supply growth caused by the ratio of the velocity of circulation and real incomes.

The reason why this equation is important is not for the maths itself, but rather because it suggests a direct relationship between money supply growth and the rate of inflation. It is at the heart of monetarist thinking about inflation.[7]

A monetarist government therefore has to keep control of the money supply in order to control inflation. The only way of doing this is to reduce aggregate demand. As you will remember, aggregate demand consists of consumption expenditure, investment expenditure and government expenditure.[8] Fairly obviously, a government will have most control over its own expenditure; indeed, because of the political philosophy often associated with this school of economic thought, a monetarist government is likely to want to allow markets to operate freely in the public sector, including in traditional areas of high government spending like health and education. And it is unlikely to want overtly to restrict the expenditure of either households or businesses in the private sector.

But government expenditure, measured through its own borrowing requirement (in Britain, this is called the PSBR, or Public Sector Borrowing Requirement), is an excellent target of monetary policy. By restricting its own spending a government does two things:

1 Reduces aggregate demand.
2 Convinces individuals that it is determined to 'beat' inflation.

This last point is especially important for monetarist policies. If the government sets a target for money supply growth and combines this with a strategy to reduce public sector spending (i.e. its own spending), then businesses and individuals will see that it is committed to its anti-inflationary policy. They see that price increases are going to slow down. Individual workers reduce their wage claims and businesses modify their price increases in the market place accordingly. The anti-inflationary policy works because expectations of price increases have *adapted* to the levels anticipated by the government. Indeed, Milton Friedman argued that the power of these *adaptive expectations* is so strong that the government needs only to show itself firmly committed to the policy and expectations will change after a relatively short time lag (about 18 months).

Another school of thought within monetarism is even more positive about the nature of expectations. The *rational expectations* school, led by economists such as Professor Patrick Minford of the University of Liverpool, argues that the time lag will be negligible if the government shows itself absolutely determined to eradicate inflation through stringent money supply targets and severe cuts in public spending. The more severe these are, the more likely are people's expectations to adapt immediately and rationally to the new level of inflation. Thus, if a government announces that it will achieve a level of zero inflation next month, people will immediately believe it and alter their wage strategies accordingly. In fact, this school of monetarism is critical of both the British and the American governments for not being firm enough over anti-inflation targets.

To a monetarist, then, there is no alternative to removing inflation entirely from the economy. In defence of this policy stance, the monetarists, as mentioned in chapter 9, use the Phillips curve to support their case. But instead of arguing that there is a trade-off between inflation and unemployment, they argue that this relationship only holds in the short run. In the long run, they argue, there is no policy trade-off or correlation at all. The economy will always revert to its 'natural' rate of unemployment because this is consistent with equilibria in savings and investment and in labour markets (which function like the market for any other product).

This position is illustrated in figure 10.5, called the *expectations augmented Phillips curve*.[9] Expectations, as we have already seen, will adapt to downward prices, but, argue monetarists, they will adapt to upward price trends as well. This causes wages, and ultimately prices, to rise.

Let's look now at how this works if the government is following a demand management policy to eradicate unemployment. It is following fiscal policies which affect the perceived level of income that people have and, hence, the level of aggregate demand. At the moment there is no inflation in the economy at all and unemployment is at its 'natural' rate of say, 10 per cent. This is illustrated by the curve P_1 in figure 10.5.

We can follow the route by which the government injects inflation into the economy through people's adaptive expectations by looking at the numbered points in figure 10.5.

Figure 10.5 The expectations augmented Phillips curve showing the natural rate of unemployment.

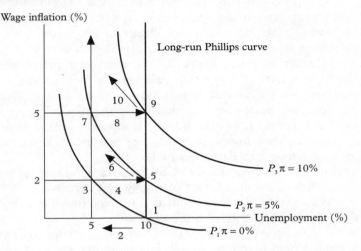

1 Here, the economy is in long-run equilibrium. There is no inflation in the economy and unemployment has settled at a 'natural' rate of 10 per cent of the workforce. This 'natural rate' represents those people who are short-term unemployed – frictionally, seasonally or regionally. It is inevitable that there will always be a percentage of people out of work even in an economy in equilibrium because there will always be some between jobs.

2 A government committed to low unemployment is elected to power and begins to follow through policies to reduce unemployment from the perceived unacceptable rate of 10 per cent. It aims for a rate of 5 per cent.

3 In achieving a rate of unemployment of 5 per cent, the government is prepared to tolerate a level of inflation of 2 per cent.

4 However, the forces of demand and supply in the economy will interact. The economy cannot operate in the long term at a level of unemployment of less than 10 per cent because of its current capacity national income. As the forces of supply and demand interact the economy reverts to the natural rate of unemployment.

5 However, it does not go back to zero inflation. With 2 per cent inflation in prices of goods in the shops, employees see their real wages reducing and start to put in inflationary wage claims: their expectations have adapted. Thus the economy has reverted to 10 per cent unemployment but is now experiencing higher inflation

(this is analogous to effects of policies to increase aggregate demand discussed in chapter 9).

6   The government is still determined to pursue the policy of 5 per cent unemployment and, unperturbed, continues to boost demand. Meanwhile, the increased wage claims of employees have been passed on to customers through increased prices.

7   These increased prices mean that the short-term policy trade-off results in a level of 5 per cent inflation – a higher increase than was previously tolerated. The reason why the rate is higher is because expectations are constantly adapting upwards: people see their real income devalued and so put in claims which more than recompense their losses. Because there is high employment they are in a strong negotiating position.

8   Again the economy will revert to its natural rate of unemployment through the interaction of supply and demand.

9   The natural rate of unemployment is re-established, but this time with 5 per cent inflation in the economy.

10   If the government continues to persist with policies to eradicate unemployment it will go on injecting more demand-pull inflation into the economy. As inflation gets higher it spirals – thus the third short-run Phillips Curve is consistent with 10 per cent inflation.

So, argue monetarists, the government is powerless in the long run. Market forces will prevail and any attempts to override those market forces through intervention will result in spiralling inflation. In turn, this spiralling inflation creates instability and hardship for the very companies and individuals that the government was trying to help by reducing unemployment. Ultimately the only macroeconomic policy that a government can follow through is an anti-inflationary one: although expectations have adapted upwards in this model, they will adapt downwards if government resolve is strong enough.

5.2   What Are the Policy Tools of a Monetarist Government?

A government seeking to squeeze inflation out of the economic system has both monetary and institutional methods which it can use. These are listed briefly below. It should be stressed, however, that this is only a reference list. The best documentation of policy methods to control inflation is given in the commentaries on the period since 1979 in the British and American economies.[10]

The primary method that a government might use to control inflation is to control the money supply. In fact all the tools of monetary policy are designed to alter the *liquidity base* of the financial sector of the economy; in other words, the relationship between the amount of money that banks have in reserve (deposits and 'securities') and the amount they lend out. Control of the money supply is the logical policy conclusion from the Fisher equation above.

There are many different definitions of the money supply. At the simplest level, 'narrow' money is simply the notes and coins in an economy plus any non-interest bearing bank accounts (M0). While an additional three definitions of the narrow money supply are used, control of M0 has been central to British government policy since it was introduced as a measure of the money supply in 1982. 'Broad' money includes deposits of private sector wholesale and retail companies as well as currency earnings from abroad.

The main way of controlling the money supply has been to control money demand, since the two must inevitably always be equal. Money demand comes from a number of sources.

1   The public sector – particularly government expenditure or the PSBR. As we have seen in earlier chapters, the government intervenes to ameliorate inequalities and reduce externalities. In so doing it spends money, which, obviously, has to be supplied. A government seeking to control inflation will reduce its own expenditure, thereby also reducing the money supply.

2   Overseas. Money comes into the country for two reasons. First, if the government (central bank) maintains an artificially low value of the currency by keeping the market flooded with sterling by buying up foreign currencies. It might do this in order to make domestic exports more competitive (if the pound is cheap it makes British goods cheap abroad). By ending a policy of supporting the currency in this way a monetarist government can prevent money from coming in from abroad. Second, if the interest rate is high, this will make speculators invest in the 'broad' money supply of the country (interest bearing accounts) in anticipation of profits while interest rates are high. By bringing the interest rate down it will prevent this flow of funds into the economy.

3   The banking sector. Banks can create credit for their customers if they keep a certain ratio of money in reserve to insure against default on loans. This has been a major source of money creation since 1981. In order to control this form of money supply, the government can impose minimum reserve assets ratio on banks,

meaning that they must keep a given percentage of their liquid assets back to guarantee the loans they are making. As this *special deposit* regulation was abolished in 1981, it has not been a tool of UK government policy.

4 The private sector. Consumers will demand less money if the 'price' of money is high. The 'price' of money is the cost of holding money (say cash) rather than putting it in a bank account. If the interest rate is high, holding cash will be expensive relative to saving, so this will reduce 'narrow' money supply measures. Paradoxically, though, in an economy with easy access to credit facilities (such as the UK or the US economy), as interest rates fall and money becomes cheaper to hold, it also becomes cheaper to fund current expenditure by increased debt (loans and credit cards in particular).

Perhaps this last point demonstrates the difficulty of running a monetary policy through attempting to control the money supply. As soon as attempts are made to control one form of money, people switch to using another type of money, so it becomes both difficult to control and an unreliable indicator of the nature of money demand. This is called *Goodhart's law*.

6 Are Businesses Right to Be Worried about Inflation?

Anyone who borrows money on a large scale stands to gain from inflation because, in real terms, the value of the debt owed reduces as prices rise. Thus, for example, many individuals in Britain gained from the house price boom of the mid-1980s: they borrowed money to buy a house, say of £35 000, in 1987 which had more than doubled in value by 1989. And anyone who borrows on a large scale also loses out if prices fall as they did in the British housing market after 1989. The person who bought a house in 1989 for £80 000 and borrowed most of the money for the purchase suffered if the value of that house fell subsequently to below £80 000, as was frequently the case. Additionally, if interest rates were high on the amount that was originally borrowed then the amount that the individual was paying for the loan might be disproportionately high.

As both governments and businesses borrow money on a large scale it might seem perverse that they appear to be the main protagonists in the fight against inflation. After all, they would appear to be the ones that would gain most from any inflation and lose most from an anti-inflationary policy, especially if it took the form of high interest rates. Yet the main reason why businesses and governments worry about inflation is that it is not always possible to predict the rate at which prices will change and, therefore, to adapt expectations accordingly.

It is the fact that unanticipated inflation interferes with the operation of the market that bothers business. Anticipated inflation, by definition, can be built into the economic system. It is indeed a monetary phenomenon and it can be insured against through index-linking any long-term savings schemes – like pensions and insurance policies. Unanticipated inflation affects different markets in different ways: a hike in public sector wages, for example, will increase costs in the public sector, which will trickle down through the rest of the economy slowly and unevenly, affecting some areas more than others. This creates environmental uncertainty – an area which businesses are keen to avoid. Further, once an inflationary spiral sets in, it becomes increasingly rapid, as we saw in figure 10.2. As inflation gets higher, it becomes harder to predict and, critically, harder to bring down. The result for business is even greater uncertainty.

Much of the debate about inflation and its effects is about this unanticipated inflation. Much of the *fear* of inflation is because of the perceived problem that it brings. As we saw in chapter 4, expected revenues and expected costs are a central part of a company's production decision: without these it cannot predict its level of profitability for different levels of output. The danger with inflation lies in these expectations of price increases, which then become a self-fulfilling prophecy as companies seek to ensure their profitability. Monetarists argue that only with zero inflation will this vicious circle be resolved.

However, the policies to cure inflation *can* present a serious problem to companies if the government places a heavy reliance on interest rate policy to restrict the money supply and reduced public spending to decrease aggregate demand. You will remember that the interest rate was viewed by the classical economists as the means by which the equality between savings and investment was restored. If savings fell, so too would the interest rate, making investment more attractive and restoring the equilibrium in the market for loanable funds (the deposits and securities mentioned above). However, if interest rates are high, companies are disinclined to invest. Further, as aggregate demand declines, so too, by definition, does expenditure, again reinforcing the disinclination of companies to invest. Indeed, the evidence of the 1980s suggests that savings fell and, rather than being pulled up again, investment itself fell to restore the equilibrium.

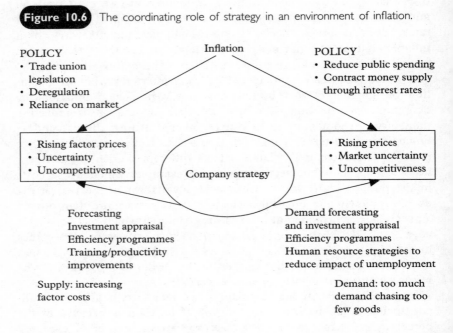

Figure 10.6 The coordinating role of strategy in an environment of inflation.

Figure 10.6 re-examines strategy as a coordinating mechanism given these concerns about the uncertainty that inflation causes *and* the uncertainty that policies to cure inflation can cause. Inflation causes on the supply side rising factor prices, uncertainties in supply markets and, ultimately, product markets as well and, if costs rise persistently, uncompetitiveness. Government policy to deal with cost-push inflationary pressures is limited and focuses on infrastructural changes like trade union legislation and deregulation. This may bring down wages but may also make markets more competitive.

Cost-push pressures are most easily dealt with by company strategies themselves and, in a deregulated and free-market environment, this would be the natural source of pushing down cost-push inflation. For example, through efficiency and productivity improvements companies can offset the effects of inflation; by reviewing any investments made companies can ensure that they produce real returns relative to the rate of inflation. Ultimately, though, the key to insuring against the uncertainty that inflation causes is effective forecasting. While the merits and demerits of forecasts are well documented, not least by quotes at the heads of chapters in this text, a company needs to have some assessment of market trends, even if it is subsequently taken with a pinch of salt.

Demand-pull pressures are a danger to companies if they become unanticipated and uncontrollable. Arguably this was the case in the middle of the 1970s in Britain. Potentially, they again create rising prices (which will feed through into factor markets), market uncertainty and uncompetitiveness if allowed to continue. If expectations adapt rationally, then there is no need for companies to worry about the impact of government policy, as any 'pain' will be short-lived. However, the evidence presented at the outset of this chapter suggests that inflation takes a very long time to bring under control – expectations adapt, but slowly.

This being the case, the effects of anti-inflationary policy for business have also to be considered. First, 'If it isn't hurting, it isn't working'[11] and 'Unemployment is a price worth paying to get inflation down'.[12] In other words, an anti-inflationary policy will always cause a recession and companies need to formulate defence mechanisms accordingly. Second, the impact on capital investment and expansion of high interest rates is potentially lethal to competitiveness – again companies need to have a means of ensuring competitiveness after demand has recovered. The history of the past 20 years has shown that economic forecasts, asset management and investment appraisal, 'human resource management'[13] and efficiency drives have become part of the industrial landscape, not just in Britain but elsewhere too. These are the strategic responses to both inflation and anti-inflationary policy.

7 Investigation (2) and Further Reading

Trevithick (1980) is an old text, but is still one of the best easy-to-read guides to inflation and monetary policy. It also provides a useful comparison with Keynesian policies. Hutton (1995) provides a critical analysis of monetary policy, particularly the impact of the years since 1979 on the financial sector while Michie (1993) provides an overview of the impact of government policy on the macro economy. The first episode of Dieter Helm's Radio 4 Series *UK PLC* (October 1995) examined carefully the relationship between government policy and its impact on the economy.

Having encountered these approaches to inflation and anti-inflationary policy, you should also look at some monetarist critiques of British and US policy. Samuel Britten in the *Financial Times* provides lucid explanations and analyses of government policy. Flemming (1979) is an old, but excellent source of pro-monetarist perspectives on inflation. Minford (1990) will also provide a solid monetarist account.

Stewart (1993) provides an easy-to-read Keynesian critique of monetary policies. Bootle (1996) is a readable and entertaining critique of zero inflation policies. Jenkinson (1996) provides an overview of many macroeconomic issues, including inflation. Michie (1992) provides a wide perspective of many issues of micro- and macroeconomic management during the Thatcher decade. Hutton provides a useful critical polemic.

After reading these polarized approaches to inflation and after thinking about the material covered in this chapter, you might like to answer the following questions.

1   Can the government effectively control inflation in the long run?
2   What is the impact on business of (a) inflation and (b) anti-inflationary policy?
3   As a business, how might you insure against high and volatile inflation?

Bootle, R. (1996) *The Death of Inflation: Surviving and Thriving in the Zero Era*. London: Nicholas Brearley Publishers.
Flemming, J. (1979) *Inflation*. Oxford: Oxford University Press.
Hutton, W. (1995) *The State We're In*. London: Jonathan Cape.
Jenkinson, T. (ed.) (1996) *Readings in Macroeconomics*. Oxford: Oxford University Press.
Michie, J. (ed.) (1992) *The Economic Legacy 1979–1992*. Harlow: Harcourt Brace Jovanovitch.
Minford, P. (1990) Inflation and monetary policy. *Oxford Review of Economic Policy*, 6(4), 62–76.
Stewart, M. (1993) *Keynes in the 1990s: a Return to Economic Sanity*. Harmondsworth: Penguin.
Trevithick, J. A. (1980) *Inflation: a Guide to the Crisis in Economics*, 2nd edn. Harmondsworth: Penguin.

8 Conclusions

We have concentrated on the British example with references to America in this chapter because it presents the best case of monetarism in practice. Attitudes towards inflation in the wake of monetarist policy have modified on both sides of the political spectrum: we now see monetarists arguing for low rather than zero inflation while Keynesians tend to accept that high and volatile inflation is extremely damaging to business because of the uncertainty it creates.

For business, the implications of all this are clear. It is not the inflation itself that brings problems but the *anticipation* that inflation will be higher in the future. Anticipation of higher prices feeds into the *expectations* of consumers, making their expenditure patterns erratic and often pushing up wage claims as well. Only by effective forecasting can a company minimize the damage caused by inflationary expectations. This is shown in the adaptation to the strategic matrix of previous chapters in figure 10.7.

Notes

1 For further reading, see, Bootle, R. (1996) *The Death of Inflation: Surviving and Thriving in the Zero Era.* London: Nicholas Brearley Publishers; Stewart, M. (1993) *Keynes in the 1990s: a Return to Economic Sanity.* Harmondsworth: Penguin.

2 Macroeconomic data since 1990 for Germany take into account the effects of reunification and the creation of a single German mark for the whole of Germany. This was highly inflationary and this, combined with high public borrowing and worldwide recession, has caused the German economy to waver in the 1990s.

3 Source: *Financial Times Exporter,* 10 October 1996.

4 Bootle, op. cit., note 1, provides a good and easy-to-read analysis of this perspective.

5 For a detailed discussion of this see McCallum, J. (1986) Unemployment in OECD counties in the 1980s. *Economic Journal,* 96, 942–60.

6 See also, Jenkinson, T. (1996) Inflation policy. In T. Jenkinson (ed.), *Readings in Macroeconomics.* Oxford: Oxford University Press.

7 This represents a vast over-simplification of the theory (and the practice!) of monetary control. Monetary control is itself dependent on the definition of money supply; and the definition of money supply has become extraordinarily complex as financial markets have developed. However, the point made simply here, that money supply growth stems from increased government expenditure (and hence government borrowing) and increased consumption, is sufficient to understand the means by which governments attempt to control inflation. It is also sufficient to understand the resultant impact on business.

8 The international dimension is dealt with in chapter 11.

9 This analysis rests on two assumptions. (a) Expectations will adapt rationally after a time lag – if prices are seen to be rising, then people will expect prices to rise further and will make purchasing and wage decisions accordingly. This was also covered when we looked at expectations as a component of the demand function in chapter 2. (b) There is no empirical long-term link in the post-war period between inflation and

Figure 10.7 The strategic matrix and inflation.

	Pricing/output	Product development and technology	Competitor analysis	Impact of regulatory environment	National income and macro economy	Unemployment and human resources	Inflation forecasting
Small companies	Dependent on competitors and demand	Vital	Vital	High – impact on costs	High impact	High – training expensive and impact of skills shortages significant	Essential but expensive. Impact of inflationary expectations high
Large companies	Price interdependency	NON-PRICE COMPETITION	Strategic interdependency	Low – can be taken up within slack and turned to competitive advantage	Potential high impact	High – loss of revenue and skills shortages. Can be reduced through specific training	Essential. Impact of inflationary expectations high but can be insured against

unemployment. This assumption is based on Milton Friedman's statistical analyses, analogous to that conducted by Phillips.

10 See, for example, Michie, J. (ed.) (1993) *The Economic Legacy: 1979–1992.* Harlow: Harcourt Brace Jovanovitch; or Jenkinson (ed.), op. cit., note 6.

11 Rt Hon. John Major MP, then Chancellor of the Exchequer, 1989.

12 Rt Hon. Norman Lamont MP, then Chancellor of the Exchequer, 1991.

13 'Human resource management' covers a variety of management tools to create an efficient workforce – including skills training, employment policy (including the core/periphery model discussed in chapter 9), working practices and collective bargaining. This is a hugely complex area and no value judgement on the nature of changes to this area of industrial relations is being made. The points about strategy are intended only to explain why companies have reacted in the way they have and to illustrate the government policy origins of some of these changes.

The International Dimension

11

Public debate may still be hostage to the outdated vocabulary of political borders, but the daily realities facing most people in the developed and the developing worlds – both as citizens and consumers – speak a vastly different idiom. Theirs is the language of an increasingly borderless economy. A truly global market place.

(Kenichi Ohmae, *The End of the Nation State*. London: HarperCollins, 1996)

One can only call the political impact of 'globalization' the pathology of over-diminished expectations. Many over-enthusiastic analysts and politicians have gone beyond the evidence in over-stating both the extent of the dominance of world markets and their ungovernability . . . In this case we have a myth that exaggerates the degree of our helplessness in the face of contemporary economic forces.

(Paul Hirst and Grahame Thompson, *Globalization in Question*. Cambridge: Polity Press, 1996)

1 Introduction

So far in this text, we have looked mainly at companies and the interface between those companies and the macro economy. We have seen that companies formulate strategies in order to compete. Those strategies are a function of the market conditions in which the company is operating as well as the internal cost structures that it faces. Among those market conditions we have included factors like the number of competitors, the closeness of substitute products and macroeconomic conditions and policies. Until now, however, we have assumed that all this happens in a 'closed' environment with no role at all for the international economy.

Yet you will remember from chapter 8 that the components of national income include an allowance for the 'balance of trade': the mysterious exports (X) minus imports (M) that we have hitherto left well alone. The reason for leaving it until the penultimate chapter before considering the implications of the 'open economy' is that, as we will see, it is a complex area that requires a picture of the relationship between the micro and macro economies (and the corresponding coordinating role for strategy) in order fully to understand it.

This is the case because international economic activity as it manifests itself in the late twentieth century is not simply a matter of how countries as a whole trade with one another. Models of international trade have traditionally concentrated on 'absolute' advantage, 'comparative' advantage and 'relative factor endowments', and we discuss these in more detail below. But they tend to treat national resources as given and distributed optimally by the 'market mechanism', as covered in chapter 3. The extension of this is that freely operating markets in international trade will allocate resources through specialization optimally throughout the world. However, as we saw in our discussion of imperfect markets, it has always been the case that individual companies allocate resources. This becomes particularly important as companies, on the back of advanced communications and manufacturing technologies, can begin to allocate resources globally. They can circumvent and override the international markets even if these are increasingly free of trade restrictions. We need, then, to examine first how international trade works in theory, and second how companies themselves can create organizations and strategies to take advantage of a free trade environment.

1.1 Global versus International: Is the Distinction Important?

That the 'world is becoming more global' is one of the clichés of management literature and business commentary generally in the 1990s. The world has always been 'global', in so far as trade has always taken place between different regions and countries with different resource endowments and comparative advantages.[1] However, this latest phase of economic development is argued to have begun during 1980s, and it recognizes no geographical boundaries; and ranges from changes in the way in which individual firms are organizing their production and transactions, and the growing attention now being given to cross-border alliances and spatial networks, to the globalization of economic activity and its impact on the role and policies of national governments and of supranational institutions.[2]

It is, then, a new phase and has unique characteristics. Dunning identifies two areas which make the word 'globalization' a more appropriate term than 'internationalization', which has been used in economics literature hitherto. First, market forces can no longer be relied upon to allocate resources efficiently and innovation becomes the catalyst for competitiveness and growth. Second, institutions are not independent but have to be viewed as a *system*. In this, the role of the firm and its organization is central, both within a country and across borders. Technology and innovation have to be viewed as *endogenous* to the firm and not *exogenous*.[3]

In other words, the role of company strategy in dealing with this type of change in world markets is critical. In this type of international market place, companies have to locate their operations around the world in order to take advantage of cost (and tax) structures in different countries. They also have to organize and coordinate these mechanisms to ensure that they create competitive advantage and not competitive disadvantage. Global operations require global strategies.

Further, the central role of technology cannot be isolated from this latest phase of globalization. Microelectronics technology has arguably facilitated the process of globalization as defined by Dunning above. Indeed, perhaps the most enduring and important changes affecting the survival of companies are technological. The introduction of microelectronic technologies in industry has altered cost structures, altered work organization and decision-making processes, changed methods of production and created requirements for new types of skills and attitudes from the entire workforce of companies. Companies successfully implementing these new technologies have had, in sum, to rethink some, if not all, of their approach to production and their relationship with their competitive environment.

To look at the link between technology, which affects cost structures, as we saw in chapter 4, and globalization, a number of points can be summarized from the debate in the literature.

1   *The process of globalization is causing national and corporate structures to change.*[4] At a corporate level, the change is towards more strategic alliances, mergers and acquisitions or, more generally, increased interdependence, both strategically and economically, between firms. At a national level, infrastructures change in response to the needs of companies while governments become aware both of the power of international business and of the importance of supranational organizations, like the IMF[5] or the EU.[6]

2   *Companies increasingly operate on a globally networked basis and the management of these 'global webs' is critical to success and survival.*[7] Rather than activities being duplicated in different countries, in the latest 'global' phase there is increased geographic integration of

activities and strategies which, if effectively coordinated, reduces total costs.

3 *Despite the importance of the global management process, the nation state is still a potent force in the competitive advantage of nations.* This is perhaps the most contentious assertion about the latest phase of international development because many management theorists, such as Ohmae, argue that the 'nation state is a dinosaur waiting to die'. However, as economists, 'we can argue that national systems will adapt to reflect the requirements of the global economy and provide a supportive infrastructure (through the structural policies mentioned in previous chapters towards education and training, transport, regional development and so on).

Arguably the biggest challenge facing companies, large or small, is how to cope with the international dimension. Can companies rely on a single country to provide competitive advantage and sufficient market demand for their products or, as Lucas found in the early 1980s, do they have to look abroad to foreign markets and structures? What impact do the economic policies of a national government have on companies exporting products and importing supplies? How do large supranational institutions like the EU affect company decisions: for example, if European legislation affects working practices in one country (say Germany) but not another (say Britain), how does this affect a company's location decision. And the burning issue of the late 1990s is: how will a single currency affect businesses large and small?

2 Aims and Objectives

There are so many issues concerned with the international dimension in business and economics that it really would be impossible to concentrate all of these down into a short chapter like this. However, as we move towards the next millennium, the 'open economy' is a major talking point among policy-makers, business and academics alike. We could not afford to ignore it. Although our coverage in a one semester framework is likely only to be cursory, we can see why the area is important and point to some extra reading.

With this limitation in mind, then, the aim of this chapter is simple: to use economics to explain some of the current events in the international economy and, hence, to evaluate their impact on business. The specific objectives, as ever, are more detailed.

1 To introduce you to the reasons why countries trade with one another.
2 To look at the price of trade as represented by the exchange rate and, hence, to look at the determinants of the exchange rate.
3 To review the impact that governments can have on international trade and investment.
4 In the light of 2 and 3, to discuss the importance of the EU and the single currency.
5 To examine the interface between the international dimension and company strategy.
6 To point to further areas of investigation through provision of reading suggestions.

3 Investigation (1)

CASE 9

Rich Grazing for Food Groups

Roderick Oram examines a European upheaval as companies are becoming increasingly cosmopolitan

If you go down to a Monoprix supermarket in Paris today, you can buy a bacon, lettuce and tomato sandwich for FFr18(£2.30). For such a fresh product, it has come a long way. It was made yesterday morning by Booker, a British food company, 50 miles north-west of London. Its lettuce was still growing in southern Spain on Friday.

As trade barriers fall and cultures borrow promiscuously from each other, has the day of pan-European foods arrived? There are attractions for both buyers and sellers. Consumers want varied and convenient food; manufacturers want high-margin products and big brand names to combat competition from the 'own-label' products of supermarkets; retailers want wide sourcing to cut costs and enhance their in-house brands.

However, for all the new-found ease in moving goods across Europe, the effort is still extremely testing for the few attempting it. Diverse consumer tastes alone are enough to put them off the quest. Establishing a pan-European product is 'something of a Holy Grail', says Mr Michael Jary, head of consumer industries at OC&C Strategy Consultants in London. Of the 100 largest European food processing companies surveyed recently by OC&C, half operated in only one or two EU countries. Only nine companies sold in at least four of the five biggest markets of Germany, France, the UK, Italy and Spain.

Many operate largely in domestic markets despite rising competition and thinning margins. They think neighbouring European markets, dominated by local producers, are too complex to crack.

Parmalat, the Italian UHT milk producer, is more interested in North and South America and Asia than Europe. 'These are more attractive than trying to push into mature western European markets,' says Mr Domenico Barili, managing director. 'We can still build a global business without being pan-European.' Europe excluding Italy accounts for only 10 per cent of its turnover.

But the rising power of retailing chains that drive hard bargains with manufacturers is forcing many companies to look to neighbouring markets. Those that learn how to operate abroad may survive better.

'A lot of companies see themselves as only national,' says a London investment banker in the food sector. 'But the only protection for them is if their products are extremely national.'

Should a producer set its sights on foreign markets in Europe, finding the right product is the first problem.

What manufacturers call 'lifestyle' foods are some of the best products for winning new consumers. Whether promoting healthier diets or minimal cooking, the likes of low-fat spreads and prepared meals are fast-growing categories across Europe.

A desire for health and convenience is 'pushing urbanised western European consumers into similar products', says Mr John Campbell, a market analyst with Paribas Capital Markets. Breakfast habits are changing rapidly, for example, with American-style cereals replacing traditional foods such as sausage and cheese.

Others promising targets are 'impulse purchases' such as soft drinks and snacks that respond well to intensive advertising. But the advertising is expensive, so it needs large sales volumes from international brands to justify it. Foods hard to make at home are another good bet; Chinese meals and tiramisu are typical examples.

But food manufacturers say it is getting expensive to experiment in the search for rare winners in these areas and then to establish them in multiple markets. An alternative is to sell 'ethnic' and speciality foods.

'It is hard to put numbers on it but we believe the speciality makers or the speciality brands of large companies are the winners, not the expensive attempts to achieve pan-European products,' says Mr James Ensor, managing director of Strategic Vision, a food consultant.

The next problem is manufacture. As demand for a food rises across Europe, the pattern of production can shift dramatically. Northern Foods makes chilled ready meals in Sheffield, northern England, for Marks and Spencer, the British retailer. They are trucked daily to M&S stores in Paris and Madrid. Nestlé and Unilever, Europe's two biggest food producers, have begun to rationalise national plants, concentrating on larger ones producing for several countries. Ideally, Nestlé would want to halve the number of its plants across Europe, Mr Campbell of Paribas believes, but is constrained by national sensibilities. But the shift is well under way at Cereal Partners, Nestlé's breakfast food joint venture with General Mills of the US.

Changing technology also means it is more efficient to produce larger quantities of a particular product than can be absorbed by one national market. Thus August Oetker can sell German-made frozen pizzas at a profit to Tesco, the UK supermarket chain, despite Germany's higher wage costs.

Specialisation creates some surprising trading relationships. Hillsdown Holdings of the UK began canning beans for the UK stores of Aldi, the German discount retailer. Pleased with the low cost and efficient service, Aldi asked Hillsdown to supply its German stores too. But consumers there wanted different beans, so Hillsdown imports the beans from the Continent, cans them in the UK and ships them to Germany.

The next problem is branding products. Typically, a large manufacturer will deploy a dual strategy – using an international brand for food with wide appeal and regional, national or even local brands for more limited products.

The brand, of course, has to be right. An interesting case study, consultants say, involves Mars and its Chinese meals. They sold badly in Germany because consumers did not know the Suzi Wan brand and assumed it was too Chinese in taste. In contrast, Nestlé outsold it with 'Taste of Asia' meals under its established Maggi brand. 'Consumers perceived the recipes were adapted to German tastes and so were less of a gamble to buy,' one consultant says.

Even if a manufacturer goes for the same recipes and brand across Europe, national variation in advertising is essential. Nestlé, for example, found that 'Italian' meant different things to consumers in different countries. Thus, for its Buitoni brand products it fixes the packaging style and the music for its advertisements centrally; but it leaves the national branches

of its advertising agency to create advertisements to fit. In the UK the Italian story line revolves around romantic dreams; in Spain, it relies on fashionable clothes and fast cars.

Getting the goods to markets is quicker and easier since many frontier controls were abolished, encouraging the shipment of foods with a shorter shelf-life. Logistics specialists such as Tibbett and Britten of the UK are typical of companies setting up dedicated distribution systems for manufacturers.

But who is to sell the food? In some countries such as the UK, France, and Germany retailing power has become more concentrated in a few hands. Southern European countries are much further behind in the trend, and European manufacturers still have a lot of clout in their negotiations with retailers. The top three supermarket chains account for only 15 per cent of European food sales; in contrast, 40 per cent of snacks and 36 per cent of biscuits are made by the three biggest companies in each sector.

Yet the pressures on food makers are increasing. One of the greatest threats comes from consortia of supermarket chains. There are at least eight in Europe. One of the first and largest is AMS, based in Switzerland. Four years old, its members include Ahold of the Netherlands, Argyll of the UK and Casino of France.

AMS members do little collective buying but they do share information on producers and their prices. 'We ask them to justify the differences,' says Mr Dick Roozen, commercial manager of AMS.

Food manufacturers' strategies to cope with these challenges are evolving rapidly. In many ways smaller, speciality companies have it easiest. They can push their unique, usually ethnic, products through supermarket chains and consortia. AMS members, for example,' help small companies – say a Parmesan cheese maker or an own-label canner – expand abroad by introducing them to other members.

Life is more frustrating for large companies creating international products and brands. 'They are moving away from centralised, European strategies to relatively decentralised strategies,' says a leading consultant. 'But they are reverting only to the regional level, not back to national markets. Through cross-border teams in their organisations they are trying to find synergies, cut costs and share innovations in products and manufacture.'

Even if ambitions are more modest than they were, the goal is the same: food companies have to become more cosmopolitan to meet demands from consumers and retailers. The forces are creating a tremendous upheaval.

'My father said this was the worst crisis he'd known in his career. Everything was changing and he didn't understand,' says Mr Guido Barilla, whose father built the family's pasta empire and died in 1993.

'But he did say to me: "I've dedicated my life to growing an Italian business. Your goal is to do something different and international."'

Read the global pizza case (case 9) and then answer the following questions.

1 How has the food industry adapted to changes in the international market environment?
2 Would the individual companies in the food industry be unduly affected by a significant downturn in one country's market? What evasive action might they take?

4 Absolute and Comparative Advantage and International Trade

For the time being, let's leave companies and governments out of the equation altogether and focus on trade between 'countries' as a whole. The theories of why countries trade with one another go right back to the classical economists of the eighteenth and nineteenth centuries. It was Adam Smith who first put forward the idea of why companies and countries can gain from specialization through the operations of the market, and David Ricardo who developed these first analyses of the advantages of specialization into models of trade.

| **Table 11.1** | Comparative advantage of Germany and Britain in the production of lager and sausages |

	Kilograms of sausages	Litres of lager
Germany	8	4
England	1	2

There are two important concepts in the simplest approaches to international trade.

1 *Absolute advantage* is where one country can produce a good with fewer resources than another. Say, for example, that England is particularly effective in its production of lager, and can produce it more cheaply than Germany. It is said to have an absolute advantage in lager production. If Germany, on the other hand, can supply hot dog sausages more cheaply, it has an absolute advantage in the production of sausages. A major football tournament is being staged in London and, rather than trying to produce lager *and* sausages for ardent supporters, it pays England to concentrate on the production of lager and import its sausages from Germany. Both countries will gain through specialization and trade.

2 *Comparative advantage.* If Germany, in this example, can produce both lager and sausages more cheaply than England, the countries may still benefit from specialization and trade, if the *relative* costs of producing the goods differ between the two countries as shown in table 11.1.

The countries will gain from trade as follows:

- Germany, if it specializes its production, can produce *either* 8 kilograms of sausages *or* 4 litres of lager. The *opportunity cost* of producing 4 litres of lager is 8 kilograms of sausages, or 4 : 8 (or 1 : 2).
- England, if it specializes, can produce either 2 litres of lager or 1 kilogram of sausages. The *opportunity cost* of producing 2 litres of lager is just 1 kilogram of sausages, or 2 : 1.
- England, therefore, has a comparative advantage in the production of lager: it has to forgo less than Germany in producing an equivalent quantity.
- By specializing and trading, the two countries can gain: Germany produces sausages and England produces lager.

4.1 The Hecksher–Ohlin Model and Comparative Factor Advantage

Usually countries tend to have a comparative advantage in products that utilize an abundant factor. The model developed by Eli Hecksher and Bertil Ohlin argues that some countries benefit from rich factor endowments: Russia, for example, has a rich supply of raw materials such as natural gas, Canada a rich supply of land, European countries a rich supply of capital, America a rich supply of land and capital, Australia a rich supply of raw materials such as coal and land and so on.

They argued that it pays a country to specialize in production of goods and services that utilize that abundant factor. Countries then trade the goods they produce using their abundant factor for goods produced overseas with factors of production in which they are less well endowed. Thus, the 'tiger' economies of South East Asia, such as South Korea, have developed and traded on the basis of their rich endowment in relatively cheap labour, while one of the major exports of the Australian economy is coal. America and Western European countries tend to export a large quantity of capital goods.

The benefits for the world from all this are twofold. First, they argue, it will increase the overall level of consumption in the world economy, thereby increasing growth worldwide. Countries rich in labour produce goods accordingly and import the capital-intensive goods that they are less able to produce efficiently. The second advantage, then, is that through international trade, factor prices equalize and income disparities between nations level out: everyone wins through this type of specialization.

4.2 How Do Companies Make Use of Comparative Advantage and Relative Factor Endowments?

There are several points to be brought out here in relation to company strategy.[8]

1   The post-1945 stage in international economic activity has been associated with the desire to minimize so-called *transactions costs*.[9] Put simply, transactions costs are the opportunity costs of keeping an activity inside the hierarchy of the firm (and thus accountable) versus tendering that activity out the 'market'. Oliver Williamson, who first coined this phrase, argued that firms will keep 'core' activities within the hierarchy of the firm and tender subsidiary activities out to the market place. For example, a company like Amstrad

keeps its R&D, assembly and marketing activities within its own hierarchy, and subcontracts out manufacturing to the cheapest bidder. It grew into a multinational company on the basis of this strategy during the 1980s, subcontracting the manufacture of its goods to developing economies with very low labour costs.

2   Thus, companies seeking to operate in the international market will locate their operations to take advantage of the very comparative advantage and factor endowments of the 'host' nation. Up until the mid-1980s, however, it was argued that companies kept their core activities in their domestic base. Thus technology (or R&D) was kept close to home, while other activities such as manufacture were undertaken abroad.[10]

3   The latest microelectronics and 'global' phase, argue authors such as Ohmae and Reich, has involved a change in this structure. It is companies, rather than nation states, that increasingly take advantage of factor endowments to ensure transactions cost efficiencies and decentralise decision-making globally. Thus a company like Ford has several central pillars, each with areas of strategic autonomy and responsibility and coordinated by an overall, integrated strategy enabled by microelectronics technology.

4.3   Investigation (2)

CASE 10

Going Global Is Nothing New

Many carmakers have chosen to avoid the problems of worldwide manufacturing, by Haig Simonian

Forty years ago, the great majority of the new cars bought in Japan were made by manufacturers from abroad. At much the same time, Volkswagen inaugurated its first factory in Brazil. And as early as 1911, Ford opened its first foreign production site when it started building cars in the UK.

Globalisation, it seems, is nothing new to the world's carmakers. But while many manufacturers have expanded far beyond their original homes, it has recently become necessary to distinguish between car companies which are merely 'multinational' and those with 'global' pretentions.

The difference is one of philosophy rather than semantics. Being 'global' means not just building cars from São Paulo to Shanghai, but adopting an integrated approach to how that far-flung empire should be run.

A 'global' car company, for example, would centrally plan its entire model range, which would be built on a limited number of basic 'platforms'. Although the metal skins attached to them may differ to suit local tastes, the basics, such as wheelbase, width and key engineering details like the location of the central pillar, would be identical.

Globalisation, in the sense of integration, embraces manufacturing and marketing as much as design and development. Although a truly 'global' car may be built in different countries, it would be made by the same processes and, quite possibly, involve similar marketing campaigns in different territories.

Purchasing, another important function in view of the fact that about 60 per cent of a car's value is comprised of components bought from outside sources, would also be given treatment as a single, worldwide activity.

Lower costs, improved use of resources and faster development times have been the reasons behind globalisation. Combining international resources can let a multinational car company make the most efficient use of its skills. Linking stylists and development engineers can accelerate development programmes, reducing the 'time to market' for a new model. By working internationally from the outset, a new car can, if necessary, be introduced in a global marketing blitz, maximising the impact and avoiding the staggered launches of the past.

But to reap the greatest benefits, globalisation requires a big upheaval in a company's structure. Most corporations will have subjected themselves to the consultants' rule over the years. But their internal organisation will probably say more about patchy organic growth and opportunistic acquisitions to expand rather than the thorough going rethink globalisation requires.

So in spite of the apparent advantages, not all the world's biggest carmakers have chosen to go 'global'. Ford and Volkswagen have been the two most active converts. Ford 2000, the name for the ambitious globalisation strategy unveiled by Mr Alex Trotman, its chairman, last year, has turned into a symbol of one carmaker's determination to adapt.

Ford's decision to tear up its geographical divisions and reorganise around five 'vehicle centres' (VCs) marks the most radical attempt to adopt a global approach. The VCs, covering different types of car from small front-wheel-drive models to hefty pick-ups, have become almost independent corporate entities charged with a specific task on a worldwide basis.

VW has moved in a similar, but less radical, direction. Mr Ferdinand Piëch, its chairman, has pushed through an ambitious strategy to axe the large number of 'platforms' on which its different models are made around the world.

Although less ambitious than Ford 2000, the VW group's approach is complicated by the fact that it involves integrating four different companies. And while VW and Audi are at least based in Germany, Seat and Skoda are both relatively recent acquisitions with headquarters abroad, complicating integration.

Mr Piëch aims to reduce VW's 16-odd platforms to just four. These will form the foundation for all future models to be built by VW, Audi, Seat and Skoda. For example, the platform for the next generation Golf, Europe's best selling car, will be shared by the new Audi A3 hatchback and other group models. To confuse matters further, the European platforms will also be used, and, if necessary, modified slightly, by VW's free-standing manufacturing subsidiaries in south America, South Africa and China.

General Motors, Ford's bigger US rival, has gone about globalisation more cautiously. Instead of opting for an all-out reorganisation, it has devolved most of the responsibility for co-ordinating its international expansion to its Opel subsidiary in Germany. Although many of the Opel-originated or designed GM cars sold outside the US and Europe are badged as Chevrolets (the group's main US brand), Opel has to co-ordinate their development.

No other manufacturer has been as radical as Ford or VW. Japan's big carmakers have steered well clear of the management and organisational implications of globalisation. Toyota, Nissan and Honda now all have substantial production facilities outside their home market, Yet in spite of devolving some design and product development functions to their new operations in the US, UK, and, in some cases, elsewhere, the buck stops firmly in Japan. This regional, rather than global, approach is reflected in the cars themselves, which are predominantly geared towards distinct markets, with little cross-fertilisation between the foreign factories and minimal flows of vehicles from one non-Japanese operation to another.

Fiat has taken a very different tack. Although appreciably smaller than Ford or VW, let alone GM or the main Japanese carmakers, is has been examining its structural options to reflect its strong international ambitions.

Cars built in Italy will continue to form the backbone of its product range, supplemented by selective sourcing from Poland and very limited imports from its big subsidiary in Brazil.

But next month will see the introduction of the group's Palio 'world car'. The Palio, which comprises three-and-five door hatchbacks, a saloon, estate and pick-up, marks Fiat's response to the challenge of globalisation by providing a sturdy but stylish car for motorists in industrialising countries.

To be launched in Brazil, the Palio will eventually be produced in Argentina, Turkey, India. Morocco, and Poland. If Fiat's executives achieve their ambition of adding China to that list, the group could be building more that 900,000 Palios a year by early next century.

Fiat's strategy requires none of the wrenching upheavals involved in Ford 2000 and entails the much more modest aim of building multinational teams for the Palio. Its caution reflects the attitude of many motor industry bosses, who say Ford has failed to take account of the risks involved in convulsive change and will suffer as a result. Others, however, argue that hesitation today will only make the inevitable task of restructuring more difficult tomorrow.

Read the case on the global operations of Ford and other car makers (case 10), and then try answering the following questions.

1 To what extent has Ford taken advantage of regional comparative advantages in its location decisions?
2 To what extent has Ford utilized regional factor endowments in its 'global' strategy?
3 Can you distinguish between the 'global' strategy that it now has and the 'multinational' strategies that it has had before? How do the theories of international trade help us to understand the distinction?

5   The Exchange Rate

Why is it that a company such as Toyota UK argued at the beginning of 1997 that it was essential for Britain to be part of a single European currency? The exchange rate is the price of trade between nations and between companies within those nations. As companies operate increasingly on a 'global' basis, they have to be concerned about the price of the supplies they purchase as inputs and the price at which they can sell their outputs. If these differ substantially between countries, they too represent 'transactions costs' to the companies in terms of both forgone profit and the currency conversion costs.

Let's look more carefully at this and go back to the reasons why companies trade. To return to the example in table 11.1, if Germany and England were bartering products, they would want to find a 'rate of exchange' which reflected the relative opportunity costs that the two countries had incurred. In other words, England would want to trade 2 litres of lager for 1 kilogram of sausages and Germany would want to trade 8 kilograms of sausages for 4 litres of lager. The rate of exchange will lie somewhere between 1 : 2 and 2 : 1. The 'fair' outcome under which both countries gain is to trade at a ratio of 1 : 1. In other words, Germany trades 1 kilogram of sausages for 1 litre of lager.

In reality, of course, countries do not barter but price goods and services in terms of their domestic currency. The value of the currency will still reflect the endowments of the country. An indicator of the endowments is often taken to be the macroeconomic health of the nation and its trade performance, reflected in the balance of trade[11] (or exports minus imports, in the equation for national income).

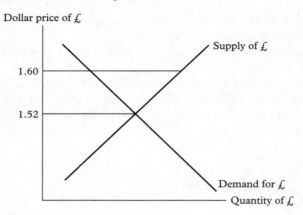

Figure 11.1   Supply and demand of sterling: determination of the rate of exchange.

Currencies are bought and sold on international markets so that overseas produced goods can be bought and domestic goods can be sold.

The price of a currency is always in relation to other currencies, a fact which most foreign travellers will have already encountered. Thus, for example, £1 sterling might buy US$1.52: for every £1 that you give to the bank, you will receive $1.52 back. As currencies are constantly being bought and sold on international markets, the exchange rate fluctuates daily – you will hear prices updated on news bulletins throughout the day.

We can explain how the exchange rate fluctuates using the model of supply and demand. In this case, demand for a currency, say sterling, comes from overseas, and supply of £1 sterling comes from UK investors wishing to sell pounds and buy overseas currencies. For the time being, let's keep this discussion to the rate of exchange between the US dollar and pound sterling, as illustrated in figure 11.1.

Figure 11.1 shows how the pound is demanded and supplied on the foreign exchange market. The analysis and the determination of the equilibrium price is similar to the determination of prices through supply and demand covered elsewhere in this text. The only difference is that the 'price' of pounds is the number of, in this case, dollars that investors are willing to spend in exchange for £1. If the rate is too high, say $1.60 has to be exchanged for £1, then there will be a surplus of pounds on the market. This will have the effect of bringing the rate down to an equilibrium where supply and demand are equal: here, at $1.52. In other words, at this rate, $1.52 has to be exchanged for every £1.

5.1   Government Policy, Exchange Rates and the Balance of Payments

If exchange rates were determined simply on the basis of investors' purchases of currency, there would be no need for any government intervention into exchange markets at all. However, as we saw above, the exchange rate of a currency, say sterling, is itself determined by the comparative advantage of the domestic economy, here Britain. This 'comparative advantage' is reflected in the country's trade performance, what it imports relative to what it exports.

This is the balance of payments which we referred to above: the total exports minus total imports in the equation for national income. It is comprised of two parts: the current and the capital accounts.

The *current account* is made up of two parts:

1   *Visible trade.* Any country trades goods and services. Trade in physical goods is called *visible* trade and the balance of trade (which you will often hear referred to in news items) is the export of goods minus the import of goods.
2   *Invisible trade.* A country will also trade money (or *invisible*) items, such as insurance policies and bank accounts. Where an overseas investor buys a UK insurance policy, this is a 'credit' item; where a UK citizen buys an overseas policy, this is a debit item. The invisible balance is the credit items minus the debit items.

The *capital account* is all trade in external 'liabilities and assets'. That is, it is all capital money (or investment and financial flows) coming into and going out of the economy.

The balance of payments is the sum of the current account and the capital account and is highly technical. However, two points are of particular importance here. First, as was mentioned above, the balance of payments is, effectively, demand and supply of the currency. In other words, the value of the currency is determined by the ratio of the money required to buy the goods and services produced in the economy (demand) and all the currency needed to buy goods and services produced abroad (supply). As we saw in figure 11.1, the interaction of this supply and demand will determine the equilibrium value of the currency. The balance of payments, therefore, must always balance: the money spent on imports must always equal the money spent on exports – otherwise there is a surplus (or deficit) of supply over demand for the currency.

A government has two principal means of affecting the balance of payments: one 'real' and one 'monetary'. 'Real' methods are those employed to affect the competitiveness of domestic industry. Restrictions on imports (such as tariffs and quotas) are one method of ensuring that competitive strength is built up within a domestic economy before trade is undertaken with the rest of the world. Consumers have a price disincentive to buy overseas produced goods as these are made more expensive relative to domestic goods, either by the imposition of import taxes or by their relative scarcity. Other methods include those covered in chapter 9: to encourage investment and competitiveness among domestic companies.

'Monetary' methods are a direct by-product of monetary policy in an economy. You will recall that a powerful method of controlling the money supply is to raise interest rates and thus encourage saving. If interest rates are increased, the currency becomes more attractive – overseas investors wish to take advantage of high returns, say in the UK, and buy sterling accordingly (this manifests itself as an increase in credit items on the capital account). The result is that the currency becomes relatively scarce and its rate against other currencies rises.

If currencies are allowed to 'float' freely against other currencies, then this will occur automatically through the interaction of supply and demand in the currency market place. The trend in the world since the end of the 1970s has been towards freely floating rates, as this allows currencies to find their own relative value, and hence takes away the need for government manipulation of the exchange rate in order to balance the balance of payments. The downside is that freely floating rates tend to fluctuate on a daily basis and, as a result, create uncertainties for businesses attempting to sell their products abroad.

It is perhaps paradoxical, then, that against this backdrop of freely floating exchange rates and free trade generally, the European Union has operated a monetary system which 'fixes', or pegs, currencies against one another. Britain was a member of this Exchange Rate Mechanism (ERM) between 1990 and 1992, and it is worth dwelling a little on how it worked. The value of a currency is agreed by the central monetary authorities to reflect the relative trade balances in the countries, and the central bank will intervene, buying and selling the currency in order to sustain the equilibrium value. The argument in favour of fixed rates is that they create stability so that companies know what price their goods will be selling at in overseas markets and know the price of competitors' goods coming into the home market. The theory is that this stability helps companies to forecast events and formulate strategies accordingly.

Figure 11.2 shows the central rate about which sterling was fixed in the ERM – at 2.80 Deutschmarks (DM). In order to prevent the rigidities of a fixed system caused by the need for constant central bank intervention to support the value of the currency, sterling was allowed

Figure 11.2 The exchange rate mechanism 1990–1992.

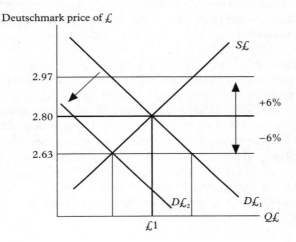

to fluctuate within a broad band of plus or minus 6 per cent of this central value (the upper limit of DM2.97 and the lower limit of DM2.63).

Supply of a currency is through the central bank of the country: for Britain, the Bank of England. Exchange market dealers buy the currency if interest rates are high – effectively they are buying investments in a country in anticipation of profit. As they buy the currency, this makes it relatively scarce, pushing up its price. Similarly, by buying up the currency, central banks can make it relatively scarce and, hence, push up its price. For the Bank of England this meant running down its foreign currency reserves.

Britain entered the ERM in 1990 when interest rates were on an upward trend to control domestic inflation. There were many who also argued that the central value of sterling at DM2.80 was too high, making British goods relatively expensive abroad and imports cheaper. Two difficulties affected the performance of sterling in the ERM:

1   Recession in Britain in the early 1990s along with inflationary pressures in Germany from reunification made potential foreign investors in Britain wary of buying sterling and strongly supportive of the Deutschmark. In order to support the value of the currency and to support government anti-inflationary policy, interest rates rose further.

2   The Bank of England continued to have to buy sterling despite increases in interest rates as demand slipped (from $D\pounds_1$ to $D\pounds_2$ in figure 11.2). This meant that its foreign currency reserves were significantly depleted: the Bank could not continue the policy indefinitely. Interest rates continued to increase.

By 16 September 1992 ('Black Wednesday') demand for sterling had fallen so significantly that despite efforts by the government to increase interest rates, the currency would remain within the lower 6 per cent margin of the ERM. Britain was forced to withdraw, along with Italy. Immediately the value of sterling fell and interest rates fell too.

Britain had moved to a freely floating exchange rate where the value of the currency reflects more accurately the competitiveness of indigenous industry. Since 1992 the value of the currency has been more volatile, but the government has had more power over monetary policy, particularly over interest rates, and as a result real interest rates have fallen.

5.2   The Implications for Companies and Strategy

We can now bring companies back into the discussion. From the discussion we have undertaken in this chapter there are two principal areas in which the international economy will have an impact on business. Both relate very simply to the interface between the company and its market which we have stressed throughout this text. The impact is depicted in figure 11.3.

First, the international economy will affect costs and, hence, supply. Companies with international operations locate in order to minimize their transactions costs and thus assess the comparative advantages of each potential host nation. This has become particularly important towards the next millennium as the 'world has become more global'. But even for small companies that operate in one domestic economy, the international dimension can have a profound impact on input prices. If that company is heavily reliant on imports for supplies these prices will be volatile if the exchange rate fluctuates, creating cost and market uncertainties.

Second, on the demand side of the model, the 'open economy' will affect a company in terms of the size of its market demand and the numbers of competitors in the market place. But perhaps the most important area affecting the operation of the market and the stability of the environment in which the company is operating is the impact of the exchange rate on prices, which in turn affects its capacity to

Figure 11.3 The coordinating role of strategy in the international dimension.

compete in its domestic market and overseas markets. This was demonstrated at the beginning of 1997, when a high value of the pound increased imports of cars and reduced the number of cars being exported. Why is it that a high value of a currency makes imports cheaper and exports more expensive, thus rendering more volatile overseas markets?

The answer lies in the exchange rate. If a British company exports, then other countries have to buy sterling in order to buy its goods. This means that the pound becomes relatively scarce and its price is pushed up. On the current account this would not matter, as the imports into the country would offset the temporary imbalance. If the government simultaneously operates a high interest rate policy (thereby making British investments more attractive), this has the effect of further pushing up the value of sterling. The result is that more marks or dollars or francs are required to buy £1 of sterling, making British goods expensive abroad and foreign goods relatively cheap in Britain. Further, if the exchange rate is floating, the price of imports and exports can vary substantially over time, creating market uncertainty and volatility in terms of both input prices (factors of production) and output (or market) prices.

It is this uncertainty that is the main aspect of the international dimension that companies need to build into their strategies. Market uncertainty is a characteristic of imperfect markets and international markets are no exception to this. Oliver Williamson (see note 9) argued

Figure 11.4 The strategic matrix and the international dimension.

	Pricing/output	Product development and technology	Competitor analysis	Impact of regulatory environment	National income and macro economy	Unemployment and human resources	Inflation forecasting	International economy
Small companies	Dependent on competitors and demand	Vital	Vital	High – impact on costs	High impact	High	Essential but expensive. Impact of inflationary expectations high	Damaging. Impact of interest and exchange rates
Large companies	Price interdependency	NON-PRICE COMPETITION	Strategic interdependency	Low – can be taken up within slack and turned to competitive advantage	Potential high impact	High	Essential. Impact of inflationary expectations high but can be insured against	Global strategy to prevent excessive reliance on one economy

that companies will have transactions cost minimization as the central pillar of a strategy designed to ameliorate these uncertainties.

This is especially relevant for understanding the means by which companies expand globally. By having operations in more than one country and by coordinating strategy across these international operations, the company has 'eggs in more than one basket'. For example, UK companies 'globalized' to a substantial degree during the 1980s in order to withstand the pressures of recession in the domestic economy. A brief comparison with Germany further highlights this point. Faced with rising domestic labour costs and uncertain domestic market conditions, German companies are now beginning to globalize in the same way that their British counterparts did ten years earlier. As Lucas documentation said then, 'We were over reliant on one market.' This is proving to be the case now for German companies.

6 Investigation (3)

In order to establish for yourself how important the international economy is for business you may find it useful to look at British balance of payments figures. The Central Statistical Office (CSO) Blue Book provides data yearly on this and is a useful source for trade figures. The National Institute Economic Review, OECD reports and Eurostat will provide data on comparative real interest rates. You may like to think about the following questions.

1 In what years was Britain's trade performance worst?
2 Is there any relationship between real interest rates and performance?
3 How might a company with global markets insure against exchange and interest rate fluctuations?

7 Conclusions

Into our strategic matrix we can add one final column, that of the global economy (see figure 11.4). Globalization is a whole area in its own right and it would not be possible to do it justice in the context of this book. However, as technology develops, pressures on costs increase and domestic economies become too uncertain a base for stable operations, no business text would be complete without mentioning this as an increasingly important trend.

This chapter began with a discussion on this globalization and pointed to a debate in the literature about the role of the nation state. In the light of the material we have covered in this chapter, we can summarize this as follows.

1   Classical economics views the nation as the central source of competitive advantage. Resources are allocated through the market mechanism both nationally and internationally through specialization. The role of the 'company' and its strategy is minimal in this perfectly competitive world, as we saw in chapter 5.

2   In the 'golden age of international economic activity',[12] which lasted until the mid-1980s, companies grew large in response to the desire to widen markets, thereby achieving economies of scale, and reduce costs by taking advantage of the factor endowments of a host nation. Trade blocks, or 'common markets'[13] were responses to this trend – free trade between members of an economic community (such as the European Economic Community (EEC), as it was called) with a common external tariff on goods from outside that community. The main advantage of such blocks was the creation of large but competitive markets for companies within the whole region. This process still continues.

3   Since the mid-1980s, companies' international strategies have responded to two things: the increasing ease with which companies can communicate and manage information on a global scale and the developing strength of 'regions' rather than nations (such as the relative strength of the European Union). Companies such as Toyota which fall outside trading blocks have been able to circumvent tariff barriers by trading from within as a European (or more specifically British) company.

4   This has led some commentators, such as Reich or Ohmae, to argue that countries are less important than regions and companies in determining the form and direction that international economic activity takes. Thus a single European currency, for example, is simply a way of further reducing transactions costs and reducing market uncertainties for these global companies.

5   Equally importantly, these very global companies still wish to take advantage of factor endowments in a country. Taking Porter's[14] arguments here, the 'competitive advantage of nations' lies not just in company strategy, but also in the structure of the domestic economy, the competition between domestic companies, domestic demand conditions, the infrastructure and the development and enhancement of factor endowments (for example, through education

and training). Thus countries determine the international allocation of resources through their own specializations.

So are companies or countries more important in determining the
future direction of international economic activity? There is no 'right'
or 'wrong' answer to this question and your answer will depend to a
large extent on the evidence you have had presented to you. As you
will have no doubt already encountered in discussions on European
Currency Union, 'hard' arguments are often sacrificed to emotive
issues like sovereignty. In truth, as Lazonick[15] argues, the path is
probably somewhere between the two positions. Global strategies are
important in determining the international allocation of resources,
but it would be ridiculous to discard centuries of economic history,
as this would disregard the importance of nations in developing the
factor endowments that these global companies seek to exploit.

8   Further Reading

Dicken, P. (1992) *Global Shift: the Internationalisation of Economic Activity*, 2nd
    edn. London: Paul Chapman Publishing.
Goodman, S. F. (1993) *The European Community*, 2nd edn. London:
    Macmillan.
Hill, C. W. L. (1994) *International Business: Competing in the Global Market
    Place*. International Student Edition. Burr Ridge, IL: Irwin.
Hirst, P. and Thompson, G. (1996) *Globalization in Question: the International
    Economy and the Possibilities of Governance*. Cambridge: Polity Press.
Jenkinson, T. (ed.) (1996) *Readings in Microeconomics*. Oxford: Oxford
    University Press. Contributions in parts II and III of this text are of espe-
    cial relevance to this chapter.
Ohmae, K. (1996) *The End of the Nation State: the Rise of Regional Economies*.
    London: HarperCollins.
Porter, M. (1990) *The Competitive Advantage of Nations*. London: Macmillan.

Notes

1   The laws of comparative advantage and absolute advantage in inter-
    national trade are central to the analysis of international markets, and we
    explore these in some detail below. For now, it is sufficient to note that
    if a country has a comparative advantage in the production of a particu-
    lar good – for example, cars – then it will be able to produce them more
    cheaply than other countries. It will pay the country to specialize in cars

and trade them for goods and services in which it does not have a comparative advantage.

2   Dunning, J. (1995) Re-appraising the eclectic paradigm in an age of alliance capitalism. Paper presented to the EMOT Workshop, Technology and the Theory of the Firm: Social and Economic Perspectives. University of Reading, 14–16 May 1995.

3   Technology and innovation are areas of economic theory which fall outside the remit of this text to a large extent. However, it is important to mention technology in the context of globalization, as many commentators would argue that it is technology generally and microelectronics technology in particular that has driven this latest phase of globalization. Advances in communications have made cross-border operations easier and more efficient, and companies have developed systems which are appropriate to their own organizational needs. Neo-classical economics viewed technology as *exogenous* to the system – that is, it stemmed from research undertaken outside the market place and was not undertaken by firms themselves.

4   Kozul-Wright, R. (1995) Transnational corporations and the nation state. In J. Michie and J. Grieve-Smith (eds), *Managing the Global Economy*. Oxford: Oxford University Press.

5   International Monetary Fund.

6   The European Union, consisting of a network of alliances between the member states: Austria, Belgium, Denmark, Finland, France, Germany, Greece, Ireland, Italy, Luxembourg, the Netherlands, Portugal, Spain, Sweden and the UK.

7   Three references will help you to understand the debate about the role of the nation state in international economic activity: (a) Porter, M. (1990) *The Competitive Advantage of Nations*. London: Macmillan. This is a major study of 12 countries, arguing that country-specific infrastructures create competitive advantage for companies based in those countries. (b) Reich, R. (1995) Who is us? Originally appeared in 1991, but reproduced in W. Lazonick and W. Mass (eds), *Organisational Capability and Competitive Advantage: Debates, Dynamics and Policy*. Aldershot: Edward Elgar. Argues the opposing view – that countries are less important than the global webs of information, strategy and distribution that are created by global companies. (c) Lazonick, W. (1993) Industry clusters versus global webs: organisational capabilities in the American economy. *Industrial and Corporate Change*, 2(1), 1–24. Provides a synthesis of the two approaches.

8   For more detail on this see Kozul-Wright, op. cit., note 3.

9   Transactions costs economics are another whole area of industrial economics which cannot be covered in any depth here, but which are critical to understanding the nature of international economic activity. There is sufficient in the text to allow you to understand the importance of transactions costs, but for further reading see: Williamson, O. E. (1975) *Markets and Hierarchies: Mergers and Antitrust Implications*. Cambridge,

MA: Free Press; or Dietrich, M. (1994) *Transactions Cost Economics and Beyond: towards a New Economics of the Firm*. London: Routledge.

10   See, for example, Patel, P. and Pavitt, K. (1991) Large firms in the production of the world's technology: an important case of non-globalisation. *Journal of International Business Studies*, 22, 1–22.

11   To be precise, demand for a domestic currency will be determined by the positive (or credit) items in the balance of payments account. In other words, it is the money coming in, say to the UK economy from the rest of the world – very broadly, money spent on exports. Any money going out of the balance of payments represents expenditure on imports, i.e. money UK citizens spend on goods produced overseas. This represents supply of the currency.

12   Kozul-Wright, op. cit., note 4.

13   Vast amounts are written on the economics of 'customs unions' or trading blocks. You may be interested to look specifically at Europe, in which case two books may be of interest in addition to those listed in the reading section. Artis, M. J. and Lee, N. (eds) (1994) *The Economics of the European Union: Policy and Analysis*. Oxford: Oxford University Press. Nugent, N. and O'Donnell, R. (eds) (1994) *The European Business Environment*. London: Macmillan.

14   Porter, op. cit., note 7.

15   Lazonick, op. cit., note 7, provides an excellent synthesis of the two arguments from the perspective of an economic historian.

12 Conclusions

Economics is an inexact science, if indeed it is a science at all. It operates in a fog of uncertainty.

(Rachel Lomax, interviewed in Dieter Helm, *UK PLC*,
BBC Radio 4, October 1995)

1 Introduction

This book started with a very simple question: 'Has anyone told you *why* economics is central to the study of business?' Eleven weeks of your one semester course will have passed by the time you reach this chapter (unless, of course, you have been reading ahead) and it is hoped that you could start to answer this question independently. Most courses, however long, end with a revision session designed to consolidate the material covered. This text is no exception, and we will go through the whole book in summary form, with the ultimate aim of deriving a proper answer that you will be able to carry through into other areas of study on your business course.

2 Aims and Objectives

The aim has already been stated: to derive an answer to the question, 'Why is economics relevant to business?' There are a number of specific objectives that can be listed in addition to this:

1 That you will understand the importance of the link between the neo-classical economics covered here and specific company strategies that you will cover elsewhere in the course.
2 That you will understand the importance of the macroeconomic environment for businesses both large and small.
3 That you will, at the end of the complete course, be familiar with the economic approach to analysing problems and that you understand that this approach is ultimately very similar to that used in business.

Two rather presumptuous objectives might be suggested in addition to these explicit ones. First, it is hoped that at the end of this course you will realize that the economic method of approaching business problems is very similar to that used by businesses themselves. To that end, the methods and techniques of investigation and analysis covered in this book will help the reader to approach problems set in other subject areas. Second, the book has attempted to make the subject simple and interesting through the use of real cases and through the discussion of current issues. It is hoped that readers have found this approach rewarding and would therefore feel both willing and able to tackle other areas of the discipline.

3 Investigation (1)

As usual, this chapter starts with a point for reflection, discussion and investigation. Before reading on, try formulating an answer by yourself to the question that has been posed in this text. Do you think economics is useful to business and why? After all, my answer is only a personal view!

In addition to this, as you read through the summary given below, you may find it useful to draw the diagrams and then check back with the relevant chapters. This will serve two purposes: it will make sure that you have understood each model and will help you to revise.

4 Summary of the Chapters

As this chapter is a support to a revision session, we will quickly look through each chapter, drawing out the main points. For simplicity, these have been listed below. If, on reading through any of the points, you feel uncertain about an area, refer back to the chapter concerned.

Chapter 1 covered the basic problem of economics – the allocation of scarce resources. It argued that the fundamental problems of economics and of business are exactly the same – to determine the most effective way to distribute income in the interests of maximizing personal gain. For companies this means the maximization of profits. Some simple analytical techniques were used, again identical to those often used in business, and the distinction between normative and positive analysis was discussed.

Chapter 2 covered the two basic models of economics – that of supply and that of demand. It was shown that, for a normal good, demand increases as the price falls and supply increases as the price rises. The rate at which either demand or supply changes in response to changes in price was called its *elasticity* or price responsiveness. The relationship between price and quantity was seen as central to the marketing function of any company.

Chapter 3 further developed the role of marketing in a business through an analysis of the interaction between demand and supply in the *market place*. It was demonstrated that demand and supply will interact with one another to determine an equilibrium price of the product that is being made. The model of the market (or price) mechanism tells us that if prices are too high, too much will be supplied and not enough demanded. There will be downward pressure on prices until an equilibrium is reached. Conversely, if prices are too low, too much will be demanded and not enough supplied. This will put upward pressure on prices until an equilibrium is reached. It was argued that companies need to know how demand will change in response to price in order to fix a level of production that will be profitable.

Chapter 4 took the supply curve and looked specifically at how it is affected by costs. Three types of costs were covered.

- *Total costs* were, as the name suggests, the total amount that it costs to produce a level of output; this will include all the overhead costs of running the factory, the supply chain and the distribution network (*fixed costs*), as well as all those costs that are directly related to the level of output (*variable costs*). The total cost curve is S-shaped and its slope illustrates the rate at which costs increase relative to output.
- *Average costs* (often referred to in business as unit costs) are the total costs of production divided by the level of output. In economics and in business these costs are particularly important because they are an indication of the efficiency of the company. Where a company is producing at the minimum point on the U-shaped average cost curve it is reaping all possible *economies of scale* and is therefore as efficient as it can be given that scale of output.
- *Marginal costs* are the rate at which costs are changing as output changes. Formally defined, marginal costs are the incremental increase in costs for a one unit increase in output.

The chapter argued that a company in the real world cannot compete without having a detailed knowledge of its cost structures. It was pointed out that the average cost curve in particular gives a company an indication of its competitiveness compared with other companies. If a company has lower unit (or average) costs then it is more competitive.

Chapter 5 discussed perfect competition and monopoly. Under a perfectly competitive market structure, with a large number of buyers and sellers and a homogeneous product, it was demonstrated that the company would have very little control over its level of output and no control over price: it would have to accept the price given by the market. Under a monopoly, in contrast, the company would have complete control over both price and output, being the only supplier of a particular product and, thus, effectively being the industry. The models are highly theoretical, but they were seen as relevant to us as analysts of business because they allowed us to predict how companies might behave under different competitive structures, particularly in relation to pricing and output decisions. It was also argued that, for business, competitor analysis is a central part of strategy and that these models allowed us to see how important other players in the market place were for companies.

Chapter 6 developed the models of chapter 5 into models that bore more resemblance to real industrial structures.

- A *Lorenz curve* was drawn to show that concentration of industrial power is never equally shared between all suppliers of a product or concentrated in the hands of one supplier. Even a monopoly supplier of trains, it was argued, is competing with other methods of transport.
- The model of *monopolistic competition* was constructed to analyse the behaviour of the large number of small firms producing a differentiated product that often only command a small percentage of total market share over which they compete fiercely. These companies will face downward sloping demand curves and thus will be able to command a degree of monopoly power, at least in the short term. This means that they will make excess profits which they can invest in innovation and new technology. The example of the biotechnology industry demonstrated how important these small companies are in driving forward innovation in new areas.
- The model of *oligopolistic competition* related to the few large companies that often control the majority of the market. It was demonstrated that these companies often do not compete in terms of price because they have too much to lose in market share and profitability if they do. Instead, they will compete through non-price means – particularly costs, technology and product differentiation. The case of the biotechnology industry again was used to illustrate how these companies create market share for themselves by using their excess profits to innovate in product technologies.

Imperfect competition is the area of economics where it comes into closest contact with the real business world. In both types of market, monopolistic and oligopolistic, the role of technology is central.

Chapter 7 went on to discuss the role of government intervention in the economy. It summarized the case for and against intervention. It discussed two areas of intervention: the amelioration of inequalities through provision of facilities to which everyone has access; and the reduction of the negative externalities caused by the operation of the market. It looked at the relevance of this for business strategy, particularly in relation to the delineation between provision of basic services (like education, training and scientific research) and development of specific competencies (task-specific in-house training or new product development). It was argued that a rule of thumb in funding was for the government to fund basic services, with industry funding specific competencies. The same principle was applied to responsibility for the environment.

Chapter 8 introduced the area of macroeconomic management. It looked at the *circular flow* of income between households and firms. On the basis of this it demonstrated how national income is calculated and, therefore, how companies are central to generating the nation's wealth. Two measures of national income were covered: gross domestic product (GDP), which is all consumption, investment and government expenditure; and gross national product (GNP), which includes the balance of trade (exports minus imports). From this, aggregate demand and aggregate supply curves were developed. It was argued that for business these represent key indicators of the macroeconomic health of the economy, and the importance of economic forecasts for business was stressed.

Chapter 9 looked at the policy issue of unemployment. Four types of unemployment were covered: unemployment caused by excessive wages, regional unemployment, demand-deficient unemployment and structural unemployment. Policies to cure unemployment were discussed and it was argued that the 'cure' depended upon the policy-maker's perceptions of what the cause of the unemployment was. Unemployment is an important issue for business for two reasons: first, it represents a misallocation of resources, i.e. resources lying 'idle'; second, where there are simultaneously a large number of job vacancies, it points to a structural problem in the economy. This skills mismatch is a real problem for business and has presented 'human resource' strategies with major challenges as technology has changed.

Chapter 10 looked at the policy issue of inflation. It was pointed out that businesses and governments who borrow have the most to gain from inflation because their debts are devalued if there is an inflation in the economy. However, since 1979, economic policy in Britain and the USA has been directed at the reduction of inflation, so it was deemed important to understand the policy measures that have been taken. The main method of inflation control has been through control of the money supply, as there is a direct link between the amount of money in an economy and the price level. To control the money supply in the UK the main policy instrument has been interest rates. UK business both large and small have been affected by high interest rates, which have increased total amounts repayable on loans and affected the value of sterling. Again, the importance of forecasting trends was stressed. This was seen as being the case because if a company knows about inflationary trends it can alter output and cost calculations accordingly.

Chapter 11 looked at the internationalization of the world economy and pointed out that this is the major economic environmental factor with which companies in the 1990s have to deal, be they large or small. It was argued that the boundaries between firms, countries and regions are becoming blurred as resources are increasingly internationally allocated. This international resource allocation was seen as a means of overcoming market uncertainty stemming from exchange rate fluctuations and as a means of achieving competitive advantage by utilizing different factor endowments of host nations. However, it was also argued that countries themselves remain potent forces of competitive advantage through the development and enhancement of their own factor endowments.

5   Microeconomics and Business

It is clear from all this that we have covered a massive amount of material in a relatively short time, and you would be forgiven for thinking that you had been caught in a whirlwind! In order to take stock of the whole course now and its relevance for your studies, we are redividing the subject into micro and macro, as this makes a review easier. Accordingly, we will divide our strategic matrix into two as well.

Neo-classical microeconomics is about scarcity and choice, and the market mechanism as an allocator of those scarce resources. The main tool of microeconomics is the model of supply and demand. Through this model it is predicted that the market will efficiently allocate resources throughout the economy through the process of demand and supply interaction and specialization. In such a 'perfect' form of competition, individuals act on the desire to maximize their 'utility' and, in so doing, create the maximum good for the maximum number of people: 'Every man thus lives by exchanging, or becomes in some measure a merchant, and the society itself grows to be what is properly a commercial society' (Adam Smith, *The Wealth of Nations*, 1780).

Of course, there are some major limitations to this. Not least of these is the fact that markets do not operate perfectly in a real world dominated by 'imperfect competition'. So microeconomics as it has been presented here tells us about the internal operating environment of the company (or more specifically, its costs) and tells us a lot about how companies behave given the nature of the market they are operating in.

Microeconomics can really inform us about three areas of company operations:

1 All areas of demand and supply analysis tell us about how the company interfaces with its external, competitive, environment. It tells us how effective pricing strategy can be, given the price responsiveness of demand, and it tells us how companies can alter supply in response to changes in demand. This is the marketing column in the strategic matrix of figure 12.1.

2 Cost analysis tells us about how efficient the company is. Effective management of total costs is a central pillar of logistics strategy: operations management is centrally concerned with creating unit costs that are industrial best practice through process and product technologies and improvement programmes. This is the second column of the strategic matrix.

3 Finally, the competitor analysis of competition theory tells us a lot about how companies will behave in different market structures. For a company, the behaviour of competitors is central to formulating any strategy at all because, especially in imperfect markets, firms are interdependent. Perfect competition and monopoly, although theoretical, tell us about pricing and output. Imperfect models tell us (and company strategists) about the importance of non-price competition and, in particular, technology and product development. The total strategic aspect of this analysis is represented in columns 3 and 4 of the matrix.

This matrix has been used throughout the text to show you where economics is relevant to understanding the types of decisions that businesses make. It is not intended as a definitive statement on company

Figure 12.1 The microeconomic strategic matrix.

	Demand and supply: marketing	Costs	Pricing/ output	Product development and technology	Competitor analysis
Small companies	Critical in creating a market 'niche' with degree of monopoly power	Will have to be efficient in order to remain in business	Depends on number of competitors and elasticity of demand	Centrally important: creating market share and creating innovation base to new industries	Vital: especially costs and new products
Large companies	Marketing a central part of activity – pricing, advertising, product development	Can use any slack to gain short-term advantage but importance of cost competition increasing	Price inter- dependency at industry level, but pricing to increase market penetration	NON-PRICE COMPETITION Essential, although large companies will hold back from new industries	Strategic inter- dependency: firms depend on each other's behaviour for market share and R&D strategy

strategy. However, the above 'micro' matrix does provide some insights into market structure and the types of decisions that companies will have to make.

6 Macroeconomics and Business

Macroeconomics provides us with a knowledge of the external economic context within which companies operate. It cannot tell us directly about the types of strategies that companies will follow through, nor can it give us definitive answers about how the economy should be run, as the quote at the top of the chapter suggests.

However, the macroeconomic environment determines the effectiveness of company strategy. No company operates in a vacuum: the rate at which prices are changing and the number of people out of work are central to any company's analysis of its markets. And, as we saw in chapter 11, the increasing internationalization of the world economy combined with new technology is creating a new pressure to companies large and small to operate in more than one national market.

Figure 12.2 The macroeconomic strategic matrix.

	Impact of regulatory environment	Impact of the national economy	Role for forecasting	Unemployment and human resources	International economy
Small companies	High – impact on costs	High impact	Essential but expensive. Impact of inflactionary expectations high	High	Damaging: impact of interest and exchange rates
Large companies	Low – can be taken up within slack and turned to competitive advantage	Potential high impact	Essential. Impact of inflationary expectations high but can be insured against	High	Global strategy to prevent excessive reliance on one economy

Very broadly, then, the macroeconomics and policies of chapters 7–11 provide companies with the following 'inputs' into their strategies.

1 Government intervention can take the form of policies to affect the operations of markets and to ameliorate inequalities and externalities caused by them. In particular, government training and R&D policies and the regulatory environment (for example, legislation on pollution control or health and safety legislation) present direct costs to industry. This is the first column of the macro matrix in figure 12.2.

2 The role of economic forecasting cannot be understated. Companies need to predict trends in aggregate demand and inflation in order to see how their own markets will respond to any changes (for better or worse) in the macroeconomic climate. Inflation forecasting is particularly important because it will give an indication of how costs and demand might change. This is the second and third column of the matrix in figure 12.2.

3 Unemployment will affect a company's human resource strategies directly in two ways. First, large numbers of people unemployed may put downward pressure on wages. Second, where there is a skills mismatch companies will be under competitive pressure to increase expenditure on training in order to have adequately skilled employees. This is column 3 of the matrix.

4 The increasing importance of the global economy is felt by business in two ways – through the price at which exports can be sold and through increased competition in domestic markets. Pressure on small and large companies will be for cost reduction and improving competitiveness through technology and investment generally. This will not be helped if interest rates are high, although adequate forecasting can help to cushion companies against interest rate rises as these can be built into expectations.

7 Conclusions

The simple answer to the question, 'Why is economics relevant to business?' is that economics and business are fundamentally seeking to address the same problem: how best to allocate resources. In a modest way, it is hoped that this text has helped you to understand not only how economics works but how business works as well. While you will undoubtedly have many unanswered questions, the aim of this book has been to make sure that the question of why economics is relevant is not one of them.

At this stage of a textbook there is little more to be said without doubling the length of the text. If you have been interested by the material covered, try other approaches to economics as well. In any event, it is hoped that this approach will at least underpin everything else you study on your business course. Good luck!

Index